POETS TEACHING

Longman English and Humanities Series
Series Editor: Lee Jacobus
University of Connecticut, Storrs

POETS
TEACHING

The Creative Process

Edited by ALBERTA TURNER
The Cleveland State University

LONGMAN
New York and London

POETS TEACHING
The Creative Process

Longman Inc., New York
Associated companies, branches, and representatives
throughout the world.

Developmental Editor: Gordon T. R. Anderson
Editorial and Design Supervisor: Joan Matthews
Design: Antler & Baldwin, Inc.
Manufacturing and Production Supervisor: Kris Becker
Composition: American–Stratford Graphic Services, Inc.
Printing and Binding: Fairfield Graphics

Library of Congress Cataloging in Publication Data
Main entry under title:
Poets teaching.
    (Longman English and humanities series)
    1. American poetry—20th century—Study and teaching
—Addresses, essays, lectures.   2. College verse,
American—History and criticism—Addresses, essays,
lectures.   3. Poetics—Addresses, essays, lectures.
I. Turner, Alberta T.   II. Series.
PS306.P6   811'.5'409   79-9303
ISBN 0-582-28105-9

Manufactured in the United States of America

9 8 7 6 5 4 3 2 1

"Perhaps Here" by Marvin Bell. From *Field* #18, Spring, 1978. Copyright ©
1978 by Field Magazine/Oberlin College. Reprinted by permission of the
publisher and the author.

"Fear and a Rose" by Daniel Van Riper. From *Intro* 9 edited by George
Garrett and Michael Mewshaw. Reprinted by permission of Hendel and
Reinke, Publishers and the author.

"December in the Terminal" by Linda Monacelli. From *Lacing the Moon* by
Linda Monacelli, Cleveland Poets Series, No. 17. Copyright © 1978 by Linda
Monacelli. Reprinted by permission of the author.

"Confusing But Not Confused" by Albert Goldbarth. From *Field* #18, Spring,
1978. Copyright © 1978 by Field Magazine/Oberlin College. Reprinted by
permission of the publisher and the author.

"Astronomy I: The Void" by Rosalind Neroni. From *The Porcupine's Princess*
by Rosalind Neroni, Cleveland Poets Series No. 18. Copyright © 1978 by
Rosalind Neroni. Reprinted by permission of the author.

"Wading Horses" by Susan Shetterly. From *The Poetry Miscellany*, 7 (1977).
Copyright © 1977 by The Poetry Miscellany. Reprinted by permission of the
publisher and the author.

ACKNOWLEDGMENTS

"Waking on Deck" by Sarah Brownsberger. From *Dark Horse* #8, Summer, 1976. Copyright © 1976 by Sarah Brownsberger. Reprinted by permission of the author.

"A Portrait of the Day" by Bill Sloan copyright © 1977 by Bill Sloan. From *The Great Lake Review*, Spring, 1977. Reprinted by permission of the author and the publisher.

"The Minuet: Sidling Around Student Poems" by William Stafford. From *Field* #18, Spring, 1978. Copyright © 1978 by Field Magazine/Oberlin College. Reprinted by permission of the publisher and the author.

Excerpt from "Asphodel, That Greeny Flower." William Carlos Williams, *Pictures from Brueghel and Other Poems*. Copyright 1954 by William Carlos Williams. Reprinted by permission of New Directions.

"On the Making of Three Poems" by Jane Cooper, includes "Stumbling Around the Woods: Draft 1" by Reine Hauser, "Stumbling Around the Woods: Draft 2" by Reine Hauser, "Stumbling Around the Woods: Draft 3" by Reine Hauser, "Anatomy of an Embrace: Draft 1" by Donald Bell, "Anatomy of an Embrace: Draft 2" by Donald Bell, "Five Women in a Café: Draft 1" by Kathie rue Hoyer, "Five Women in a Café: Draft 2" by Kathie rue Hoyer. From *Field* #18, Spring, 1978. Copyright © 1978 by Field Magazine/Oberlin College. Reprinted by permission of the publisher and the authors.

Excerpt from "Distance" by Peter Everwine. From *Keeping the Night* by Peter Everwine. Copyright © 1973, 1977 by Peter Everwine. Reprinted by permission of Atheneum Publishers.

"Tall Ship" by Dave Fantauzzi. From *Bits*, 7 January 1978. Copyright © 1978 by David A. Fantauzzi. Reprinted by permission of the publisher and the author.

Excerpt from "Aphrodite as History" by Robert Francis. Reprinted from *Robert Francis: Collected Poems, 1936–1976* (University of Massachusetts Press), copyright © 1960 by Robert Francis. Reprinted by permission of the publisher.

CONTENTS

Acknowledgments   v
Preface   xi
Introduction   1

GROUP I   16
"My Grandfather, Dying," Martha Moody   16
"The Outline of My Head," Hank Davis   18
"Waking on Deck," Sarah Brownsberger   19

   Commentators
   David Young   20
   Stuart Friebert   25
   Alberta Turner   30
   David St. John   35

GROUP II   40
"A Portrait of the Day," Bill Sloan   40
"Brother and Sister," Michael Pauly   42
"Window—we do not see," Barbara Stafford   43

   Commentators
   William Stafford, "The Minuet: Sidling Around Student Poems"   43
   Lewis Turco, "Poetry: the *Art* of Language"   49

GROUP III   53
"Mother's song of strangers," Paul Minx   53
"A Second Visit to Miller's Grave," Mark Jones   54

   Commentators
   Sandra McPherson   55
   Henry Carlile   59

GROUP IV 63

"Anatomy of an Embrace," Donald Bell 63
"Stumbling Around in the Woods," Reine Hauser 64
"Five Women in a Café," Kathie rue Hoyer 67

Commentators
Jane Cooper, "On the Making of Three Poems" 68
Thomas Lux, "Hoof and Paw: Working Over Some
    Student Poems" 73
Jean Valentine 81

GROUP V 83

"Sicilian Semaphore," John Gabel 83
"Tall Ship," David Fantauzzi 85
"Cowtale," Joan Nicholl 86

Commentators
Hollis Summers, "Shaking and Carving" 87
Robert Wallace, "And Praxiteles Was Not First" 93
John Haines 103

GROUP VI 109

"All Ugly Scarred People," Brenda Bochner 109
"My Mother Dyes My Father's Hair," Zena Krall 110
"Mother's song of strangers," Paul Minx 111

Commentators
Marvin Bell, "Perhaps Here" 112
Richard Shelton 116

GROUP VII 120

"Fear and a Rose," Daniel Van Riper 120
"In the Terminal," Linda Monacelli 122
"Grandfather's Funeral," Nancy Ring 122

Commentators
Albert Goldbarth, "Confusing But Never Confused" 124
Stanley Plumly, "Reading and Writing" 132

GROUP VIII 139

"Her Daughter," Bob Vance 139
"Progeny: A poem from David," Anonymous 141
"Astronomy I: The Void," Rosalind Neroni 141

Commentators
Donald Justice 142

Judith Hemschmeyer   145
John Woods   149

GROUP IX   152
"An Autumn Drowning," Bruce Cohen   153

Commentators
Steve Orlen   154–168
Mark Halperin
Boyer Rickel
Jon Anderson
Bruce Cohen
Michael Collier

GROUP X   169
"By His Stripes," Helen Williams   169
"Walking over Rochford Burn," Dave Cole   170
"Looking for Winter: A Seasonal Change," Doreen Schmid 171

Commentators
Dave Smith, "Passion, Possibility, and Poetry"   173
Heather McHugh   191
Cynthia Macdonald   197

GROUP XI   203
"Sonnet," Larry Rapant   203
"Wading Horses," Susan Shetterly   204
"The Vanishing Mailmen," Charles Agvent   205

Commentators
Philip Booth   206
Larry Levis   210
Jay Meek   214
Lawrence Raab   217

PREFACE

Because I both write poetry and teach it, I have often been caught in the crossfire between poets who say that to make poetry writing an academic discipline will stereotype American poetry and academics who say that teaching anything as subjective as poetry writing will make a mockery of academic discipline. This hostility has existed ever since the Romantic Movement took the Muse out of the classroom, took away her book of classical rhetoric and shut her inside the poet and the poet inside a garret. For a while the two sides ignored each other: the academic taught literature and wrote poetry as a hobby—if at all; the poet put in a full day at the clinic or the insurance office and entertained the Muse at home after hours. But since World War II, and especially since the late 1960s, young American poets have tended increasingly to begin their careers by taking a degree in a college or university writing program and earning their livings by teaching there. By now creative writing is in the curriculum of most American colleges and universities, and degrees in creative writing are offered in about fifty M.A. and nine Ph.D. programs. The Associated Writing Programs have their newsletter and their annual convention. The Modern Language Association job listings offer a substantial number of positions in creative writing. And in 1978 three of the five National Book Award nominees for poetry were teachers in writing programs. Though the poets still can, and many still do, teach themselves by reading, imitation, and rejection slips, a very considerable number get an M.F.A., publish in little or literary magazines, in the Wesleyan or Ecco or Pitt series, compete for the Whitman or Juniper or Devins awards, and teach either part-time or full-time at colleges, universities, or writers' conferences, with time out at Yaddo or MacDowell or on NEA grants or Guggenheims for creative work.

This book is a sample of what actually happens when the professional teaching poet sits down with the student poem. It allows the reader to look over the shoulder of thirty-two poets while they are teaching. Those who will want to look over the poets' shoulders will probably be other teaching poets or teachers-in-training, whether from high schools, colleges, or private noncredit workshops; students of teaching poets who want to compare what they're getting with what other students are getting; and nonacademic poets who are teaching themselves and who want to know if there's something more they need to look for in their own work. Literature teachers will want to see what differences of poetic theory and process lie behind the differences between, say, Kinnell's *Book of Nightmares* and Eliot's *Wasteland*. And of course any reader interested in contemporary poetry will want to look in order to understand what criteria contemporary poets use to judge each other.

All thirty-two teacher-poets in this book are "established"; more than half have graduated from writing programs themselves. Their work and theory are near the center of contemporary poetics, and the poets themselves represent a range of age, sex, geographical location, kind of poetry written, and teaching temperament—certainly a sample large enough and representative enough to show in broad outline *how* student poems are being criticized and students taught to become their own critics.

This material is also sufficient for starting other investigations. For example, if several teachers have themselves had the same teacher, does this make their teaching noticeably more uniform than the teaching of poets from more widely different backgrounds? Is the workshop more helpful than the individual conference? Does the beginner's poem receive as careful and sympathetic attention as the advanced student's? Do poets' specific criticisms illustrate their stated poetic theories? How is the teaching of poets similar to or different from that of sculptors or painters? . . . or a dozen other questions which the grouping of poets and poems in this collection suggest.

Enough for my present purpose if those poets who say that teaching poetry writing will make poetry rigid and uniform and those academics who say that it cannot really be taught will reconsider.

A.T.

INTRODUCTION

The assumption behind these essays, an assumption so basic that it is not even stated, seems to be that poems have an almost metaphysical existence inside students and that only if students listen very carefully and transcribe very skillfully can they tease them out of themselves without damaging them. Studying writing, therefore, becomes a process of sharpening perception: awareness of all the connotations of a word, of all the rhythms of an emotion, of all the possible clashes among images, awareness of clichés and how to avoid them or use them so that they become effective allusion, ability to perceive glibness and superficiality in oneself, to know when one is being honest. Such study means learning how to become a whole person from poets who are still teaching themselves to be whole persons. They hesitate to say they can do it or even that it can be done. But even if their answer to the question, "Can a poet be made?" is a qualified no, it is so qualified that it amounts to a guarded yes. No—but one can be taught to recognize and respect poetry, one can be taught to read it (Haines)*; no—but a beginner can be taught to become his own teacher: "To get beyond what workshops can teach you is what workshops are finally for" (Booth); no—"talent" or "inspiration" can't be taught, but students can be taught to recognize sources in themselves (St. John). If the students are "serious," if they are willing to continue the process that has begun in the workshop or class or conference, the habits of reading and self-criticism they have learned and practiced there, they may be able to make themselves into poets, and the teacher can help them do it.

The necessary talent is therefore an attitude: "a love of language and word play" (St. John); having been "moved by the poems of others"

* Citations refer to the teacher-poets in the body of this collection.

to want to write (Wallace); "a matter of character, as well as luck and a passion for the medium" (Cooper)—in other words, the passion that creates both awareness and persistence in any artist.

The necessary talent for teachers is also an attitude. They must win the students' respect and confidence so that they will ask questions, listen more closely to sounds and rhythms, try new techniques; and they must respect and have confidence in the students so that they do not make them disciples or grotesques or pale imitations of their teachers, on the one hand, or, on the other, rejected failures who give up. Since these poets are fairly confident and successful in their own work, they find it hard not to say, "This is right, this is wrong, this is the way to do it." Several speak of the temptation and take pains to counter it: Wallace warns against the tendency to expect discipleship. Cooper reminds herself that no matter what happens in the workshop some students come with an already strong talent and their own voice; Halperin confesses, "The easiest thing for me to do is to rewrite someone's poem, and that has no value for them." Again and again they remind themselves and their students that they may be wrong. As Carlile puts it, "Any poet teaches a set of prejudices. For that reason I always warn my students in advance that I can only teach my own ways of writing, which may not, finally, help them to find their own best voices." And Bell: "The teacher can be wrong. I myself am often wrong."

Before teaching can begin, therefore, a relationship between students and teacher must be established which will enable the students to start on the long process of becoming their own teachers. This relationship ranges from the teacher as sympathetic listener, whose teaching consists of barely whispered questions which will hopefully lead the students to realize their poems' possibilities, to the teacher as firm guide, who measures the student poem against his own standards of what a poem should be. Stafford and Turco represent the ends of this range. (By coincidence and unknown to one another, they worked on the same three poems.) Stafford says that his first impulse is "to become steadfastly evasive until some signal from the student indicates a direction where the student is ready to go." His method is wholly inductive: "the first move is the student's move, not mine. . . . If I charge into the poem, I might either take it over or alienate the writer; . . . and I might enhance rather than decrease that dominance implied by teacher-student conferring. Surely our direction is to be toward the writer's own taking over of the writing." He never reaches the stage of overt judgment: "This succeeds, this fails, this is what you really mean."

Turco gives more direction. He measures the poem by whether the author is "aware of structure and how it operates to release meaning and pleasure." He uses the term *structure* broadly, to include both metrical and free-verse forms. It means a conscious and controlled use of thought and language patterns "that the reader can follow," not private, not confused. When he finds such a poem he says, "I knew I had stumbled upon a poet with a capital P."

Mostly, however, the teacher's approach to the students is neither as tentative as Stafford's nor as authoritative as Turco's. On the "hard" side are Haines ("I don't believe in making things easy for people"), Bell ("I am very much opposed to teaching poetry writing by making bad student poems slightly better"), Shelton ("I'm not sure the poem is salvageable"). On the softer side are Summers ("My comments are considerations, not edicts"), Carlile ("The teacher's role here is passive. In the end the student and the poem must find each other"), and Cooper (students should learn that "there's no such thing as authority"). And most often the teachers modify a soft or hard approach according to the temperament or sophistication of the student. Bell says, "If the student can take some kidding, I'd suggest the poem be retitled *The Blue Sink at Midnight,* and directed by Alfred Hitchcock. (And if the student cannot take kidding, that's important, too.)" And Valentine says, "By the time we were working on that poem, I could be as opinionated as I wanted; he had a healthy skepticism, and a real survivor's stubbornness."

Once a comfortable working relationship has been established, students and teacher join to increase the students' self-awareness, a recognition of what they really feel and believe in reaction to specific experiences, so that when they leave the workshop they will be able to detect for themselves where the nucleus of a poem is and the direction in which it is going before they try to refine its technique. Haines starts perhaps farthest away from the finished poem. He would have the students ask themselves if they really need to write. To win Haines's respect, poems must be written from "some real and earned attitude toward life and death." Levis wants "a concept that evolves necessarily from fully imagined or real experience." Cooper believes that "only when the experience is there to respect can one begin to ask whether it should be clarified, carried further." The poets agree that the first step in helping any student poem is to discover the experience that the poem is growing out of and the student's emotional reaction to it, even if the student himself doesn't realize what it is. Summers and Bell call this a process of teaching students to be their own readers. Others call it finding the poem's "center" or "what the poem is saying" or, more rarely, it's "intention."

In teaching this first step some poets walk on eggs. They hesitate to interfere lest the interference deform the poem or stop it entirely. Stafford says, "I might wildly misread some main current in its actual or potential development." Valentine cautions, "The poem seems to be at some midpoint, moving toward its impulse. If I were working with this writer, I guess I'd wait." But others infer an intention or assume that there is none and pronounce judgment on the poem accordingly. Turco, confused by two poems, says that the poets do not know what they are doing. Anderson says that if the teacher states first why a poem doesn't work for him (that is, makes clear what he thinks it's doing), then *any* suggestions that will move it in that direction are legitimate. The methods for getting the student to realize or clarify the poem's center range from the direct question, "What were you trying to say?" through teacher hypotheses about what the poem probably means, through indirect questions pointing in various possible directions the poem might be taking, to having the student review the steps of his initial creative process.

Before actually revising student poems, both students and poets need criteria of what a poem should be. Young and St. John would establish these jointly with the students; Turco gives them "Turco's Principle and Corollary." Most make no initial statement about criteria, but assume them. However, no student would be long in doubt about what these were, for the comments on the poems tend to be more specific than general, and praise and blame are awarded for the ideas, words, and rhythms which fulfill or violate the poets' criteria.

Whether stated or implied, the criteria are fairly uniform. They consist of the critical theories of postmodernist poetry. Most often the poets seek for ingenuous or at least unpretentious *sincerity* rather than posture or preaching. Levis distrusts "a slick poem in a prevailing style"; Booth, a poem that is "typically bad rather than individually bad"; Anderson, anything that doesn't seem "earned." Several also mention *significance.* St. John would have the poem create for the reader a "familiar and intimate anxiety." Halperin wants surprise, "the kind that hits you somewhere that it hurts." Haines insists that the poet "have something to say."

Perhaps because of their predominantly inductive teaching method, their need for a comfortable relationship with the students, or perhaps because of postmodernism's distrust of academic labels, these poets seem almost deliberately to avoid using many of the standard critical terms. For *theme* they tend to say *center* or *impulse*. For *persona* or *point of view* or *tone* they tend to say *voice*. They use colloquial and slang terms, such as *gut, cute, quirky, schmaltz;* moral terms, such as *self-indulgent, earned, committed;* metaphors, such as the poem that *disintegrates,* the *view that takes breath;* euphemisms, such as *this bothers me,* instead of *this is cacophonous* or *this is a mixed metaphor.* And they use abstractions which have been worn smooth in lay language to perform some very important value judgments—for example, *interesting* to mean *significant* or even *profound; surprise* to mean the effect produced by the most skillful fusion of theme, image, rhythm, and diction. Only rarely do they speak of *tension* or *texture* or *irony.*

Most of the poets are working toward finished, even publishable, poems. Wallace speaks of helping the student "realize one of his possible poems," and Friebert says, "I strongly believe in helping students realize finished texts, if possible." But the teachers are realistic. They know that few poems written in a class or workshop will reach professional level. Carlile says, "When the teacher makes specific criticisms recommending minor additions, deletions, or rewrites, the student can be pretty sure he or she is finding the poem." But he also cautions, "Any teaching poet knows how seldom one can help a beginner to write an adult poem. Usually we settle for more modest accomplishments." Beyond the single finished poem, they aim at the farther goal of the independent poet. As Cooper puts it, "In teaching it's the direction of a student's writing that counts, and the life-giving energy, how a series of poems adds up, what it promises." And Stafford says that the development of the student's "appetite, confidence, inventiveness, flexibility— these are much more important than whether this poem ever gets off the ground."

The writing class generally takes the form of a workshop, supplemented, especially on the elementary level, by exercises for the whole class, to develop such specific skills as concreteness or rhythm or awareness of voice, and on all levels by individual student-teacher conferences. Texts on creative writing are available, but the poets in this book, when they help a student edit a poem, most often refer directly to other poems. They themselves have read widely, not only other poets, but also what these other poets have said about the craft, and they expect their students to do the same. Haines begins by asking the students what they have been reading and then assigns a reading list, both historical and contemporary, to make up the deficiencies. St. John goes so far as to ask his advanced students to do imitations to find what makes up another poet's "presence" or "persona." And Goldbarth says, "I believe strongly in providing outside examples (have, despite the classification 'creative workshop,' in many situations asked for formal critical papers.)"

Even those who don't mention a program of reading continually refer their students to specific poems and lines of poems to illustrate principles or show them how what they have tried to do could be done more effectively. Booth, for example, helping a sonnet, refers the student to Cummings's "next to of course god" for its individual voice and Yeats's "Leda and the Swan" for its fresh, dramatic use of familiar narrative. They are equally ready to show that the weaknesses of student poems also occur in the work of professionals. Booth cites Millay's sonnet "On Hearing a Symphony of Beethoven" to illustrate just how bad a sonnet can be.

The actual editing of the student poems in this collection might well be expected to vary widely from poet to poet, student to student, poem to poem, and even from draft to draft of the same poem. The subjective criteria, vocabulary, and methods of contact leave room for wholly different interpretations of a poem's central impulse; and individual differences in perception and personality leave room for both thoroughness and superficiality, vagueness and explicitness, rewriting the poem for the student, inducing him to rewrite it, or even for leaving him in utter confusion. To determine the kind or extent of help that the same poem is likely to get from different teachers, we need to look at what actually happened to several of the poems.

"My Grandfather, Dying" by Martha Moody is a poem by an advanced student in the Oberlin College writing program. It is criticized here (Group I) by four poets who know each other and each other's poetic preferences well but who criticize it independently (Stuart Friebert, David St. John, David Young, and I). Independently they all agree that the poem is nearly finished, and each would suggest finishing touches.

MY GRANDFATHER, DYING

But still alive, in that green chair,
with eyes that are bluer,
blinder than they've ever been.

He hasn't had a bath for weeks
but his body
smells clean. His skin is clear,
thinner than a membrane and we see
it's holding nothing
but light.

When he rises, slowly,
to place his hands on his wife's shoulders
and walk
we step aside.
Not because his hands are quick enough to
    touch us,
or that they'd try,
but because we know our place—

apart, the relatives who make
a reluctant pilgrimage
to his home three times a year.
We're not what matters.
What matters is the family left in Sweden,
the ones he never knew,
what matters are the men he taught the courage
to buy Pepsi and not beer.

What matters is the view
from the steeple of the church he built near
     Paxton.

What matters is the salvation of Edna,
who would have died alone, years ago,
if he hadn't taken her seventy years
and married them to his.

What matters finally
is the soul, the baby soul,
unfolding like an icon in his chest,
filling him with the light
that will soon break through his skin,
surround him like an eggshell as his body
fades away,

the light around the grave that starts us
     crying
because we've been left behind.

St. John suggests the fewest changes. After praising the poem's central success, that of "recreating a familiar and intense anxiety," and the poem's "authority of voice" and its structure ("We are taken by its movement through the practical to the spiritual. . . . The ending of the poem returns us to ourselves"), he praises the phrase "what matters," which helps establish this movement, and the right choice of the particular details. For revision he mentions only "occasional missteps in tone," giving as an example only the stanza beginning "What matters is the salvation of Edna." He makes no specific substitutions.

Friebert feels that the poem is so close to finished that the best way to help its author perfect it would be to pretend it's his own and talk aloud while making final revisions—"not to write her poem for her, but to make sure she sees and feels it get airtight. Sees me follow it along one line of resolve. . . . In the middle of all this, if it didn't feel right to me, I'd rip it out of the typewriter and start again. Even do that if one word felt wrong, like a helpless piano student starting the piece again, however far along he got, at the first, slightest intuition of a mistake."

Friebert's revisions are frequent, specific, and technical. They are chiefly compressions, such as removing "He" from the fourth line to establish "visual line rhythm" and keep "the internal couplet alive," as well as "but because" (line 16) "to keep this tone clipped that we've taken pains to establish in the last two lines of stanza 1." The first three lines of stanza 4 (the "reluctant pilgrimage") should go because "the apposition is awkward and unclear." That part of the anaphora ("what matters") in the second-to-last line of that stanza should go in order to emphasize the antithesis "We're not what matters / what matters are." He'd cut the last line because the next-to-last line completes the poem, "joins the two parts we've been anxious to keep separate . . . till now and flies over the whole text with elegy for its emblem." Finally, he singles the "icon" image for special praise, calling it a risk, but a successful one: "The icon forces us below the surface to a sharp pain, the *metal* force, underneath. A dive under."

Young, in keeping with his stated principle that the teacher should "not deluge a student writer, in conference or in workshop, with too many reactions and suggestions," selects only to reduce the "explanatory" elements in this poem and to strengthen the rhythms. Like St. John, he begins with praise: for its "ring of truth," its "familiar but powerful subject," and the "images and details that convey the emotional complexity of the experience to the reader." To reduce the explanatory quality, he would remove the last line; he'd then ask the author to find and remove other examples of editorial interference and would make sure that by one means or another the last three lines of the third stanza, the phrase "We're not what matters," and "the cluttered effect at the end of the next-to-last stanza" would go.

In editing rhythm Young first praises lines which he believes work well rhythmically, such as "is the soul . . . in his chest," and contrasts them with "what matters . . . Edna," which he considers "almost comically flat," then asks the student to reconsider the effectiveness of the very short lines. He doesn't suggest specific changes, just asks the student to reconsider this because the matter is so subjective that he really doesn't "have hard and fast answers." He goes only so far as to say, "There are rhythms in our living and our dying, rhythms in our attempt to speak of such things, that a poem like this needs to track and respond to, dance to. It has begun this process through the stanzas and in many of the lines, but my sense of its successful movement comes and goes, an intermittent music."

In my own commentary I also find the poem close to finished and detect its center: "the poem's 'point' seems to be its tone, and that tone is well enough controlled so that a first reading reveals it—at least to me." Editing would be a joint effort, but I give some very specific suggestions for the student to accept or reject. First, the emotional rather than intellectual thrust of the poem seems to me to require the jerkier rhythm and syntax of emotion. I then suggest three specific changes, including the removal of several of the repeated "what matters." Next I suggest removing several details which seem to direct attention to the viewer rather than the grandfather. I also question the image of the icon as conflicting with that of the eggshell and finally suggest six specific changes in diction which would extend the number of simple, Anglo-Saxon words and reduce the number of Latinate ones.

The four commentators on this poem have agreed on essentials: the poem is nearly finished; it has found its center and dominant tone—it *is* a poem. Three agree that the last line is wrong. Three agree that there is something wrong with the line "What matters is the salvation of Edna"—Young because of its rhythm, I because of its Latinate diction, St. John because of an unexplained "misstep in tone." Friebert and I would cut the relatives' reluctant pilgrimage, Young and Friebert and I all find need to shrink the last three lines of the third stanza, "Not because . . . our place." All, in other words, are clearly operating out of the same poetic principles: that feeling is best revealed and created by "show not tell," that emotion has a different rhythm from exposition, and that a poem should be as lean as possible.

But there are significant differences. Only I find any trouble with the icon image. St. John thinks the long series of anaphoras ("what matters") is a strength, I, a weakness; Friebert would remove part of it to emphasize antithesis. St. John likes the way the last line "returns us to ourselves"; I think the emphasis on ourselves detracts from the focus on the grandfather. But on the whole one is left with the distinct impression that the differences among the four poets' advice to this student are less significant than the similarities. Whichever one the student conferred with, she would be made aware of the same basic strengths of significance, tone, structure, and detail; given some specific suggestions about diction, rhythm, and conciseness; and made to realize that it was up to her to decide which suggestions to take—if any. She might have to fight a little with Friebert and me; she might have to ask St. John and Young a few more questions about specific lines and words; but she would know that however much or little of our advice she took, we would respect her decision.

This kind of uniformity is more common than not in this collection, but there are cases in which discrepancies are both greater and more fundamental. In one workshop the poem "An Autumn Drowning" by Bruce Cohen produced differences of opinion so fundamental that discussion left the poem and went back to the poet's creative process. The poem is by an advanced student at the University of Arizona, and the discussion transcribed here (Group IX) includes three poet-teachers (Jon Anderson, Mark Halperin, and Steve Orlen), the author (Cohen), and two other advanced students (Boyer Rickel and Michael Collier). All six have discussed poems in this way before, are familiar with one another's work and are relaxed and comfortable together.

AN AUTUMN DROWNING

```
The ocean collapses into itself, swelling like
    a blowfish,
or how the breeze behind the bathhouses
might be a genetic means of becoming human.

Most things bounce off themselves in different
    directions:
the first chill from Canada speaks in soft
    French
and your hands release a yellow box-kite on
    the breakers.

Maybe you just got too human too fast
and it tightened around your finger like your
    father's ring.
```

Maybe you lost it. What you mistook for a
    flaw

was illusive charm: you could have been
    handsome,
but your profile swims like your ancestors,
back to the ocean, half evolved . . .

The shirt and pants you left on the beach
scampered in the breeze,
giving your body new shapes, as if to tease.

It's annoying how the afternoon dissolves
separating each grain of sunlight,
but not related to the way people live.

It never occurred to anyone
that people would have to live separately:
why you spent your childhood here,

opening clams under the hallucination of
    pearls.
The rain's become a hairline pleasure,
the dream that returns where rust is
    favorable,

But your father's ring is not lost after all.
It taps your shoulder and says thanks for
    coming.
But you've already drowned and are coming into
    a new life.

This time your own.

The workshop begins with praise for the authentic but controlled voice and for the strong sense of location, and for the vivid imagination, the surprise (Orlen). Then it moves to the poem's chief problem, the lack of center. The poets begin to grope toward this center. Orlen asks what the poem's latent form is. Perhaps it should start with big general statements or progress toward them. Halperin says that perhaps it should juxtapose the fragments so that "they become something extra that makes them larger than just chance sayings." Anderson suggests, "You can play content off content, instead of image off image." Halperin says, "I think the statements in the last stanza, those two lines about your father's ring and 'taps your shoulder saying thanks for coming' are potentially the real heavies in the poem." But the poets realize that their groping isn't getting very far toward a finished poem. The student, instead of lighting up like a hundred-watt bulb, says, "I think only in the first line did I really have an idea of what was going on." Finally, Orlen asks, "What's your writing process, Bruce?"

As Bruce describes the process, it appears much like the process described by a large proportion of the poets who answered questions on their working habits for *50 Contemporary Poets* (David McKay, 1977). It begins with a phrase which strikes the author as a neat statement of a fresh idea: "I sat down with two lines that I liked—something a friend said in a conversation—because I thought there was a poem in them: 'Maybe you just got too human too fast. . . .'" By free association he let the statement touch off a series of jottings ("It must have hit other things"). Some of these he can account for (he's lived by the sea; he's had recurrent and anxious dreams about losing his father's ring), but not all. The next step was taking the poem out of the free-associative material (the original jottings were twice as long as the workshop version): "Anything that didn't touch on more than one level I tried to get rid of." To Anderson's suggestion that an especially telling line might serve to focus or order the others, he replies, "I thought that might be bad because it would call attention to itself."

What emerges from the discussion of process is that the student states and defends a fundamental difference in poetic theory. All three agree that the poem must speak to the individual *I* in order to reach the universal *I*, and that the individual *I* must originate in the poet. Bruce adds (and a fellow student supports him) that the *I* must not seem to be too private, too singular, lest it exclude the universal *I*. "In some

way you've got to hide it, undercutting as much as you can—always."
Bruce and the poet-teachers differ chiefly on how to universalize the
personal experience. It has to do with the level of consciousness at which
the happening of the experience, the emotional involvement with it,
gives way to the more objective crafting of it into a poem. Anderson be-
lieves that crafting should take place at a very deep level, part of the
first, preconscious stage; Orlen sees it as taking place in the second,
conscious stage, as a very deliberate process; and Halperin is some-
where between the two. Bruce grants the necessity of the preconscious
step, saying, "I think that's . . . how I get the stuff. But once I get it I
try to organize it. . . . I'll write a lot, and then I'll circle whatever
seem to be the good lines. Then I look for two lines that could go next
to each other, that would make good couplets. I do that first. And then
from that, usually I get one or two *new* lines. So eventually, even though
the order is originally arbitrary, I get some kind of order, I have to have
that order." This organization, as he describes it, seems to the poets too
mechanical, as if it had taken place before the emotions had had a
chance to fuse attitudes and images into the beginnings of a poem. In
Anderson's words, "It lacks a sense of commitment . . . a commitment
to an emotional state, an attitude, a pure intelligence. . . . The poem
keeps beginning again, rather than following through." The workshop
ends with the poem's center still unfound.

At first reading, this discussion seems confusing. Points are made,
dropped, and picked up later; the poets interrupt each other, even con-
tradict each other and themselves. But when one considers further, that
which has actually happened is a demonstration of honesty, humility,
good teamwork, and considerable restraint. Each of the teaching poets
knows and lets the student know that he could find a center and a
structure that would complete the poem. Each talks enthusiastically
about how he himself faces and resolves the same kind of problem in his
own work. But in the end they all make Bruce do it. Without saying, as
they might, "You aren't yet perceptive enough to see the poem in your
raw material," they suggest, "Here's a structure you might try, here's a
theme you might find central, but only *you* will be able to tell when
you've found the poem. It has fine parts, but no whole, and only you can
make it whole."

The analysis of any poem in this book gives us, of course, only a
partial view of the teaching process. The complete view, as the poets

frequently remind us, would let us see each poem in several stages, probably spanning a semester or more. We'd see the poem grow both in workshop sessions and in successive conferences with a teacher in a writing program—perhaps even more than one teacher and program. (Cooper specifically encourages working under several different teachers, and it is not unusual for writing students to take an undergraduate writing major, then an M.F.A., then even a Ph.D. at different institutions.) But even this partial view reveals attitudes toward poets and poems, basic assumptions about where poems are to be found and how to find them, and theories about technique. I am impressed again and again by the poets' recurrent agreement on the fundamentals of teaching method and poetic theory. The differences seem to be relatively minor: the result of (1) differences in specific strategies to teach the same principle, such as Justice's advice that students avoid confusion or over-explicitness in a poem by putting expository matter in the title, compared to Halperin's advice to avoid the same thing by putting large, general statements in the form of questions; or Friebert's asking that a very poor poem at a very early stage be rewritten "out of sight of the original piece" in order to find its center, compared to Anderson's rebuilding a poem around one of its large general statements. Or (2) the differences are the result of applying the same principles to the same lines according to the poet-teachers' differences of ear, emphasis, tempo, or literary background (such as the differences of opinion about the anaphora in "My Grandfather, Dying" or about the rhythm of several lines in "Sicilian Semaphore").

But the effects of these differences are nearly always tempered by the reluctance to be dogmatic, the refusal to finish a poem for a student; a desire to be inductive, even when the temptation to give up on a poem or to finish it is great. To the student-poet as artificer the teacher-poets give (or rather offer) advice from their own experience as artificers; to the student-poet as person, perhaps as visionary, they only ask quite literally searching questions, whose answers will require the student to grope and probe and so become inevitably a more perceptive poet.

Group I

DAVID YOUNG
STUART FRIEBERT
ALBERTA TURNER
DAVID ST. JOHN

These four poets worked independently on three poems by students in the Oberlin College writing program. Friebert and Young teach in the program; St. John was then teaching in it (he is now at Johns Hopkins); and Turner is a former colleague of Young and Friebert who teaches poetry writing at nearby Cleveland State University. All but Turner knew the students, and Friebert and Young had worked with them on these poems before.

MY GRANDFATHER, DYING
Martha Moody

But still alive, in that green chair,
with eyes that are bluer,
blinder than they've ever been.

He hasn't had a bath for weeks
but his body

16

smells clean. His skin is clear,
thinner than a membrane and we see
it's holding nothing
but light.

When he rises, slowly,
to place his hands on his wife's shoulders
and walk
we step aside.
Not because his hands are quick enough to touch us,
or that they'd try,
but because we know our place—

apart, the relatives who make
a reluctant pilgrimage
to his home three times a year.
We're not what matters.
What matters is the family left in Sweden,
the ones he never knew,
what matters are the men he taught the courage
to buy Pepsi and not beer.

What matters is the view
from the steeple of the church he built near Paxton.

What matters is the salvation of Edna,
who would have died alone, years ago,
if he hadn't taken her seventy years
and married them to his.

What matters finally
is the soul, the baby soul,
unfolding like an icon in his chest,
filling him with the light
that will soon break through his skin,
surround him like an eggshell as his body
fades away,

the light around the grave that starts us crying
because we've been left behind.

Martha Moody was born in 1955 and received her A.B. from Oberlin
College in 1977. She studied creative writing with Thomas Lux, David
Young, Stuart Friebert, and David St. John and went on to study medi-
cine at the University of Cincinnati.

THE OUTLINE OF MY HEAD
Hank Davis

the outline of my head
makes an irregular gap
in the line of light fixtures
reflected on the library window

outside, through my head
it is deep blue
a tiny shirt travels
inward from the left ear
a boy running the track

my face has no features
he runs what i think
in the failing dusk

cars pass
their headlamps
break through the reflection
i watch them
enter my head
from both sides

garish jewelry
where is the runner?
a man carries a suitcase
up the reflected aisle

i've lost him
he may have left

is he getting stronger?

Hank Davis, born in 1949, received his B.A. in ethnopoetics from Oberlin College. He studied poetry writing with David Young and has led poetry workshops on junior high school and college levels. He lives in Bloomington, Indiana and may go on to graduate studies in West African oral poetry.

WAKING ON DECK
Sarah Brownsberger

I saw a woman in red skirts
Crush cactus in a stone bowl.
I woke, and felt salt tears drying on my skin,
And cirrus in the skies.
Now I know how life is a fragile flame
But I guess I just might live until I see you again.
When this rolling world unfurled my sails
I woke,   and saw
An egret
Poised in red mangroves,
And fragments of bone and tooth
Shifting in sand.
A man with ropes of muscle
Drove a stake into the ground.
I heard my bones moving inside of me
And the northern breeze brushed off my tears
And lifted up the cirrus clouds.
My dream of you had burst;
I woke,   and was healed,   and saw
A woman making breakfast on the beach.

Sarah Brownsberger was born in 1959 and is a student in the Creative Writing Program at Oberlin College under Stuart Friebert and Diane Vreuls. On graduation, she plans to study further in writing and historical linguistics.

DAVID YOUNG

These comments will be brief, partly to reflect my feeling that one should not deluge a student writer, in conference or in workshop, with too many reactions and suggestions—it's better to single out one or two problems that a new version could concentrate on—and partly because no conference or workshop exchange should be one-sided, a teacher's monologue; what should happen, that can't be represented here, is a mutual finding out of subject, theme, intention, strengths, and weaknesses. My purpose here is thus to suggest how I might *start* a conference or a workshop discussion on each of these poems, rather than to predict all the conclusions it might reach or all the issues it might raise as it went along.

The three poems form an interesting group because they seem to represent three levels of accomplishment. The writer of "My Grandfather, Dying," is experienced and writes with a clear sense of purpose and a good control of diction and tone. The writer of the poem that begins "the outline of my head" shows some sophistication of technique and a sense of subject and structure, but doesn't seem nearly as close to having a finished and successful poem. And the writer of "Waking on Deck" is pretty clearly a relative beginner. I'll discuss these poems in that descending order of accomplishment.

"My Grandfather, Dying"

It's trite but useful to begin with some praise, and that is not difficult in the case of "My Grandfather, Dying." It has a ring of truth about it, it takes up a familiar but powerful subject, and, again and again, the author has found images and details that convey the emotional complexity of the experience to the reader. In keeping to my principle of finding one or two aspects to stress for revision, I would (after making it clear that I think the poem isn't far from being finished and successful) argue for change in two areas: a reduction of the "explanatory" elements in the piece; and a strengthening of the rhythms.

My first example of explanatory material that actually tends to limit rather than enhance the meaning of the poem would be the last line; when it is removed and the next-to-last line becomes the close, then the "reason" given in the last line *as well as* other reasons for the crying can be present. I'd argue for the experiential truth of this; when we cry at a funeral, the causes are multiple, not single. And I might also use the example to make the general point that it's as important to know when to let go, to shut up, as it is to know when to take hold and speak. A writer must know how to calculate, probably more from intuition than from any rule or guideline; that to tie that next-to-last line down to any one "because" is to keep the image from gathering its fullest meaning and power in the imagination of the reader.

That example seems clear enough; others may be harder. At this point I would ask the author, if it was a conference, or the class, if it was a workshop, to help find other examples. I suspect we'd want to work on the last three lines of the third stanza ("Not because his hands . . . we know our place"); that we'd go after the phrase "We're not what matters"; and that the cluttered effect at the end of the next-to-last stanza, while not precisely a problem of extraneous explanation, would also get whittled away at. Before long, I think, some brisk editing would have this poem both trimmer and richer in implication.

The rhythm problem is not so easily described and resolved. I'd start by pointing out a strength; that the lines "is the soul, the baby soul, / unfolding like an icon in his chest," take part of their power from their strong, firm movement. I'd contrast them with the line "What matters is the salvation of Edna," which to my ear is almost comically flat, and suggest that more attention to rhythmic weaknesses would strengthen the poem. We would need to consider the effectiveness, if any, of the very short lines: why they are there, whether they work, how what they seem to seek—a sense of emphasis and a hesitation in the poem's movement and thus in its voice—might be more fully accomplished. Here I don't have hard and fast answers, just a strong conviction that the poem will benefit from a going-over in terms of its rhythmic strengths and weaknesses. There are rhythms in our living and our dying, rhythms in our attempt to speak of such things, that a poem like this needs to track and respond to, dance to. It has begun this process through the stanzas and in many of the lines, but my sense of its successful movement comes and goes, an intermittent music.

"The Outline of My Head"
I find it more difficult to diagnose the problems of the second poem. When I first read it, it took me a moment to figure out what was going on. When I did, I thought the use of the window as mirror and see-

through to set up an interplay of mental and physical realities was a
clever and intriguing idea, somewhat similar to the "conceits" of seven-
teenth-century poetry that play with microcosms. The tension between a
solipsistic self and a world that threatens to inundate or extinguish it is a
legitimate subject for poetry, which, since it so often stems from and
reflects that tension, ought to have the license to look straight at it,
though the danger of narcissism will always lurk around attempts to
say "this is what it's like for me when I'm writing, or thinking about
writing, a poem."

But there's something wrong with this poem that keeps my ad-
miration for it theoretical rather than actual. To try to get at that, I
might begin by describing my mixed feelings, my sense that the idea for
the poem is more attractive at the moment than the poem, and then try
to settle on some areas of strength and weakness. I would note that the
middle of the poem—the second, third, and fourth stanzas—strike me as
most successful, while both the beginning and the end seem not to work
very well. Surely the beginning feels clumsy and prosaic; "necessary"
exposition that is neither winning nor graceful. And the end? It seems
to strike a note of melodrama (though that may not have been the
author's intention) that is quite out of place in the poem.

I'd suggest, then, that a concise, graceful beginning be sought, and
the subsequent poem be built around the strengths of the current ver-
sion, the image of the runner and maybe the images of the cars and
the man with the suitcase. I say "maybe" because I have a hunch that
they don't advance the poem significantly over the first image. I think
one good principle of revision is building from strength, trying to iden-
tify the parts of a rough draft that work best, that are truly imaginative,
then reorganizing the poem around them, reducing *and* discovering on
the basis of having learned where the true center of the poem seems to be.

That might be a start for dealing with this poem, but I don't know
whether it would be enough. I think the poem also raises the question
of whether there is enough there, in bemusement with seeing the world
through one's reflection, to make a good poem. I suspect the poem is a
fairly straightforward transcription from experience, which would sug-
gest that its author has not paid enough attention to the fact that what-
ever relation poetry bears to experience, it is to the reader an experience
in itself, a little world of words that does or does not take hold of our

imaginations. A workshop discussion, then, or a conference, might profitably turn to the question of how this poem might go on, how its scope might be widened. And an answer might lie in the principle of imaginative transformation. This poem makes one such transformation: a head turns into a world beyond a window, a world of dusk and occasional light. Does it need to stop there? Might it not go on? That, finally, is a question the author must answer, for at that point the teacher would have to begin writing his/her own poem. But the teacher might be able to think of a useful analogy—a poem which is similar enough that one can point out how it goes on from one imaginative transformation to a series. I can't, at the moment, think of one which is very much like this poem in situation or imagery, but I could discourse endlessly on the general notion of imaginative transformation as a principle of movement and structure in poetry. I might begin by contrasting the "conceit" style mentioned above, which would develop one comparison to its limits, as in Donne, to what someone has called a "nibbling" style, as in Shakespeare's sonnets, where an image gives rise to another image: for instance, "That time of year thou may'st in me behold," which starts with autumn, moves on to twilight, then changes to a dying fire—three images clearly related (and with smaller transformations inside, e.g., trees as ruined churches) but giving way to each other in a restless, expansive sequence. One can find examples of this everywhere. Some of my current favorites are in Hopkins (e.g., "The Starlight Night"), Mandelstam, surrealists like Benjamin Peret, and Rilke, especially in the *Elegies*.

Perhaps my enthusiasm for this principle is too general to have much immediate use for the author of "The Outline of My Head." But immediate use is not the only kind we should offer, and it's terribly important, I have found, to make students understand that while poems must originate in the experiences of their authors, they must eventually achieve independence, with energies of their own that result from the interactions of words and images rather than simply from the feelings that begot them. This was probably easier to understand when poetry seemed less subjective and reportorial. I say "seemed" because I think that poetry that may appear to be simply "confessional" or "documentary" is, if it's good, what poetry has always been, a machine, as Williams himself, whom many take to be a documenter, put it: a machine made out of words.

"Waking on Deck"

The third of these poems, "Waking on Deck," strikes me, as I said
at the outset, as the work of a pretty thorough beginner, and I'd be
disposed to be gentle with it without obscuring the fact that the writer
has a long way to go. I argued earlier for finding something to praise by
way of getting started. That's not easy here, but one could begin by
contrasting the relative effectiveness of the image "fragments of bone
and tooth / Shifting in sand," which is vivid and real, especially in com-
parison with "the northern breeze brushed off my tears" and "a man
with ropes of muscle." The language in these latter images, because of
inexactness and overfamiliarity, simply doesn't work as the writer hopes
it will. Even less effective, to my mind, are the lines which seem to bear
the influence of popular songs: "Now I know how life is a fragile flame /
But I guess I just might live until I see you again." This writer is clearly
willing to try anything! And the result, of course, is a hodgepodge of
possibilities. The images don't connect, the movement is erratic, the
tone is a blur. Even if the language of the pair of lines just quoted was
adequate, they still wouldn't follow in a satisfying way from the first
two images. The effect of the poem, finally, is of a subjectivity and
privacy, mixed with the problems of tired metaphor and "pop" senti-
ment, that fail to include the reader. An attempt to help the writer would
have to be based on the discovery of the poem's background: what locus
of emotions, what dream or dreams, what relationships lie behind this
poem? When that was established, it could be followed by a considera-
tion of how to communicate these things effectively to a reader. In other
words, the poem's ineptness drives us back to the most basic considera-
tions: the language of poetry, form, diction, sequence, consistency,
movement, the power of imagery. I had a teacher once who called cre-
ative writing "bonehead aesthetics," and in a sense that is what it
always is, since the teacher and student need to measure the distance
between whatever the student has produced and an ideal that both can
agree to share. The value of being willing to admit the need for "bone-
head aesthetics" is that it involves one not only in the inadequacies of the
work at hand, but in a consideration of what poetry ought to be, a
question that all of us ought to be able to take a vivid interest in. So
"Waking on Deck," for all its shortcomings, is grist for the mill where the
rude grain of daily language is ground into the marvelous flour from
which we make poetry.

David **Young** was born in 1936. He teaches at Oberlin College and was educated at Carleton College and Yale University. His books of poetry include *Sweating Out the Winter* (1969), *Boxcars* (1973), and *Work Lights* (1977). IIe has also published two studies of Shakespeare and a translation of Rilke's *Duino Elegies* (1978). In 1978 he was the recipient of a Guggenheim Fellowship and an Individual Artists Award from the Ohio Arts Council.

STUART FRIEBERT

I strongly believe in helping students realize finished texts if at all possible. So I usually decide early on if any given piece is far enough along before I'm willing to give very specific criticism. Otherwise I've found myself writing the poem for the student. If it's not far enough along, I try to suggest various broad approaches for looking at the whole landscape of the text again, with a view toward discovering what the poem is about, where it lies. Always a young writer needs to rewrite (at such an unfinished level) the whole text, out of sight of the "original" piece.

"The Outline of My Head"

The second text under consideration, "The Outline of My Head," is just such an unfinished text. It's simply not substantial enough, realized enough to be taken seriously at this point. I'm both confused and bored by its turns. So I'd try to get the writer to start all over again, perhaps with the "runner." In fact, the more I reread it the more I realize I'm really most interested in that runner and his relationship with the man carrying the suitcase, so first I'd cut out all the nonsense about where the narrator's head is in all this, and show the student the following subtext, or collection of phrases I'd drained from the poem:

```
A boy running down a track
my face has no features
he runs what I think
in the failing dusk
........................
where is the runner?
```

```
a man carries a suitcase
..........................
i've lost him
he may have left
is he getting stronger?
```

Now these are nothing more than phrases, but with some glueing and sanding they might stick together well enough so something else can be set on top: the *real* subject of the poem should emerge from this early separation. For me it'd have something to do with the relationship between the runner and the man. On the other hand, I don't give a damn about whether or not they enter the head of the narrator, or how they look when they get there (worst is the phrase, because it's so poeticky, distracting, and gratuitous: "garish jewelry"—awful!). But the sense of loss toward the end of the text seems important, and I as reader but also as writer want to find out something more of that loss, when and how it occurs, what it has to do with (idea of "increasing strength" is not bad!).

"Waking on Deck"

Using what I call the X-ray technique (i.e., what's underneath the text), I come to this on a second reading:

```
A woman in red skirts crushes cactus in a bowl.
When this rolling world unfurls we wake and see
an egret poised in red mangroves and fragments
of bone and tooth in the sand.  A man with ropes
of muscle drives a stake into the ground, bones
move inside him and the wind lifts the clouds.

..........................................................

..........................................................

and see a woman making breakfast on the beach.
```

The man and the woman in the text are more interesting to me than anything the "I" says or does, so I would restrict it, collapse it maybe into the "we" I've introduced in line 2 at best. This "we" might recur in the second stanza to frame the little scene of the man and woman on the beach. There's more life in the first part so far, and I would work hard to balance it in the second stanza, perhaps with a kind of mirror scene, before the woman makes breakfast. That is, something else must still happen before she makes breakfast; it may have to do with healing, but if so, then we as readers must be much more involved in the healing. Otherwise we have another "Take it from me" situation on our hands, and I for one feel cheated.

Notice, too, that on second reading I've come to a much longer line. I felt as the text pulsed along that the whole action of crushing cactus, driving the stake, the movement of bones and clouds, begs for a longer line. One last thing: the title is awful, in no way focuses the poem. It must be a perfect title for this kind of text, something that can't perhaps be said in the text but through which we can look at the little scene still a different way, because so much is going on.

"My Grandfather, Dying"

The pleasure in working with this text comes from an immediate sense that, basically, "it's all there"! Usually, in dealing with undergraduate writing, one is faced with having to ask for more, much more: to get the student to go round and round again, dig up more so a clearer pattern may emerge. Try this, try that, stand it on its head to see if anything else falls out. Anything to generate more material so really splendid choices can be made. As a last resort, do what painters do: look back at the text through a mirror, over your shoulder, anything to get clearer lines, more substance, more life before settling for a "last" version.

Here, however, it is equally important to get the student to stay with *just* this material, not let the hand that writes nervously add distracting material. The text is too rich for that, too far along, too resolved, and anything else of great moment would tip the scales. Which is not to say that final suggestions won't be important. They will, crucially. Because one's goal now should be to help the student write something so perfect at this stage in her development as to insure further work at this level. Something so fine she can draw on it for many other texts, write a whole series as it were, have a "Blue Period." Once done, I mean, and done superbly, this text should generate others of similar and similarly handled material so that she will never forget how to build *this* kind of piece: one that is central to her life, one she has a real stake in, one that is more hers than anyone else's.

On to those final, crucial decisions, then! What I would do now is pretend the poem is mine and let the student watch me rewrite it while I talked aloud about what I was thinking while revising. Martha, in the first stanza I'm changing the last line to read "blinder than ever"— that will make room for a fuller line, enabling the "talking voice" to assert itself where and when it really needs to. And insures that the preceding line, "with eyes that are bluer," has a couplet cousin to itself. In other words, just the tiny bit of slack in "they've ever been" is going to start a wobbling that will topple the poem if allowed to form this early. I would want the second stanza to continue without a subject ("He"), and cut back to

```
    Hasn't had a bath for weeks
    but his body smells clean.
```

That establishes visual line rhythm and keeps the internal couplet alive. The second part of stanza 2 I would change to "His skin is clear, thinner than a membrane, / it holds nothing but light." Likewise, in stanza 3: "and walk / we step aside" should change to "When he rises, slowly, / to place his hands on his wife's shoulders / we step aside"— the *he/we* internal rhyme locks the lines in place. Notice I am insisting on very specific changes. Not to write her poem for her, but to make sure she sees and feels it get airtight. Sees me follow it along one line of resolve. In the middle of all this, if it didn't feel right to me, I'd rip it out of the typewriter and start again. Even do that if one word felt wrong, like a helpless piano student starting the piece again, however far along she got, at the first, slightest intuition of a mistake.

The second half of stanza 3, starting as it does with "Not because . . . ," keeps the major strategy going: "But still alive"—"Hasn't had a bath for weeks"—"Not because his hands are quick enough." The clipped, breathless afterthought, correcting our impressions as we go. To keep this tone in place, that we've taken pains to establish in the last two lines

of stanza 1, I'd try this for the last lines of stanza 3: "or that they'd try. /
We know our place."

The fourth stanza has problems starting; the apposition is awk-
ward and unclear. My first impulse is to drop the first three lines alto-
gether, starting the stanza simply with "We're not what matters," which
nicely cuts across the original voice, the *buts*, and can now carry the
poem on down to the final turn. To strengthen this chance, I'd take out
"what matters are" in the second last line and deal then with the queer-
ness in the final two lines something like this:

```
We're not what matters.
What matters is the family left in Sweden,
the ones he never knew;
his buddies at the lodge
buying Pepsi and not beer; the view
from the church he built near Paxton.
```

I wouldn't touch a word in the second last stanza, it seems just right,
but as for the last stanza (not counting the final couplet), it has some
of the same problems the fourth has. It stutters, is crowded. *But* it is *all*
there, and I'd let the student look over my shoulder now while taking
it apart and putting it back together like this:

```
What matters is the soul, the baby soul,
the icon in his chest,
filling him with the light
that will break through his skin,
wrap around him like an eggshell,
his body fading away:

the light around the grave that starts us
    crying.
```

About that last line, first of all: cutting "because we've been left behind"
restores that beautiful line to its fullness, joins the two parts we've been

anxious to keep separate till now (see couplet talk above) and flies over the whole text with "elegy" for its emblem.

Perhaps the riskiest, but also the most interesting "move" in the whole poem has to do with that "icon." I'd argue that it's a breathtaking extension or deepening of what would have been an acceptable, though tame, ending—gentle, all right, but tame. The icon forces us below the surface to the sharp pain, the *metal* force, underneath. A dive under. It comes up like a lost treasure. And feels good in the chest, the cross buried in all of us.

Stuart Friebert was born in 1931. He directs the creative writing program at Oberlin College and holds a Ph.D. from the University of Wisconsin (Madison). He has published four collections of prose and poetry in German and four collections of poems in English, the most recent of which are *Up in Bed* and *Uncertain Health*. In addition to his poems, he has published translations from the Czech, German, Polish, Spanish, and Italian.

ALBERTA TURNER

If three of my students brought in these poems, I'd rejoice at "My Grandfather, Dying." It knows what it's about. Its intense feeling and dramatic structure would let me suggest fairly specific adjustments of sound and phrase. I could help Davis's poem, too, though less easily, because though the dominant metaphor is clear and fresh in the first half of the poem, he seems to lose it toward the end. Also, the emotional thrust which should control that image seems to be weak or absent, almost as if the poem were written from nothing more than a fascination with the image itself. I wouldn't at this stage know just what to help the poem *become*. "Waking on Deck" is the weakest of the three and the hardest to help. The urge behind it seems to be to write something "poetic," without the emotional force necessary to turn occasion into poem. Each of these illustrates the central problem of the writing teacher: he must start by trying to identify what the poem is trying to be. Only then can he decide what is standing in its way and suggest to the student-poet specific ways to satisfy his poem's need.

"My Grandfather, Dying"

The most nearly finished is "My Grandfather, Dying." The feelings of tenderness, wonder, almost exaltation that come through this early draft are already embodied in the controlling image: light, supported by other images that imply clarity or simplicity and so make irradiation possible. *Blue, blind, clean, clear, membrane-thin, skin, eggshell* lead inevitably to the "light around the grave." The poem's "point" seems to be its tone, and that tone is well enough controlled so that a first reading reveals it—at least to me. I'd start by telling the student this, not in the words I've used here, but by telling her specifically how the poem has made me feel about the grandfather. If she agrees, I'll pick out the images and mention the sequence that makes me react as I do; if she disagrees, I'll ask her to show me what I've missed. In either case, she and I together can start right now to edit this poem, to discuss and eliminate whatever stands in the way of the poem's realizing itself.

Because this poem's impact is more emotional than intellectual, I would suggest that she use syntax which creates the jerks, sparks, and fragments in which emotion occurs, rather than the more connected and subordinated syntax of exposition. We need to see and hear her grandfather with tenderness and awe rather than to understand him. Two or three examples would be enough for a student whose control is already so strong. In paragraph 1 I'd suggest leaving out *with, that,* and *are;* I'd mention that the second sentence of paragraph 2 might read, ". . . His skin, clear membrane, / holds nothing but light" and that paragraph 3 might read, "we step aside, / we know our place." The heavy anaphora of "what matters," repeated six times, seems especially out of place rhythmically, like a declaration. Could it be reduced to three or even two?

I'd also suggest scanning the poem for details that don't help create the tone of radiance and wonder or that take our eyes off the grandfather. The "green chair" and "He hasn't had a bath for weeks" are not such details. Their mundane homeliness and individuality make the experience seem real and the irradiation, by contrast, a true miracle. But I wonder about the hands not trying to touch or about the reluctance of the pilgrimage. Don't these focus too much attention on the viewer, especially since they are not an actual part of this encounter? And the last line, the sudden emphasis on the speaker's self-pity; couldn't the sense of deprivation be implied by "starts us crying," which at the same time implies a vast complex of emotions which are much more than just envy? I'm not sure. It's not my poem. But I'd mention it to the poet, talk it over with her and let her decide.

I'd also question the image of the icon. The metaphor of the baby soul unfolding in the eggshell seems so consistent with the poem's tone and its purpose to identify death with growing life that *icon* seems too formally artificial—almost as if Yeats's golden bird of Byzantium were hatching in that shell. Icon and bird both unfold but not by the same kind of unfolding. Also in this paragraph, isn't "as his body fades away" gratuitous? When light becomes eggshell, hasn't body already faded?

Finally, I'd suggest a few, very few, changes in diction, chiefly to avoid heaviness and formality in a poem whose diction is mostly simple and informal. For example, *rises* (line 10), *place* (line 11), *salvation* (line 27), *surround* (line 36). Wouldn't *stands* and *put* be more consistently informal for the first two? *Salvation* could be implied by such rephrasing as "What matters is Edna / who would have died alone years ago / if he hadn't married her seventy years to his." And *surround* could become *hold,* which seems not only less formal but more accurate for an eggshell. *Fades away,* which is a sentimental cliché, would have disappeared in an earlier revision, as would the abstract and Latinate word *reluctant.*

Techniques I'd have to work on in most poems are well enough controlled in this one so that I'd not mention them except by way of compliment. Lineation is well controlled, sounds don't jar, syntax is clear, clichés are scarce and used less for rhetorical effect than for simplicity and directness, the details chosen are unique and inconspicuous, which makes them seem inevitable. I'd tell the student all this, lest she make too many changes. And I'd close our conference by saying that with very little editing this would be a distinguished poem. It's possible that this first conference would enable her to finish it.

"Waking on Deck"

But it will take more than one conference to finish the other two poems. After reading "Waking on Deck," I'm chiefly confused. What is the core, the heart, the central urge of this poem? The title suggests a sudden awareness, a sort of epiphany—from dream to waking or to a different sort of dream. The first four lines (the first two against the second two) imply such an awakening. But the next two show no relation to the first four. The image of the fragile flame is not necessitated by crushing a plant or drying tears. All are destroyed, but their destructions are of different kinds. Intention is involved in the first, natural inevitability in the second, and accident in the third, and the connection between any of the three and the fragility of the persona's life while waiting for the loved one is not clear. The image of the persona as ship is a new metaphor merely mentioned and left. The poet doesn't develop the feeling of being a ship. The physical point of view shifts, too. From the ship the poet sees the egret, as one could from a deck, then immediately the fragments of bone and tooth, which could be seen only from close by, on the beach itself, then the man driving the stake, who could be seen from the deck of the ship again. The persona then returns to the epiphany of the title and the first four lines. Bones move, clouds lift, the dream bursts. Waking is healing. Healing is returning to the mundane world of breakfast on the beach. Now I begin to see the structure of the poem—and also what's missing. The structure is dreaming, then waking to a world disoriented by the dream, then being wholly awake and totally healed of the dream. What's missing is the dream and the mood engendered by it. Without it there can be no healing and no poem.

Until the poet creates for me the dream and its mood, I can't help the poem much in matters of editing: lineation, paragraph division, rhythm, diction, appropriateness of metaphor. Any specific change I might suggest at this time, such as making the point of view consistent, might just compel the poet to keep lines and images in the poem which would otherwise disappear as she clarified her vision. Even the triteness of most of the images and their traditionally "poetic" phrasing must wait until the poet has decided just what the poem is doing. If she isn't sure, I'd ask which of the images meant most to her, what her eyes saw first on waking: the clouds, the egret, the man pounding the stake? Was she still in the dream when she woke? Did any of these images take on the emotional coloring of the dream? Just what details of the images had this coloring: the imminent flight of the egret, the height of the clouds, the savagery of the man's stroke? Given a full dream and a shocked waking, the comforting sight of a woman (in a red skirt?) making breakfast on the beach might indeed heal.

"The Outline of My Head"

Hank Davis's poem begins with a startling image (original so far as I know) which makes a dead metaphor come alive: "Thoughts go through my mind." The poet faces a window from inside at dusk. The room is lighted, and it's dark enough outside to make the window a mirror for what is inside the room: lighted lamps, a man carrying a suitcase, and the mass of the poet's own head. But the world outside the window is still light enough so that he can see through the window, within the space covered by the reflection of his head, a boy running and cars passing. What happens there seems to pass through his head from one unknown place to another. There is sequence, direction, yet mystery about whence or whither or why. So much we learn from the first three paragraphs. Then the point of view becomes double: the car headlights break through the reflection so that they seem to move inside the head, like the runner, but also to sparkle like jewelry on the outside of the head in the reflection. They are simultaneously inside and outside the head, both literally and metaphorically. Then another shift, and we are watching the reflection of the inside of the room—a man carrying a suitcase behind and to one side of the reflected head. The poet loses the reflection, presumably because the man with the suitcase is now directly behind the reflected head and so no longer reflected, or he's left the room and is out of both pictures entirely.

As a reader, I'm confused and disappointed after paragraph 3. The poet has made me want to stay inside that head, to see patterns of direction, intersection, or deflection, perhaps even explosion, to see that dead metaphor come alive as fully and complexly as possible, but I'm wrenched away to look at the container of this drama (ornamented by what goes on inside it) and then to follow the progress of a thought (the man with the suitcase) which disappears into the head instead of appearing into it like the runner. And the last line introduces a concept not dealt with earlier, the concept of increased or decreased strength. How did this confusion happen? Isn't the poet aware of the gift he's been given by that first perception of people and cars going through the head like thoughts? Is he just collecting examples of reflections and transparencies at random? He seems almost to be building a metaphysical conceit, but by the rules of surrealism.

Such a logical failure, it seems to me, is only one symptom that the poet has not yet found the poem's emotional center. Is it wonder, fear, ambivalence, or delight that accompanies his recognition that the things passing in the dusk, outside the library, outside the lighted scene, represent half-understood urges, half-thoughts going through the pre-conscious mind and separate from his normal conscious social activity? When the poet decides what his feelings about this discovery are, he can go back and decide whether he really wants to talk about lights from within as jewelry for the outside of the head, whether the man with the suitcase should function, like the "man from Porlock,"* to interrupt the inner movement or appear in the same field as the runner, and whether the last line is an expression of fear or hope. I wouldn't dare do a thing to the poem until he decides. If he doesn't decide while we're talking about the poem or convince me that I've misread the poem entirely, which I may have done, I'll send him back at dusk to the library to look longer at the world which runs through the feature-less outline of that head. Later, I can see, we'll need to work on phrasing and lineation, probably on selecting and sequencing the details so that they require less author intervention or explanation in order to take their place in the pattern of movement. But all that is part of the second or editing stage. The poem hasn't finished "happening" yet, and I don't want to stand in its way.

Alberta T. Turner, born in 1919, is a poet and professor of English at the Cleveland State University where she has taught creative writing since 1964. She is director of the Cleveland State University Poetry Center and an associate editor of *Field: Contemporary Poetry and Poetics.* Her own volumes of poetry include *Need, Learning to Count,* and most recently, *Lid and Spoon.*

DAVID ST. JOHN

I would like to begin by speaking very generally about the teaching of poetry, so that my later comments about the specific poems might have a context, and so that my prejudices will be known from the outset.

I believe that writing, the *craft* of poetry writing, *can* be taught. I feel young writers can be shown the best ways to make use of their talents, not by prescribing a formula their poems must follow, but rather

---

* Coleridge was prevented from finishing "Kubla Khan" by the interruption of a "man from Porlock."

by showing them how to be attentive to the strong points in their writing, to what seems most vital and immediate in—and particular to—their own "voice." This is not to say that "talent" or "inspiration" can be taught, and that is most likely a good thing. But students can be taught to recognize sources in themselves, the resonances of their own experiences and concerns, and it is that which provides the impulse to seek themselves, *for* themselves, in language.

With beginning writers, the process is often so simple as "show don't tell." Once a young writer begins to pay attention to the *details* of the experience rather than to the overriding (and often, for them, overwhelming) emotion of the event, a strong beginning has been made. At this point, it is easier to begin to develop with the young writer a vocabulary with which to speak about the poems. Criteria of success in regard to image, line, tone, and overall structure can be discussed. All of this happens, naturally, as a process of learning, as the young writer begins to recognize, through the reading of other poets and through the criticism, help, and guidance of both teachers and peers, those qualities of tone and particulars of image which seem to best reflect his or her interests and poetic concerns.

With students I feel to be more advanced, perhaps students who have been writing three or four years, I begin to press them to pay close attention to how, in other poets, a sense of *person,* or *presence,* or *self* is exposed within a poem. I ask them, often, to write imitations so that the relationship of tone and style in Poet X becomes clearer to them. When they see that Poet X's impact is not simply a choice of subject, a highly imagistic (for example) style, or a cold, distant tone, but rather a marriage of those and other elements as well, it becomes easier to talk about the difficulty of exposing within one's own poem the *person,* the *presence,* one wishes for the poem, whether that person or presence is the poet himself or herself or a persona.

Clearly, the degree to which I press this concern is dependent upon the progress I feel the student has made; often, such a pressure too early in a beginning writer's experience will lead, I think, only to self-consciousness or self-absorption.

Also, it seems to me that, perhaps regardless of the quality of teaching the student receives, it will be the discoveries in and illuminations of more private moments which will continue to serve as sources and motives for a young writer. And, however magical or transforming those moments, unless they are attended by a love of language and wordplay, they will never arrive in poems. As teachers, working with poetry writing as a craft, we might possibly help make the conjunction, in poetry, of speech, experience, emotion, and intelligence a clearer and more exciting act.

Of the three poems under discussion, "My Grandfather, Dying" is by far the most accomplished. "Waking on Deck," although perhaps less cohesive than "The Outline of My Head," seems to me far more promising in that there appears to be a *source,* a prevailing anxiety, from which the poem has issued.

"The Outline of My Head"

The Davis poem, to my taste, is simply the establishment of a moderately clever conceit which is then mechanically played out, without, for me, any interest being aroused about either the speaker of the poem or about the "runner" who circles the track. The poem seems to me an example of what young writers are often encouraged to do, that is, to play out a single image or idea to its conclusion. I feel not only do I know nothing new about the speaker or myself, I feel as if the poem allows me to know nothing at all. Perhaps this is unfair. I *do* know the writer of the poem is capable of noticing a visual moment and of attempting to imaginatively transform that moment. Yet in choosing an image which asks to rely so heavily on its mirrorlike and reflective qualities, to supply whatever interest and tension the poem has, I feel the poem reflects and mirrors nothing of the speaker, his needs, *anything* which might cause me to wish to enter the landscape of the poem. I am being general, perhaps, in my objections, but only because I would wish to turn this writer back toward some sense of his own ambitions for himself in the poem; the ambitions here seem to me so superficial, having only to do with writing—the "writing-out" of an image—and little to do with the speaker or a sense of life, let alone any inner life, even though in the nature of its conceit that is *precisely* what the poem advertises as its goal.

"Waking on Deck"

Although the details of "Waking on Deck" betray and violate its purpose, I am in more sympathy with its ambitions, which appear to

center around the separation of two lovers, while inviting a conjoin-
ing of the figure of the woman in the poem with the speaker and the
figure of the man "with ropes of muscle" with the "you." If these figures
do not serve as the actual elements of this equation, they still function
as tangential shadow-entities to the speaker and the "you." The poem
is loaded with clichés, lots of tears and clouds. Yet the motive behind
providing a dreamscape which will serve as context for the speaker's
resolution with the fact of separation, the healing, seems proper to the
poem. What is a problem is that we, as readers, are never allowed to be
situated to the poem. We have no real way to draw the figures of the
woman and the man into any revealing relation with the speaker and
the "you." This, it seems to me, aside from mistakes in detail which
could easily enough be changed, is the crucial problem of "Waking on
Deck."

"My Grandfather, Dying"

"My Grandfather, Dying" seems to me to be successful not only for
its intelligence in recreating for us a familiar and intimate anxiety, but
in its ability to establish quite invisibly an authority of voice. The pres-
ence of the speaker in the poem is one we recognize as an intimate to
the grandfather's affairs, the right and proper guide to a place, a land-
scape that we may not wish to enter for the memories and pain it might
hold for us as well.

The poem employs the repetition of the phrase "what matters" with
great effect. We are taken by its movement through the practical to the
spiritual. The ending of the poem returns us to ourselves, left out of
the final—and necessarily private—globe of light surrounding the body,
the grave. The details of the grandfather's personal history, early in the
poem, give us a sense of a *person*, a real person we might care about;
and through the combination of the distance occasioned by pain and
the urgency of peculiar details in the voice of the poem, we are made
to join in that caring. For its occasional missteps in tone (the "What
matters is the salvation of Edna" stanza, for example), the poem ac-
complishes a presence of self in the voice which we recognize as hav-
ing a vital concern, a painful and frightening story, and an elegiac
conversation it wishes—and we wish—to share.

David St. John was born in 1949 and teaches in the Writing Seminars at John Hopkins University. He studied at California State University, Fresno, and at the Iowa Writers' Workshop. He was awarded an NEA Fellowship in poetry in 1976 and a Guggenheim Fellowship in poetry in 1977. He is the author of *Hush,* a book of poems.

Group II

WILLIAM STAFFORD
LEWIS TURCO

These two poets worked independently on two poems provided by two of Stafford's students and on one provided by Turco from a student magazine, whose author he did not know. Stafford teaches poetry writing at Lewis and Clark College, Portland, Oregon; Turco directs the writing program at the State University of New York, Oswego.

A PORTRAIT OF THE DAY
Bill Sloan

morning, afternoon, and evening
A portrait of the day should be simple.

green morning, brown afternoon, and black evening
A portrait of the day should be simple.

With morning's green, afternoon's brown, and evening's black,
a portrait of the day should be very simple.

With morning's green painted on the edges of the day, afternoon's brown set in the foreground, and evening's black dispersed across the colors, a portrait of the day, with a suitable frame, should be very simple.

With morning's green painted around the edges of the day,
creating the impression of sunlight through curtained windows
and clothes on hardwood floors, afternoon's brown set in the
foreground, intermixing on the edges with green, turning the
morning face to brownsad afternoon, and evening's black dis-
persed across the colors, reminding the observer that the
absence of light will prevail, a portrait of the day, with
a suitable frame to complement its wild design, should be
very simple.

With morning's green painted around the edges of the day,
creating an impression of sunlight through curtained windows
and clothes on hardwood floors, that digresses into hues of
minutes and hours, through lacquered halls and coffee, through
artbooks and palettes searching for colors and symbols, after-
noon's brown set in the foreground, intermixing on the edges
with green, turning the morning face to brownsad afternoon,
trying to find the spot where green ends and brown begins,
following in the footsteps of one who went before, through
tea and conversation, throwing flowers at a singer's feet,
beginning to see that this job is not so easy, and evening's
black dispersed across the colors reminding the observer
that the absence of light will prevail, that sees the day
changing in degrees like the colors of the spectrum from ra-
diating green to blackdeath, a portrait of the day, with a
suitable frame, carved in a way that would complement such a
wild piece, that would firmly transfix the images of a day
upon the wall for all to see, should be very simple.

Bill Sloan was born in 1956 and studied at the State University of New
York, Potsdam, and at St. Lawrence University and is doing graduate
work at the State University of New York, Buffalo. He studied with Albert
Glover and Robert Creeley. He is completing his first volume of poetry.

BROTHER AND SISTER
Michael Pauly

No one was there

when I became your brother.
Just you and me and our mouths
wrapped around some scream,
some sign of first breath
or recognition.
It was so cold then. And yet
we didn't seek the house or
any shelter by the roadway,
but slid farther in our grip
hoping each white star that tore
from the blackness beyond
was the right one.

Now, years later, there is some great
coldness, some shiver in my blood that
makes me seek the place where
fire burns and forgets its ash.
And in that flame I dream
my way back to the storm and find
the snow I've always known.
Fresh, infallible,
I gaze over the absolute distance
that separates us perfectly.

Perfect distance it is . . .
the perfect distance of love.

Michael Pauly was born in 1953 and received his B.A. in English and Biology from Lewis and Clark College in 1976. He has done research in cancer and genetics and is currently studying agricultural crop science at Oregon State University.

WINDOW—WE DO NOT SEE
Barbara Stafford

Window—we do not see
shivers for wind;
push the molding away
then clutch the latch
in case it really happens.

A stone could hit;
you believe in this:
the chance
to break light like the windows of Chartres.

A cold morning might draw children
to play with thimbles against the frost cover,
or rain to make us remember.

You find in dreams
that eyes come close
and hands touch.
Condensed drops of light
hold this breath
from the image darkness reflects.
We pull curtains before the possibility.
You will never know.

Barbara Stafford was born in 1956. An art major at Lewis and Clark College, she has studied creative writing with Vern Rutsala and William Stafford.

WILLIAM STAFFORD

THE MINUET: SIDLING AROUND STUDENT POEMS

My first impulse, when confronted with a student's writing, is to become steadfastly evasive until some signal from the student indicates a direction where the student is ready to go. I want to become the follower in this dance, partly because of some principles about what can be truly helpful in such an interchange, and partly because I have learned that the area between us is full of booby traps: the writer may have many kinds of predispositions, hang-ups, quirks, needs, bonuses. How the student comes toward me across that area is a crucially important beginning for whatever dancing there is going to be.

The first move is the student's move, not mine.

Of course, even handing me the writing is a move, and I am ready to give a slight twitch in return—slight, for a reason. And now I must try to formulate something about that reason. I assume that a writing—a poem, say—is sort of like an iceberg, with only a small part of its real self visible. If I am to be helpful, I need all the signals I can get, about the deeper drifts, the potentials, the alternatives actually ready to function for the main person involved—the student.

Not my life, my knowledge, my insight, but the student's whole life and potential are the main focus in our encounter. And I have to converge. Or so I see the process.

The balance I need, early in the encounter, induces from me only minimum commitments. If I charge into the poem, I might either take it over or alienate the writer; I might wildly misread some main current in its actual or potential development; and I might enhance rather than decrease that dominance implied by teacher-student conferring. Surely our direction is to be toward the writer's own taking over of the writing. My ideal response becomes something like "Uh-huh . . . oh . . . where? . . . ummm." And ideally the writer begins to tell, assert, maybe question on particulars. On particulars I can hazard a human response. But I must rid myself of the burden of being the person who makes those decisions that must be made by the writer.

"A Portrait of the Day"

Still, once the minuet steps have begun, what positive moves can be made in consultation with a student? How would the dance continue on a poem like "A Portrait of the Day"?

I ask myself—and might even ask the writer—what main current or attraction led forward through the writing of this poem. What successive closures were making the writing process satisfying? How could the writer sense that something was developing? These questions occur to me on this poem because I see quickly that it is a sequence of patterns with increments that carry forward, part by part. A glance at the longer and longer sections of the poem will reveal this kind of pattern. And a look at the wording confirms what is happening; one of the satisfactions for the writer must have been the working out of a glimpse that showed something simple and then simply developed by means of repeated accretions of wording. For me, the search for satisfactions that carry a writer forward is an important search: I feel that one of my most valid functions is to induce the inner guides and securities that will sustain the artist through those independent, lonely encounters with the material. I remind myself that this one poem may not be the best focus for my efforts, that the development of the writer's appetite, confidence, inventiveness, flexibility—these are much more important than whether this poem ever gets off the ground.

So I hang back from quibbling about obvious oddities that might snag my attention—capitals or not, periods or not, line breaks that are acrobatic. But I am ready to raise questions about small things, if such questioning proves to be the easiest way for me to remain mobile and harmless but still engaged, in our interchanges.

In this poem I would be ambitious to explore *outward:* Why does it not continue—get even longer? Why does it not start from an even more simple beginning stanza? Could the continuity of the art element throughout (portrait, colors, palettes, etc.) be more intensified? Somehow, could there be more lightning-flickers of realization that would hint at a background validating the enigmatic "should be" of the refrain?

But I would explore such questions only if the writer showed an interest. If I could, I would keep from having any good ideas of my own. Finally, I would indicate that I follow the gesture of the poem down the page as the sections widen and deepen. I would try to lean away from evaluation. And would probably suggest we turn to further poems.

"Window—we do not see"

It happens that I know the writer of this poem well. For this reason, and in order to take up a variety of approaches, I will juggle into a new approach. But the general stance indicated for the preceding poem might very well characterize most of the moves in relation to this poem—slow approach, readiness to retreat, interest in the first moves made by the writer.

I am attracted (though I don't want the writer to know anything about my *evaluative* feelings) by a certain combination of elements in this poem—its centering definitely around "window," but its readiness to rove oddly out into fairly wild connections—stones, rain, thimbles, dreams. As a reader, I am ready for the demands put upon me by the swerve into the last line—"You will never know." But I cherish the opportunity to stay stupid a long time as I stare at the lines in the company of the writer. Somewhere in all this sequence there may lurk some organizing principles that mean more to the writer than anything so far put into the poem. I do not want to get in the way of something ready to happen in the still-evolving life of the poem.

Tugging at me are impulses to free main parts that want to become important in constructions that at first hide amid chance elements in what seems like a preliminary draft. I think that often a poem can shake down from amid nouns and verbs cluttering along in its early drafts. I would like the student to do the shaking and the recognizing that may follow. If I rush in, I may distort the main drift. My effort is to find out, while staying clear during developments, what is important to the student.

But even though unspoken, between the student and me there begins to accumulate a kind of ideal revision in my own mind. The student would never encounter this, but to indicate something of the background from which remarks would come I'll hazard the ghost poem hiding between us:

WINDOW

```
We do not see it,
it shivers for wind—
clutch the latch, lest
it really happens—

That a stone hit.  We
believe in this:
```

chance, light breaking
like the windows of Chartres.

Or a cold morning might bring
children, thimbles against
frost. Or rain
to make us remember.

We find it in dreams—
eyes come close, hands
touch, drops of light
hold our breath.

It's an image darkness
reflects. We pull curtains
before that possibility
we will never know.

I want to make the lines help. But mostly I want to find out what the student leans toward in any survey of the poem. And I do not want to make it a "good" poem. Nor say it is good—or bad. Together, we want to find out what it is.

"Brother and Sister"

All the evasions, noncommittal stances, readiness to be led that characterize my encounter with the preceding poems would be part of my usual approaches to a poem like "Brother and Sister." But some other elements might also be present.

One is a twinge of envy. I would cultivate that twinge, let it teach me that I should read student's poems with at least as much attention as I gladly give when I read Keats. Have I been adequate in my reading of earlier poems? Have I allowed myself to hover above the poems rather than plunging into them, as language among friends invites us to do? I savor my envy and prepare to let it gleam through if anything like an evaluative interchange should happen at the end of considering this poem.

Who is this student with the definite, driving, deft first sentence? How does it happen that so many of the lines break at places so helpful for keeping me leaning forward into the unfolding of a steadily implied richness of feeling? This poem elicits quite a bit of my allegiance, as I take the ride it gives. And maybe by reading it myself aloud between us or listening to the student read it aloud, I permit myself some tremendous signal of approval, like a raised eyebrow or a leaning forward at certain places. My role is an easy one, if I am permitted to take it—I want to learn what guided the writer, what not-yet-written-in portions there might be in this poem. I am interested in the choices the writer feels as the lines progress. Maybe this poem shouldn't be any better—it might turn into a fabrication not fully enough engaged with this writer's continuing motivations. I stay careful.

And there are some regrets, not just regrets about technique (I think—I'm not even sure what that is, or what fallings-off from technique might mean in this poem), but regrets about what seem to me possibly relapses from faith on the part of the writer. Maybe this writer is being corrupted already by success—why "dream"—why not just "find"? why "always known"—why not just "known"? why "absolute distance"—why not just "distance"? And "the perfect distance of love" strikes me as a dangerous last line, a sell-out.

But I remember my twinge of envy. Maybe my old teacher-balance is gone. Sustained by my confusion, I lean back into the safer—and more helpful—position: "What do you think?"

I might even get back into so good a balance I can be helpful and valid and honest and indirect: "Come on, cheer me up—I know you've got them—show me some of your bad poems."

William Stafford, born in 1914, teaches literature at Lewis and Clark College. He received his Ph.D. from the University of Iowa. His most recent books include *Stories that Could be True* and *Writing the Australian Crawl.*

LEWIS TURCO

POETRY: THE ART OF LANGUAGE

In my workshops we operate by what have come to be known as Turco's Principle and Corollary:

1. Just because you don't *know* what you're doing doesn't mean you're not doing it; and,
2. Learn what you're doing so well that you don't have to *know* what you're doing.

Only one of these student poets has discovered the Principle, which is to say, he or she is aware of structure and how it operates to release meaning and pleasure.

"Brother and Sister"

If we are to discuss two of these pieces, we might add an Axiom: The reader has no way of knowing what's going on in your head unless you put it all on paper. I am lost, in "Brother and Sister," until the last line, but the last line doesn't help me to understand the rest of the poem, which seems to me to be very private and exclusive—it just lies there and offers up a cliché masquerading as a profound statement.

Some sense of structure would have helped. This, like the other two poems, is written in prose mode, not verse mode. Verse is *metered* language, prose is *unmetered* language, which is not to say that prose is without rhythm. Successful prose poems derive their rhythms from grammatic structures—line-by-line phrasing, sentences in parallel constructions, stanzaic paragraphs, and so forth. These structures follow some sort of line of development, such as a chronology. The first two lines of "Brother and Sister" seem to set up, first, a birth and, second, a system of phrasing: each line is a phrase, the two lines together are a sentence, and each line contains three stresses.

But the next four lines are a sentence fragment—parallel structure is abandoned. The phrasing continues, but after line 4 the rhythms change: four stresses in line 5 (with overstressing through alliteration in the first two of the five syllables in the line and in the last two

through consonantal echo), and two stresses in line 6 (which con-
tinues the echo in the second syllable, but otherwise drops sonics and
introduces the first four-syllable word of the poem). The effect of all
this, rhythmically, sonically, and grammatically, is anticlimactic and
dissonant.

On the level of the sensory the poem is even more confusing. The
first vivid image of the poem is introduced ("Just you and me and our
mouths / wrapped around some scream"), but the reader begins to
wonder what's going on. Why are brother and sister both present at
the birth? Are they twins? Why do they scream simultaneously, for both
cannot be born at once? "First breath" may be all right, but "recogni-
tion"? Do newly born infants recognize? The word *some* is so vague and
offhand that it belies the specificity of the rest of the image.

The poem slips more and more insensibly into such vaguenesses
and disharmonies, until it achieves its cliché. I won't belabor the point,
except to point out that, just after the first stanzaic break even the sys-
tem of phrasing is dropped, then later reaffirmed. Clearly, the poet has
not learned his or her craft well enough to have achieved the state of
the Corollary, the Principle, nor even of the Axiom. He or she has not
taken the time or trouble to become aware of the structural premise
of the first few lines of the piece so that it might achieve unity on at
least one level.

"Window—we do not see"

"Window—we do not see" is better to a degree. It, too, is a prose
poem built on phrasing, but in line 3 of the second stanza the phrasing
begins to break down, as in "Brother and Sister," and as a result rhythm
is lost. The first three stanzas of this piece add another structural
premise: Each stanza will consist of one sentence, but this device is
dropped in stanza 4.

The unity of the poem is to be found on the sensory level: the
poem is built throughout on images. However, the images are so pri-
vate and disjunctive that the reader is as puzzled to understand the
poet's train of "thought" (in this case, visual thought) as he was in
"Brother and Sister." Furthermore, who is the "you" introduced in
stanza 2? Is it the reader, the poet, some third person, or the impersonal
one in disguise? What is the situation? How many people are involved?
There is a difference between ambiguity and obscurity—the former

amplifies meaning, whereas the latter blocks it. Both these poems are obscure because the poets have used private images and words with personal, not universal, associations. They have failed to give the reader landmarks in the landscapes of their minds.

"A Portrait of the Day"

The author of "A Portrait of the Day" has achieved the state of the Principle, quite clearly. Though he or she may not know the term, the technique used is called *prolepsis:* an expansion on a general statement, particularizing it and giving further information regarding it. Furthermore, incremental repetition is used, and, grammatically, each stanza is one sentence. There is phrasing in the first three stanzas, but we are not confused when it is dropped because the poem is so frankly a prose poem (it is not "free verse," which is a contradiction in terms, because verse is *metered;* it cannot be meter*less,* though it may be variably metered), and the phrases are so long that there is no sense of a premise abandoned, especially since the poem's rhythms do not derive from phrasing, but from repetitions.

None of these poems is by one of my students; I can therefore say, without fear of being suspected of partiality, that when I saw "A Portrait of the Day" I knew I had stumbled upon a Poet with a capital *P*. A Poet is interested in the language he or she uses to body forth his or her emotions, thoughts, and sensations. Many students believe that structure (or form) and poetry can be divorced, and that the former can be ignored. But the two things are one thing—language *is* the poem. One need not use traditional structures, but one does need to structure so that the reader can follow. "A Portrait of the Day," so far as I am aware, is uniquely structured, but the structure is clear. So is the poem, therefore, though it is dense and rich.

One can merely, it seems to me, quibble with "A Portrait of the Day." Only here and there—in single words and an occasional phrase which slip from one level of diction to another—can one point to flaws. For instance, in stanza 6 "this job is not so easy," and the word *wild* in "such a wild piece" are not in keeping with the sophisticated level of diction of the rest of the poem.

My advice to the other two poets? I don't care what you do, so long as you do it well. Begin to learn what it is you are doing.

And to the author of "A Portrait of the Day"? Keep writing.

Lewis Turco, born in 1934, received his B.A. from the University of Connecticut and his M.A. from the University of Iowa. He is director of the Program in Writing Arts at the State University of New York at Oswego. He has written twelve books, including *The Book of Forms: A Handbook of Poetics* (1968) and nine collections of poems, including *First Poems* (1960) and *A Cage of Creatures* (1978). He is a SUNY Faculty Exchange Scholar.

Group III
SANDRA McPHERSON
HENRY CARLILE

These poets are husband and wife. They worked independently on two poems contributed by one student of each, Carlile at Portland State University and McPherson at the Aspen Writers' Conference.

MOTHER'S SONG OF STRANGERS
Paul Minx

The mother like a fine-toothed comb,
the rich chocolate hair, the four steps
from her vanity to the bathroom mirror.
Mother plays her hair like a
violin. Children come to hear her.
Father plays her hair in lust.

Mother is a beautiful horse. No one
can ride her. She wears her hair
like a gown and gallops the village.
At night mother plays her hair
to sleep.

Three bold men, like night
come and sleep with her.
Mother lies with the goats and the sheep.
Mother opens the door to her womb
that speaks no secrets, only sings

in a high, thin voice
like gold wire: her song of strangers,
her song of the gifts they bring,
of being wanted by all men,

of taking her own life away from them,
for herself.

Paul Minx was born in 1953 and has studied at Indiana University and the University of California at Davis. He has studied creative writing with Sandra McPherson and Marvin Bell at The University of Iowa's Writers' Workshop.

A SECOND VISIT TO MILLER'S GRAVE
Mark Jones

Know that Winter found Miller and his blade.
I'd been there in Summer. The heavy wood
He'd stroked apart, that I violently heaped,
Still is heaped, and now burns with such slow
Flame as scarcely warms the earth. Yet it grows
Light. And amaranth skulks at every fence
To litter his dead ranch with life. The fence
Depends on it for business, as a blade
Depends on flesh to cut; flesh that bleeds, grows
As though to keep blades busy, and the wood
Is no different. The season there is slow,
Cold—deliberate, cooling the wood I heaped,
Cautious not to move a heaped
Thing too fast. Coyotes used to leap this fence,
Smirk in the field, make progress on the slow
House, circle and howl, then, fast like his blade,

Scoot. I never saw, but "In the wood!
Back in the wood, boy!" he points, and grows
Excited, shakes me, and the shadow grows
Quite still, till he races through the snow, heaped
On the field unbroken but by still fence
Shadows and him. And all's still but the wood,
Which is yellow in the gold moon and blade
Shaped, carving swerving blue tree ghosts like slow
Ceremonial dancers in the snow, slow
Like thin smoke swaying. A story grows
How Miller carving his bounty with blade,
And with soulless carcass on carcass heaped,
Went mad. Now they add, his headstone by the fence
Is no more wood than his stone heart was wood,
And carcasses by the half-cord like wood
Now tumble as kindling, blue with a slow
Burning. But it's not like that: he feared fence
And dog alike; a stand of trees that grows,
No less than flame that needs it. He heaped
Crime on crime, till no book nor compass blade
Would show him true North, but his wood still grows
Consumed with the slow snow flame that's heaped
On it, no less than fence and rusted blade.

Mark Jones was born in 1957 and is an undergraduate at Portland State University. He studied creative writing with Primus St. John and Henry Carlile and plans to continue writing as well as teach French or English.

SANDRA McPHERSON

These two poems have in common a convincing rhetoric. The poets insist in them. The rhetorical drive is consistent and constant throughout them. The poems seem to have a strong skeleton. Each poem suggests an intricate mind creating it.

"Mother's song of strangers"
Dominating "Mother's song of strangers," the repeated assertions of what mother is or does convey the power which is her province, the

hold she has on the writer and on others in her family. This is not the
first draft of the poem, but a much sounder second or third draft. The
first draft reads as follows after an identical first and second stanza:

```
    Mother's tune is this:
   "My long dark hair is short and blond."
   Go to her and say, "Cry, Godiva, cry."
   Mother is a broken bridle.


   At night mother plays herself,
   to sleep.
```

So it took the poet a while to admit outright the mother's conflict with
men. Without the current last half of the poem, we would only be
reading interesting similes. The exploration of the similes gives much
pleasure, but the real drama is in the introduction of the mother's rela-
tionship with men. The first and last halves of the poem represent two
very different tacks of writing, and it is not surprising that they were
developed separately.

My general leeriness of metaphor-switching began to dissipate
upon closer study of this poem. The mother is "like" a fine-toothed
comb, a violinist, and "is" a horse. But the comb is also a musical instru-
ment; and, according to the poet, the horse has musical hair associated
with a horsehair bow. What does not work is "the rich chocolate hair."
It suggests that she is edible—which might be another poem—but this
poem doesn't need that, indeed is the weaker for it. Though she is
sensual, she is never overpowered by others. Secondly, the visual image
of "rich chocolate hair" is cartoony and suggests an unreal smoothness
and bruinity (without, however, tying in with the two main meta-
phorical systems, music and animals, as the words smooth and bruin
do).

"Three bold men like night" reads better unpunctuated than with
commas and forced pauses. The hesitation does not go with the bold-
ness. Removal of the commas also makes less obvious the possibility that
no real men at all sleep with her, only night and its imagined males.

We can comprehend the womb singing in a high, thin voice, but
that the womb "speaks no secrets" is potentially comic. The reader may

imagine a silly sound or just find the figure fallacious. I think a poet must take special care, anyway, with negative description: investigate if it would be better to state the secret-keeping in positive terms.

The poem performs very well, I think. Care is taken to use words and phrases which have more than one dimension: "her vanity" and "taking her own life"—"away from them"—being two examples. The mother's coiffured concert is one of the more original things done with hair since *The Rape of the Lock*. Larger than that, the poem vivifies a difficult portrait—a woman's ambivalence as to what she wants out of life. William Carlos Williams has a like passage in "Asphodel, That Greeny Flower" where he begins in simile and ends in humanity:

```
        There are many other flowers
                I could recall
                        for your pleasure:
        the small yellow sweet-scented violet
                that grew
                        in marshy places!
        You were like those
                though I quickly
                        correct myself
        for you were a woman
                and no flower
                        and had to face
        the problems which confront a woman.
```

"A Second Visit to Miller's Grave"

"A Second Visit to Miller's Grave" has a formal structure as well as a rhetorical one. It is a sestina with the stanza breaks omitted. It has the energy and archaism of the young Pound. With a line like "Know that Winter found Miller and his blade," it seems to be playing for high literary stakes. A scary talent is at work here, and one that wants to credit itself with not bending any rules of the demanding sestina form. However, if expectations of those gentle bends had been set up early enough in the poem, the poet could perhaps have avoided the inversion of "carcass on carcass heaped" and could consider changing, at the end, the unconvincing "his wood still grows / Consumed" to "his *woods* still *grow* / Consumed" by the snow flame heaped on *them*. It's a possibility, to indulge in ambiguity there.

The odd thing about the repetitious sestina is that it lures the poet into overrepetition. Two lines apart we have "The fence depends on it for business" and "flesh that . . . grows as though to keep blades busy." The second time the figure is not so much fun. Later the poet writes, "and the shadow grows / Quite *still*, till he races through the snow, heaped / On the field unbroken but by *still* fence / Shadows and him. And all's *still* . . ." (italics mine). The poet should hunt around for other ways to express stillness. When near the beginning the poet speaks of the woodpile burning "with such a slow flame as scarcely warms the earth," he should want any echo of that idea to enlarge upon it, not merely mimic it; therefore, later in the poem, the carcasses "blue with a slow burning" should be blue-with-a-slow-something-else. Working out this kink demands meditating on the nature of combustion. Sometimes hunting for variants to make a richer poem can be solved in a minute at the thesaurus; other times it takes weeks of conscious and unconscious gnawing away at it.

Frequently this poem uses innovative language. I find "The heavy wood / He'd *stroked* apart," "amaranth *skulks* at every fence," coyotes *smirking* in the field, and the house described as *slow*, attractive. This poem has praiseworthy verbs. There's only one rhetorical device I find unpleasant—the euphonious alliteration. It doesn't appear until late in the poem, which suggests that it was used when the poet ran out of other ideas such as action (and good verbs) and things (and good nouns): "like *s*low / *C*eremonial dancers in the *s*now, *s*low / Like thin *s*moke *s*waying. . . ." An obfuscating music. The writer has to use the two *slows* for the form, but *snow* could become *snowbank* or *-drift* or *-field* or *-pasture* or whatever. And one of the *s* words in "smoke swaying" has to be replaced. The same advice applies to "slow snow" in the penultimate line. The poem is robust and is not served well by the mellifluous.

I like these poems because they are earnest and entertaining. They are, I believe, in tune (orchestral) and need only to be tuned up (automotive).

Sandra McPherson was born in 1943 and teaches in The University of Iowa's Writers' Workshop. She studied writing with Roberta Holloway at San Jose University and with David Wagoner and Elizabeth Bishop at the University of Washington. Her books are *Elegies for the Hot Season, Radiation, The Year of Our Birth,* and *Sensing.* She has been awarded an Ingram Merrill Foundation grant, a Guggenheim Fellowship, and an NEA grant.

HENRY CARLILE

Any teaching poet knows how seldom one can help a beginner to write an adult poem. Usually we settle for more modest accomplishments; we praise strengths and discourage weaknesses and hope the right things will happen to help a young voice to its maturity. Any poet teaches a set of prejudices. For that reason I always warn my students in advance that I can only teach my own ways of writing, which may not, finally, help them to find their own best voices. I encourage them to seek out other poets whose writing styles differ from my own.

Just as it is always easier to criticize a poem that is stylistically closer to our own work, so it is more comforting to approach a nearly finished poem. The promising but badly flawed poem usually requires more general treatment. One points out defects, suggests alternatives, and leaves much more of the rewriting to the student. The full possibilities of the poem are as yet unexplored, and too close criticism at this stage may limit the choices, perhaps prevent one of those happy accidents that can save a poem by completely changing its direction.

"A Second Visit to Miller's Grave"
"A Second Visit to Miller's Grave" may require some of both treatments. The flaws in the poem are obvious: unnecessary internal repetition, an awkwardness of syntax forced in part by the requirements of the form, and an unbalanced feeling in the lineation. It is obviously a poem written by a young, inexperienced writer—in this case a college sophomore. And yet how commendable for its ambition! Auden, in *The Dyer's Hand,* says,

> Rhymes, meters, stanza forms, etc., are like servants. If the master
> is fair enough to win their affection and fine enough to command
> their respect, the result is a happy, orderly household. If he is too

tyrannical, they give notice; if he lacks authority, they become
slovenly, impertinent, drunk and dishonest.

How to help this young writer? I would begin with specific re-
visions. First, discourage needless repetition: *heaped* in line 4, *still* in
lines 20–22, *wood* in line 30. The sestina already has enough repeating
words, and unless the internal repetition is natural or inevitable (and in
this case it is not) it should not be used. I would cut *which is* from the
beginning of line 23, *no* from line 36, to eliminate the double negative,
and *snow* from the penultimate line to correct an awkward juxtaposi-
tion. Lines 24 and 25 are especially troublesome: a Yeatsian exoticism—
conscious, unconscious, or coincidental?—from somewhere outside the
country of the poem. I'd suggest a rewrite. I might also ask why
Winter and *Summer* in lines 1 and 2 are capitalized or why the stanza
breaks are omitted. Evidently because of the run-on lines. But perhaps
the breaks should be retained, if only to relieve the structural density of
the poem, the solid block of language that to most readers might seem
visually off-puting. Despite this, I would compliment the student's initia-
tive in experimenting with the form.

More general criticisms might be made by calling attention to how
other poets have handled the form. I might compare, for example,
Donald Justice's "Sestina on Six Words by Weldon Kees" with Kees's
"Sestina: Travel Notes." I would hope the comparison might instill a
better sense of the line as a unit of speech, though, in this case, I would
also praise the student's use of interesting enjambment.

Some poet-teachers might find more to fault, but I would stop here.
Auden says, elsewhere in *The Dyer's Hand,* "As a rule, the sign that a
beginner has a genuine original talent is that he is more interested in
playing with words than in saying something original. . . ." So I am
encouraged when I find wood that is "stroked apart" and "violently
heaped," "amaranth" that "skulks," coyotes that "smirk" and then
"scoot." A willingness to experiment with language should always be
commended.

Few college sophomores come this close to a sestina; most would
rather avoid it completely. If a willingness to play with words is one sign
of genuine original talent, perhaps the attempt to master a complex and
difficult form is evidence of a young writer's commitment. As a sopho-
more I could not recognize a sestina if I saw one much less write one.

"Mother's Song of Strangers"

The other poem, written by an older, more experienced student, is closer to completion and easier to criticize. I like the lyrical voice, the play of images like a Renaissance allegory or a fable. It seems weakest to me where it becomes most explicit. The first and second stanzas are fine, but I would change *and* to *to* in the second line of the third stanza. I would cut the next line and "her womb / That speaks no secrets, only" from the following two lines, splicing the stanza so that it reads:

```
        Three bold men, like night,
    come and sleep with her.
    Mother opens the door that sings
```

The last two lines are again too explicit. It has already been said better in the second stanza: "Mother is a beautiful horse. / No one can ride her." Since the poem is a song, a refrain line might work. Why not repeat that line at the end, adding *But* to make the transition?

```
        Three bold men, like night,
    come to sleep with her.
    Mother opens the door that sings

    in a high, thin voice
    like gold wire: her song of strangers,
    her song of the gifts they bring,
    of being wanted by all men.

    But mother is a beautiful horse.   No one
    can ride her.
```

Is this tampering too much? Perhaps. But it is only one possibility. The student may want to revise more expansively.

One question seems fundamental in any writers' workshop: "How would you revise this poem if it were yours?" You always hope you can say, "I wouldn't change a thing." Sometimes you want to say, "I'd throw it away and start over." I seldom say that. If a poem is really bad I begin asking questions: "What did you mean by this line?" etc. If a student's answer is more imaginative, and it often is, I might say "Good! Why didn't you write it that way?" Sometimes just talking over a problem spot helps find other alternatives. The teacher's role here is passive. In the end the student and poem must find each other. When the teacher makes specific criticisms recommending minor additions, deletions, or rewrites, the student can be pretty sure he or she is finding the poem.

Henry Carlile, born in 1934, teaches at Portland State University and is currently a visiting lecturer at The University of Iowa's Writers' Workshop. He has published *The Rough-Hewn Table* and is the recipient of a Devins Award and grants from the National Endowment for the Arts.

Group IV

JANE COOPER
THOMAS LUX
JEAN VALENTINE

These poets worked independently on three poems contributed by one student of each. All three teach in the Sarah Lawrence College Writing Program, Bronxville, New York.

ANATOMY OF AN EMBRACE
Donald Bell

Draft 1
There's the thumbnail of love,
sometimes the entire strong hand.
This is followed by the arm up
to the shoulder, and the nape.

Yes, the small hair-sprinkled nape
is also there. Call it the mid-point
because with this classical movement,
there's a second part, too.

The second shoulder descends like an angel
into the second arm punctuated
by an elbow and wrist. And the final hand
falls into the first. The complete embrace
is in your grasp. Proceed. Proceed.

Draft 2
There's the thumbnail of love,
sometimes the entire strong hand.
This is followed by the arm up
to the shoulder, and the nape.

Yes, the small hair-sprinkled nape
is also there. Call it the mid-point
because with this classical movement,
there's a second part, too.

The other shoulder descends, an arc
down the arm, punctuated
by elbow and wrist. And this hand
falls into the first. The complete embrace
is in your grasp. Proceed. Proceed.

Donald Bell was born in 1957. He studied at Sarah Lawrence College
with Thomas Lux, Galway Kinnell, Jean Valentine, Jane Cooper, and
Jane Shore. He expects to continue studying poetry at the graduate level
and plans, eventually, to teach.

STUMBLING AROUND IN THE WOODS
Reine Hauser

Draft 1
In this forest that's so quiet
it's almost green, someone is
making so much racket I get
tremendously annoyed—until
I discover it's me, stumbling.

Look—in a party filled with
only your best, most personal
friends you trip four times
in five minutes. And everyone
there knows you're on the wagon.

The chairs fall over before
I walk into the room. It
must be preparation. I'd just
like to know who tipped them off.

All I want is for the wind
to shut up a minute;
to hold its breath long
enough so I can barely
catch what this tiny
pinecone is trying
to tell me. I know
it must be important,
because all the seventy-
nine brown tongues are
stiff with fatigue.

And all that moss growing
only on the north side
of the trees must have
something to say; managing
as it does without a
compass or stars.

Draft 2
All I want is for the wind
to shut up a minute;
to hold its breath long
enough so that I can
finally catch what this
tiny pinecone is trying

to tell me. I know
it must be important,
because its seventy-
nine brown tongues
are stiff with fatigue.

And all that moss
growing on the north
side of the trees must
be important, too;
managing as it does,
quietly, without
a compass or stars.

In this forest that's so quiet
it's almost green, someone
is making so much racket that I
get tremendously annoyed—until
I discover it's me, stumbling
in the underbrush, over roots.

Draft 3
All I want is for the wind
to shut up a minute;
to hold its breath long
enough so I can finally
catch what this tiny
pinecone is trying
to tell me. I know

it must be important
because its seventy-nine
brown tongues
are stiff with fatigue.

And that doe pawing
the ground by a bush must

be important, too;
managing, as she does,
quietly, on fragile,
fawn-colored hooves.

In this forest that's so quiet
it's almost green, someone
is making so much racket I
get tremendously annoyed—until
I discover it's me, stumbling,
in the underbrush, over roots.

Reine Hauser was born in 1956 in Niagara Falls. She went to Sarah Lawrence College and studied writing with Lawrence Kearney, Mac Hammond, Galway Kinnell, Thomas Lux, and Jane Cooper. She received an Honorable Mention in the Academy of American Poets Conference in 1977 and 1978. Currently, she works for the Lower Manhattan Cultural Council in New York.

FIVE WOMEN IN A CAFE
Kathie rue Hoyer

Draft 1

Late summer. Late evening.
It is warm, the night will drag on.

The buzzing of the fan which
had been annoying continues half-forgotten.
    Each one listens to her own breathing
        to the silences between her words, words, words.
The glasses are empty. The ice melts quick enough.
I'm hot. I'm tired. I'm so hot. Let's go.

Nothing had gone right; they missed the first act,
the bakery closed early. There's so little to say.
    The youngest one, in a white dress, reaches across
        the table, knocking over a glass of melted ice.
There is one moment, that moment before the eager
hands reach out to steady, sustain, return.

Draft 2

Late summer. Late evening.
It is warm, the night will drag on.

The buzzing of the fan fades, half-forgotten.
        Each one listens to her own breathing
        to the silences between her words, words, words.
The glasses are empty. The ice melts quick enough.
I'm hot. I'm tired. I'm so hot. Let's go.

Nothing had gone right; they missed the first act,
the bakery closed early. There's so little to say.
        The youngest one, in a white dress, reaches across
        the table, knocking over a glass of melted ice.

The pool of water spreads unimpeded towards
table edge. They sit and stare and hold their breaths.
        Hands reach to steady, sustain, withhold.
        Apologizing, the girl in white. Blushing, she wants
to contain the night, wrap it, place it inside her dress.

Late summer. Late evening.
It is warm, the night will drag on.

Kathie rue Hoyer was born in 1958 and studied poetry with Jane Cooper
at Sarah Lawrence College. Currently, she is a dancer and writer.

JANE COOPER

ON THE MAKING OF THREE POEMS

First of all, let me say that I don't think it's the criticism of any one
poem that makes the workshop experience valuable for a student. Rather,
it's the slow working through of poems week after week, the attempt on
the part of the teacher (and the whole class) patiently to discover the
student's strengths, point them out, help her or him to build on them yet
not to be limited by them. For this reason I think this kind of analysis of
only one poem is only partially illuminating. In teaching, it's the *direc-*

tion of a student's writing that counts, and the life-giving energy; how a series of poems adds up, what it promises. Without this sense, criticism is apt to get picky—and I'm afraid that is somewhat the problem of the paragraphs that follow.

"Stumbling Around in the Woods"

Reine Hauser's "Stumbling Around in the Woods" could have gone either way—toward the self or toward stillness. On the whole, I too would have encouraged her to cut out the party and concentrate on the trees, since there's a risk of self-consciousness in the first-draft stumbling into the room—a perilous cuteness. The decision to start the second draft with the original fourth stanza ("All I want is for the wind"), and end with the first stanza and the actual stumbling in the forest, then seems the best part of the revision process. I like not getting to the "I" of the poem till the very end. I like looking outward at the woods, staying still to listen, first. However, I wouldn't myself have traded the stanza about the moss (stanza 2 in draft 2) for the stanza about the doe. Two images I enjoy are the "seventy-nine / brown tongues [of the pinecone] / stiff with fatigue" and the moss "growing on the north / side of the trees / . . . managing as it does / quietly, without / a compass or stars." The doe throws me off, for the intense quiet that makes the "I" of the poem so aware of her own stumbling seems interrupted by the presence of another animal, by "pawing," however delicate. . . . Finally, here are several notes on the last draft of the poem as it stands: I would cut "tiny" before "pinecone," which seems coy, and I wonder whether "pinecone is trying to *say*" might not be better than "*tell me*," since I'd prefer to keep the speaker offstage till the end of the poem. In the doe stanza, again I jib at "*fawn-colored hooves*." I like the addition of the last line after "stumbling." I wonder what exactly is meant by "In the forest it's so quiet / it's *almost green*"? This didn't bother me for the first 65 or so readings, but once I asked the question, it kept recurring. Is this a woods in, say, March? Ah, now I see one reason why I miss that moss. The sequence of brown pinecones and then the (unspoken) color of moss (surely made more mysterious by "stars"—the idea that this landscape is perhaps being seen by night) led me easily to "almost green" in earlier drafts, but now, with the doe, that subliminal sequence is destroyed, and I'm in danger of becoming too literal. . . . I like the poem. I suppose I would have urged it along in slightly different ways. But that is the benefit of having serious students work with more than one teacher. In the end, it leaves them truly free. Both Reine Hauser and Donald Bell (whose poem follows) have studied with several different poets, and so they have learned the healthiest of all lessons for an artist: There's no such thing as authority. And, after a certain point, amicably, one develops one's own style.

In fact, I like all these poems, which is one reason—despite my first disclaimer—why it's a pleasure to write about them. The poor poem in a workshop is almost never the one about which there is specific question but rather the poem about which there is nothing much to say—the poem that hasn't come into being enough yet to make it sensible to talk of words or music or imagery. The worst part of workshop practice is that it tends to isolate technique. What's important to remember is that the poem always grows out of some total experience; only when the experience is there to respect can one begin to ask whether it should be clarified, carried further, etc.

"Anatomy of an Embrace"

One thing I admire about Donald Bell's work is its musical firmness and variety. In "Anatomy of an Embrace," each line stays in place and yet is not quite predictable; at the same time, there's a fine fluency from beginning to end of the poem. The only place I trip—in both drafts—is at the last line of stanza 2: "There's a second part, too." There is some heaviness in that end-stopped "too," but it's "part" that keeps bothering me. "Classical movement" in fact suggests a piece of music. Isn't "part" a rather blunt but also vague word, which seems grammatically to go with "movement" but which signals instead, confusingly, another part of the body? Anyway, the only further revision I'd suggest for this generally tight and accomplished poem would be the elimination of that one line. I think line 7 could read (I'm not quite sure about this) "because *from* this classical movement," and then line 9 could follow directly, without a capital ("the other shoulder descends, an arc"), and the curve of the poem would be complete. (This might also result in three stanzas of four lines each.) My favorite image is "small hair-sprinkled nape." The repetition of "nape," that quirky, minutely observed "hair-sprinkled," which is like nothing else in the poem, make this the high point, literally, from which the two halves of the poem depend. I'm glad the angel was "canned"—partly because it got in the way of the nape. But given "embrace" as the subject, I wonder if I'd have had the good sense myself to can the angel? Still, for all the positive connotations of "embrace," this is a witty, even sly poem. The two hands of one person end by embracing each other. "The complete embrace / is in your grasp." Tch! Then how can you "Proceed. Proceed"? But you must. We must. And the poem opens out again, leaving the poet with the final grin.

Rather arbitrarily, I decided to consider these three poems in reverse order according to the age of the poet. Reine Hauser was a junior at Sarah Lawrence when she wrote "Stumbling Around in the Woods," Donald Bell a sophomore when he wrote "Anatomy of an Embrace," and Kathie rue Hoyer a freshman when she wrote "Five Women in a Café" for a workshop of mine. A reminder of humility: we all need to keep telling ourselves that no matter how much may happen in a writing workshop, some students come to us already clearly talented and with voices of their own. In this case, I've chosen a poem of Kathie rue Hoyer's I consider not yet finished, but other poems of hers, written the same spring, reached a point where I couldn't add very much by further criticism. This doesn't mean, of course, that she won't continue to grow. One of the imponderables in teaching writing, by the way, is that it's impossible to tell who will go on and, specifically, who is an early and who a late maturer.

"Five Women in a Café"
"Five Women in a Café" certainly has its own voice, its own stamp, from the beginning. The beat of repetition and suppressed protest ("I'm hot. I'm tired. I'm so hot. Let's go.") is there from the first line. The poem develops, for me, quite inevitably up to the point where the glass is knocked over and the ice water spills. At the same time, there is invention ("they missed the first act, / the bakery closed early"). How much we know, how much we don't know about these five women! How adept is the movement from outside to inside—the murmured or perhaps not even spoken words—and back again. In the first draft, I felt the last two lines were inadequate to deal with the tension that had been built up, and the poem became suddenly impersonal (to "steady, sustain" whom? to "return" what?) and even a bit pretentious ("There is *one* moment"). I like the second draft better, though I still don't feel it has solved all the poem's problems. For one thing, it's always easy to end a poem by re-

peating the beginning—the oldest way to end a poem, or a song, in the
world. In the fourth stanza, "unimpeded" seems too heavy for the situa-
tion—as, in a different way, so does "hold their breaths." I'm not sure the
new "withhold" is clear. But I like "Apologizing, the girl in white. Blush-
ing, she wants / to contain the night, wrap it, place it inside her dress."
What an odd metaphor this is—and yet it convinces me, from the truth
of some disproportionate adolescent shyness we've all shared. I wish the
sliding of the water across the table could be a little more worked on—
and then that the poem could be still fuller. The fact is, enough has been
created for me here so that I want to know more. Where should the poem
end? The new draft has brought it to the point where the tension is be-
tween the "youngest one" and the other women. What does that mean?
But how interesting it all is. . . . Surely this is one secret: that the poem
should be interesting, that it can be interesting even in the way a story is.
I want just to add that, once again, musically this is a confident poem.
And the visual pattern across the page is handsome, especially in draft 2.
This poet is a dancer, and I always feel an element of dramatic per-
formance in her work, even when it is elliptical and, for that reason,
sometimes still obscure.

One last word, which hasn't to do with the three poems. Obviously,
all three poets I've discussed—Hauser, Bell, Hoyer—are gifted and seri-
ous, and they all think, justifiably, of going on. But what about the stu-
dent in a workshop who doesn't necessarily want to be a writer? Well,
why not? It seems to me writing courses, at least on the undergraduate
level, should always leave room for the unsure, the experimenters, for
amateurs who (in the old meaning of the word "amateur") are simply
lovers of poetry or fiction or plays. I learned a lot about how to look at
a painting from having studied with a good painting teacher from the
age of ten to the age of sixteen. Yet I'll never be a painter, and it was
clear quite soon that I wouldn't be. While I believe the best teachers of
writing are themselves practicing writers—for who else keeps up with
the genuinely new?—the students can be anybody, can come from any
place. To become a writer is finally a matter of character, as well as luck
and a passion for the medium. But it is surely not the worst part of any-
one's education to be left with a lifelong hunger for good writing, to be
able to read with that special joy and concentration that come from
sensing—no, actively seeing—how the thing was made.

Jane Cooper was born in 1924 and has taught writing at Sarah Lawrence College since 1950. She studied with Robert Lowell and John Berryman at the University of Iowa and with Louise Bogan at New York University. She has published two books of poems, *The Weather of Six Mornings,* which was the 1968 Lamont Award winner, and *Maps & Windows* (1974). Last year she was co-winner of the Shelley Award, and she has had grants from the Guggenheim and Ingram Merrill Foundations and CAPS. She is finishing a third collection, *A Mission with the Night.*

THOMAS LUX

HOOF AND PAW: WORKING OVER SOME STUDENT POEMS

Like my friend and colleague Jane Cooper, I'll start by saying that a one-shot critique of three poems is not indicative of how I teach a poetry workshop or of the workshop experience as a whole. The main thing missing is a dozen or so other people—the students. It is, simply, a group effort. A great deal can happen over the course of a year to the student or teacher who keeps his/her ears, eyes, mind and, lastly, mouth, open.

"Stumbling Around in the Woods"

How would I deal with them? Well, one I've already worked on with the student. Reine (pronounced *Wren*) Hauser's poem "Stumbling Around in the Woods" is a good example of her voice: there is sly understatement, a clarity, a sharp wit, and most of all, to my ear, a fine rhythmic sayability—without compromise, prosaic or otherwise. I know this poem as one of many—a style that is sure and concerns that continue to grow.

I don't remember exactly what I said when Reine first showed me this poem. I do remember that it was in a conference, so there were only three characters present: Reine, myself, and the poem. Looking at the third draft now there are a number of things I wish I *had* said. I think it's obvious that the poem improves through the three drafts, but I still see (maybe, or certainly, a year's time gives me more objectivity) three or four places in the poem where it seems to back off from some possibilities. A few places where the poet lets her marvelous tonal qualities replace some discoveries the poem might have made. In the course of reading a poem—in a workshop or in a one-on-one conference—I like to start by hearing the poem read aloud at least once and sometimes two or three times, and then start right at the top with specifics. I'm in favor of looking at, carefully, every line, word, piece of punctuation, etc. I often ask students to give the early drafts of a poem a test: isolate each line and ask yourself if something interesting is going on in it. Does it contain an image, a metaphor? Does it have some sounds, a rhythm? Is there *anything* interesting with language going on in this line, this isolated fragment? Of course, this is an impossible test to pass with every line, but it is still, I believe, a valid test. At the very least it gets the student looking more closely at what he/she has written. Everything written for a reason and everything where it is for a reason. Nothing arbitrary. I think we can arrive at a good reading of a poem's overall intent (although the real reason or intent of a poem often occurs accidentally or unconsciously) by this kind of line-by-line examination.

In other words, I don't think we have to miss the poem as a whole by concentrating (in this first reading) on its parts. In a workshop, the value of this kind of discussion is clear: the class learns to talk specifically yet objectively about something as subjective, say, as metaphor or the imaginative process. Talking about poems with sensitivity, toughness, and, hopefully, articulateness, is difficult—because the language of poetry can be difficult—but worth the effort. By "difficult" I don't mean obscure or even, necessarily, complicated. I mean simply that the language of poetry can be highly demanding of the imagination. We need to put something into the reading of a poem to get something out of it.

But enough of this aside—let's get back to the poem. Because I like it, I'm going to ask it a lot of questions. Like: why not get to the point in the first line? "I want the wind . . ." instead of "All I want is for the wind . . ." Why not? The verb "is" surely can be dropped, the "all," the "for." Even the line break becomes more interesting, I think, after this basic cutting. (—Sure, he thinks it's better, he rewrote it. But, it's *not* rewriting the line for the student. It comes as a suggestion: "What about that first line, Reine? What's the simplest and most direct way to say that?") I wouldn't meddle with much more in this stanza, but there are a number of small things which add up and bother me. The central image of this stanza is clear: the speaker wants the wind to quiet down so she can hear what a pinecone is trying to tell her. Well, we know that pinecones don't usually talk, but as the metaphor continues the pinecone's flaps (I don't know what they're really called) are compared to tongues. What bothers me are the cloying sounds of those three lines, particularly the "finally/tiny/trying" half-rhymes and then a real emptiness (by "emptiness" I mean virtually nothing is happening with language) of the last line of this stanza. "Tiny" could certainly go. I like the internal and subtler *o* sounds: "so/pinecone/know." I like the colloquial use of the verb "catch." The enjambed stanza ("I know") break calls attention and even doubts—the speaker trying to convince herself with this line/stanza break emphasis. I also like the specificity of "seventy-nine." Does a pinecone (in this poem, in the real forest) have a set number? Eighty? Are pinecones like pianos or the teeth in our mouths—a specific number? Anyway, I like knowing that there are *exactly* seventy-nine brown tongues. The logic of the metaphor—the tongues stiff with fatigue, as if they were backs that stiffen after a day of hard work—is emblematic of the sly wit of this poem. I love the first line of the third stanza because a "doe pawing the ground" is an image implying aggressiveness, or at least restlessness. It is another message, and like the tongues of the pinecone, it is an aural image as well as visual. We're certainly involved, placed in, the landscape of the poem. I enjoy the huffy, pause-loaded (done with the choice of language, the line breaks, and the punctuation) movement of the third, fourth, and fifth lines of the stanza. I can't decide about the fawn-colored hooves. Sometimes, it works OK for me. Other times, it seems too cute, the metaphorical connection easy. In a case like this—which certainly happens often enough—my response is something like: "I dunno. What do *you* think?"

The last stanza also has some problems. Suddenly the forest is quiet, the wind has shut up, the pinecones are on hold, and even the doe, presumably, has stopped her pawing. The only sound is the sound of the speaker, stumbling. I don't think she needs to be "tremendously" annoyed. I wonder if the speaker should be even more annoyed (or maybe chagrined) when she finds out she's making the racket herself. Again, this kind of reading and comments on the poem aren't suggestions for rewrites. They seem to me more like directions announced in the poem that the author might want to explore.

So—we've been through it top to bottom.

Now let's look at the whole, the metaphorical heart of the poem. This gets more theoretical, of course, and it can also slip easily into simple attempts at paraphrase. The forest the speaker is stumbling around in is trying to tell her something. And she can't hear it for her own stumbling. The poem is talking, somehow, about listening. I miss the stanza about the moss at this point. I like very much the subtle implications that moss growing on the north side of a tree (a compass created, supposedly, by nature for those of us lost in the forest without a compass) can get along without a compass or the stars (another directional aid that nature provides). I'd argue for trying to get it back in the poem. How? I don't know. We'd talk about this for a while—in conference just the two of us, in class all of us, the various readers' minds ranging with the associations and reverberations the poem allows. There seems to be a lot going on in this poem—yet it is told with understatement and an edge of humor.

All this time, by the way (in a workshop situation), the author of the poem is silent. This is common workshop practice. If the author were allowed to interject or explain the poem, that would influence the objectivity of the criticism. Also, if something had to be explained by the author that the poem doesn't explain by itself, there's a problem with the poem. Finally, we go through the poem one more time: nag, nag, nag. We'll talk about smaller technical things, punctuation, general mop-up work. Faster this time than the first line-by-line reading, but covering every syllable or letter in our alphabet that needs covering. When the class is done with its comments the author gets to speak and ask questions. To tell the class and the teacher how dumb or how good the reading of the poem was.

The teacher's role throughout this (average time: forty-five minutes) is to give his comments like everyone else and to try to direct the discussion loosely: keeping it on tracks, connecting comments, trying to entice people in who are obviously out in left field with their backs to the plate, etc. And, maybe occasionally, a joke—if it has to do with the language or the subject of the poem. Not a joke, however, *on* the poem. But, as Roethke says, a teacher has to be careful about jokes. The process of talking about and seriously considering a poem is delicate, involving, and complicated. It can also be freewheeling, exciting, and illuminating. Of course, the better the poem, the better the possibilities for discussion and actual learning: about language, about ourselves, and about the orb we walk around on. Reine's poem teaches me something and gives me something, obviously, to talk about. It's a good poem and it could be better. Hell, three drafts ain't nearly enough anyway.

"Anatomy of an Embrace"

Donald Bell's "Anatomy of an Embrace" is also, I think, a good poem. Shorter, a little more lyrical, and also capable of being a better, more realized poem. I like the first two lines very much—the image itself and the assonance in "thumbnail/love/sometimes" leading to the hard stresses on the last two words "strong hand." The next two lines don't quite have the sensory exactness of the first two but they do certainly further the poem's journey or purpose. A kind of love poem that's not afraid to make a variation, at this point, on the old song ". . . and the hipbone's connected to the thighbone . . ." (etc.). When we get to the nape we linger there for a while because it's a pivotal point in the poem, the point at which anything thrown into the air halts for a split second (though the halting is longer here) and then descends. It's the midpoint of this embrace. Now I begin to have a few problems with the poem. First of all, "classical" doesn't tell me much. What "classical" movement? What, exactly, is "classical"? I like the way, however, he follows this with the almost childlike phrase "there's a second part, too." It seems slightly awkward, somehow. Because it's childlike it doesn't have to be awkward. How to have both—if that's what the poet decides he's looking for—I dunno (the fairly frequent comment). I'm glad the poet concentrated his revision on the second stanza. The first line of the first draft is overdone. I'm glad he gave the angel a break and removed it from the poem. The angels, of course, are ever-forgiving, but poets abuse them terribly with over- and indiscriminate reference—an offense I've been guilty of many times. It was also smart to get rid of the second and third "second." I'm pretty sure the repetition was intentional, but it doesn't work, and doesn't, certainly, add any emphasis or meaning to the word. I think "arc" is better than angel but still not very specific. I'm beginning to lose the effect of the embrace. I like the verb "punctuated." What kind of literal punctuation would an elbow or wrist equal? A comma? The irony of this embrace, of course, is that it is a self-embrace. I see it almost as a dance movement, or the position, the pose, of a sculptor's model. (Classical?) Once the embrace is complete—the hands brought together —it is in your grasp. I'm not a big fan of puns but this one is subtle and certainly not a groaner. I'm not sure about the "Proceed. Proceed." Its instructional tone seems appropriate, but the choice seems easy or too obvious. I'd ask the poet how important he thought it was. It does seem to start the poem over again, a poem that has just completed a circle.

Donald Bell, like Reine Hauser, is a student whose work I know well. When I read this poem I hear many poems, poems that led to this unique voice, this technical skill, and this obviously serious intent. It's not one of Donald's very best poems, but it shows a lot. He also knows that, unless you're incredibly lucky, poems don't get written in two drafts. Two drafts to warm up, maybe; two drafts to find a direction, maybe, but not enough to write a good poem.

"Five Women in a Café"

I've never worked with Kathie rue Hoyer, but I think, I know, my approach to her poems would be the same. In fact, it might be a little easier because I don't have a number of her poems or her (poetic) voice in my mind. The first thing that's obvious to me is that her poem improves a great deal between draft 1 and draft 2. It's almost as if there are some missing drafts in between. Or it's a case of an early draft of a poem very clearly announcing its needs. I like very much the first three lines of this poem: they set the tone, the time, and the place. We get a lot of sensory information from three simple lines. The near overalliteration is broken up nicely by the "half" in "half-forgotten." "Buzzing" is also, I think, a good verb to go with fan. The next two lines let me down a little. I can't get terribly interested in the image of someone listening to their own breathing—it seems rather clichéd to me—but if the author thought the image important I'd probably suggest at least cutting "one" and "own" from the line. Listening to silence seems to me even more clichéd, and the repetition of "words, words, words" doesn't do much for me here. The notion could be interesting—of a silence, say, between each word of a sentence each one of the five women might be speaking, but since repetition already plays an important part in the structure of the poem it might be best not to employ it at this point. I'd suggest that the poet look harder at what is trying to be said here. It seems important and should be confronted more carefully. The next two lines I like a great deal. Especially the sentence "The ice melts quick enough." It sets us up for the tired, yet emphatic, yet complaining last line of this stanza with its four short sentences. We begin to get more information in the next stanza, but never so much that it becomes prosaic. The five women are sitting around: hot, tired, irritated. They were late for the play, late to the bakery. There's nothing to say. A marvelously controlled and loaded scene. A scene of edgy somnolence, until one of the women, the youngest, who is wearing a white dress, knocks over a glass. OK, perfect, and we arrive at the central point of the poem, the point where it begins to make its point. I like the first line of this stanza. It's as if this mere spilled glass of water were a broken dam about to flood an entire sleeping valley. It—the water—moves on unimpeded. But, in this poem, not because it is so powerful, but because of the spectators' (the five women) inertia. It's an edgy inertia that's been created, gradually, throughout the poem. I wish they were doing something other than staring and holding their breath, or at least I wish this were told, or implied, in a more interesting way. I'm intrigued by the next line: "Hands reach to steady, sustain, hold." It certainly seems to be referring to more than just the containment of the water. There are various implications in all these words, particularly "sustain" and "withhold." They refer also, somehow, in this context, to the youngest woman. I like very much the slightly unusual inversion in the sentence "Apologizing, the girl in white." It seems important that "Apologizing" comes first in the sentence—right after "steady, sustain, withhold." I love the next line-and-a-half. The youngest woman wants to contain not only the spilled water but also the night, placing it inside her white dress. A beautiful image. The last two lines, simply a repetition of the first two, show that the previous lines are impossible and brings the poem around (like Bell's) full circle, to where it started.

A damn interesting poem. One I've enjoyed writing about and would enjoy talking to the author about face to face or with lots of other faces in a workshop. One similar comment that I made in talking about the other two poems: not enough drafts, not enough work on this poem yet!

All these poems seem quite good to me. They're well imagined, well crafted, and are getting at some things. Of course, I might be accused of prejudice because I've worked with two of these students (although they've also worked with at least two or three other writing teacher/writers as well) and because they all attend the college where I teach. Accusation noted, but I've approached these poems in the same manner I'd approach any poem of similar quality: objectively, carefully, word by word.

By way of conclusion, let me add a few more general comments about the teaching of poetry writing as I practice it. First, there can be no serious discussion of poetry writing without the discussion of the reading of poetry. In the classroom and even more often in conference I'm always bringing up particular poems and poets I think the student can gain something from by reading: "Have you read X? Her second book might interest you, especially a poem called. . . ." Or: "Check out Y's poem on this subject. He's on to something there that you'll like." There's no writing poetry unless you read it, unless, in fact, you love reading it and read it constantly and carefully. I also think reading aloud is important—I insist on it in class and in conference. *All* poems aloud, not just our own. And again, I must stress the importance of the workshop experience as a whole. A year, thirty or so class meetings, the gradual progression and discoveries, the joys of our language and voices, the rare intelligence of metaphor and imagination.

I think I love best the last four or five weeks of a workshop—maybe because I can relax a bit—but I think more because I've seen, and the whole class has seen and experienced something. We've made at least a small dent in our study of the language of poetry, a language for which there is no substitute. There is always growth and there is always discovery. Our language and its possibilities are more accessible than they've been before—to the teacher, the students individually, and the class as a whole. It can be, when it works, an extremely valid educational experience, and it's an experience that isn't abstract or intellectual, that can have everything to do with our real lives.

Theodore Roethke, a poet who thought about and wrote about teaching a great deal, says in one of his essays that the teaching of poetry writing is the opposite of most learning processes. It's a synthesis, the process of writing a poem and of metaphor, a building up rather than the analytical breaking down of a subject. I believe that and I believe this kind of teaching, this kind of class—and I believe this to the bottom of my socks—can be important, can *matter*.

Thomas Lux, born in 1946, teaches creative writing at Sarah Lawrence College. His books of poetry include *Memory's Handgrenade* (1972) and *The Glassblower's Breath* (1976). He has also translated Dino Campana's poems in *From Orphic Songs: Versions of Campana* (1977).

JEAN VALENTINE

"Anatomy of an Embrace"

"Anatomy of an Embrace" I worked with the writer on, so these first notes will be from memory. The second draft I think is a live poem, that does what it set out to do; the last words seem freshened by their echo of Frost's ferocious "Provide! Provide!" The few revisions, all in the last stanza, are useful ones. ". . . *an* elbow and wrist" sounded disembodied, and so it edged on confusion; likewise "the *final* hand"—of how many? how many people (elbows, wrists, hands) are there? (It is an embrace.) The changes clear away those questions. But that angel gave me trouble: I couldn't see an angel being "punctuated"; but worse, I couldn't *see* the angel, much as I wanted to; or if I saw the angel, I couldn't see the rest. Could the angel be gotten into the line drawing of that poem? After a long, mulling look at the problem (this was in a conference), the writer said, "Oh, *can* the angel!" Right or wrong, it's a bright memory.

In actual teaching, how much I say (not to mention, how much I see) varies from student to student and from time to time. With the writer of "Anatomy of an Embrace," by the time we were working on that poem, I could be as opinionated as I wanted; he had a healthy skepticism and a real survivor's stubbornness. What I must be forgetting in these notes is all the wonderful ideas I had that he wasn't struck by.

"Stumbling Around in the Woods"

What I keep thinking here is that the first draft, because of the party, has something more to say, and something more moving than the second draft ends up with: this first draft of a poem about stumbling has more of the quick of experience; the room and the forest make each other, and the speaker, more real. The second draft, though it's less awkward, has lost that connection, and seems the less for it. The addition of another line after "stumbling" is good; though I'd argue with the word "roots" unless it's modified somehow out of what seems too much meaningfulness. And if the writer were to go back to draft 1, I'd have hesitations about the third stanza there, at least as such a strung-out event, and set off in a stanza by itself.

In both drafts I have trouble—it's in the language, not the notion— with that pinecone talking (the word "tiny" is part of it: it sounds fey); also about the doe in draft 2 which "must be important" (I keep finding the moss in draft 1 more interesting than the doe). I'd want something to change here; maybe if the notion was less personally and less sympathetically taken up than ". . . this tiny / pinecone is *trying* / to tell *me*." I think of Peter Everwine's beautiful passage from "Distance":

```
The light pulling away from trees
the trees speaking in shadows
to whatever listens
```

And how good, and how convincing, this is: "the seventy-nine / brown tongues / are stiff with fatigue."

"Five Women in a Café"

There's an immediacy in this poem; how well the voice shifts as it goes. And it sometimes keeps to a strong spoken rhythm, as in the first two lines, the last two lines of the second stanza, the first four lines of the third. In the first draft, a poem about the longing for something real, something alive: the "one moment" not controlled, not "steadied" by "the eager / hands."

But in the second draft, I'm confused by what seems the most emphasized new line: "Blushing, she wants / to contain the night, wrap it, place it inside her dress." It is more specific certainly than the "one moment," but I'm left unsure as to what she wants, and why: to hide the night—her shame at having broken through the dragging surface; or: to save the night—to keep it away from this empty dragging on. Or, something else . . . I lean toward the first reading, to hide the night, but I can't tell yet. The poem seems to be at some midpoint, moving towards its impulse. If I were working with this writer, I guess I'd wait.

Jean Valentine was born in 1934 and teaches at Sarah Lawrence College. She went to Radcliffe College, and has published three books of poetry, *Dream Barker and other poems, Pilgrims, Ordinary Things,* and a chapbook, *Turn.* Her latest book is *The Messenger.*

Group V

HOLLIS SUMMERS
ROBERT WALLACE
JOHN HAINES

Two of the poems that these poets analyzed were contributed by members of the Cleveland State University Poetry Center's public workshop; the third, "Tall Ship," is by one of Robert Wallace's students in his writing class at Case Western Reserve University. Summers teaches creative writing at Ohio University, Athens; Haines has taught it at the universities of Alaska, Washington, and Montana. All three worked on the poems independently.

SICILIAN SEMAPHORE
John Gabel

There is a tidiness about a ship at sea
The decks are clear
The watches come and go
And each man has his purpose
In port it is a different matter
The decks are littered
Strangers come aboard
And the crew disappears into the city

We were told to move the ship
Take her out, swing her about
And dock portside-to instead of starboard
A Sicilian Pilot arrived in time for lunch
Later we mustered a crew of cooks and messboys
To handle the hawsers

Control was from the flying bridge
An open area above the wheelhouse
The Pilot, Captain and I manned it
The Pilot to give orders
The Captain to observe and be responsible
And I to act as helmsman

The Sicilian spoke no English
Except orders to the helm and to the engine room
Those he gave were contrary to the Old Man's expectations
The septuagenarian Captain could not see beyond the bow
And did not like what he saw
Instant apoplexy
Was followed by an arm waving soliloquy
Mostly profane
The Pilot responded in kind
Made angry Sicilian sounds
And semaphored his opinion
Of the myopic Captain, his ship and Americans in general

He brokenenglish ordered the engine
From full ahead to full astern every fifteen seconds
And did not seem to understand
Triple expansion steam
That needs three minutes
For an order's relay, compliance
And the slow turning screw to show effect
Through an air scoop I could hear the Second Engineer swearing

The bemused white hatted cooks
Spent the afternoon sunning on the bow

While my two sea gulls wheeled in full cry
And I deadpanyessired them both
Steered the thing
Rang all those bells
Wrote them in a log as long as my arm
And answered the Second's phone calls
"John what the fuck are you doing up there?"
"Jimmy none of us knows"

Somehow we got it to the dock
Not where we had expected
But we didn't go aground
Or lose anybody overboard
Communication is never easy

John Gabel was born in 1922 and has never formally studied creative writing. He is presently the president of Retirement Plans, Inc., a firm of actuaries and employee benefit consultants in Cleveland, Ohio.

TALL SHIP
David Fantauzzi

A floating gallery.
Spars and yardarms
stretch blank canvas
abreast easel-masts.
Sea-breeze lashes,
splashes the rigging
with salt-water
colors. A seascape
where sails swell with breath
like sailors' white chests.

David Fantauzzi was born in 1955 and studied at Case Western Reserve University under Robert Wallace and Anne Rowley. He is now a law student at the John Marshall Law School in Chicago.

COWTALE
Joan Nicholl

Ah, miss. Those are fine-looking colored beads you've got there.
Uh huh.
See this cow? How would you like to trade this cow for those beads?
Listen fella. I've got to get home. I've got things to do.
What's wrong with you? This beautiful Gurnsey? She got a prize at
the fair.
Yeah. Well, what would I do with her? I live in an apartment on
Hampshire.
And, she gives yogurt. You could get a space for her in Lot 4.
I'd have to get a pasturizing machine; she could have TB.
Listen, she could have a lot of things, but she doesn't. Look at those eyes.
Nice, but I'm no dummy. These are good beads. And besides, blue's my
favorite color.
You probably think if you plant them they'll grow really high and you
can grab a golden egg.
Come on, that's bull shit. And besides, gold's a whole other thing.
These are blue beads.
Yeah, somebody gave you a line, stairway to heaven stuff, and you
went for it.
Well, I'm not going for any cow that gives yogurt. So lay off.
They aren't even very big. I think you got taken.
Size isn't everything. Look at the trouble you're having trying to dump
that cow on me.
Listen, I'm trying to do you a favor, dolly, trying to take those beads
off your hands.
So I see, but I'm not buying so fuck off.
OK then, beat it. Take a trip. String yourself up with those beads,
smart ass.

Joan Nicholl was born in 1930. She has never taken a writing course, but
has attended both the Cleveland State Poetry Forum and the Poets'
League of Greater Cleveland for the past six years.

HOLLIS SUMMERS

SHAKING AND CARVING

I would prefer to confront the poets . . .

I'd rather talk to the writers . . .

Already I am having trouble with the language. "I would prefer," or, "I'd rather."

It is the word *teacher* that is bothering me. I am a *reader,* one fallible reader. "Tall Ship," "Cowtale," and "Sicilian Semaphore" obviously matter to their makers. The writers have cared enough for their subjects to write about their caring. I reverence their caring. I have no right or reason to talk about the wisdom or the propriety of any subject. What right have I to analyze these poems? For that matter, who has a right to judge poetry?

I know the answers to my often asked questions. "Every right," and, "The Reader."

The Reader has not only the right but the responsibility of saying, "This poem works for me," or "This poem does not work for me." The Reader brings what he knows about being in love or out of love, alive or dead, to the words and white spaces on a page that records somebody else's experiences. The responsibile reader checks his prejudices, even his faiths, at the portal of a poem. He is willing for the time of a poem to be convinced of anything: even the virtue of rape, war, hypocrisy. His judgment centers on the poem as poem. He considers the poem for the way it says what it says. Long after the statement of a good poem holds no surprises, he returns to the poem for its poemness. I know of no other legitimate way to consider a poem. I am talking about technique, the details that compose the unit of a poem.

I like to play a painful game with a poem that has finally got itself written. The game consists of two questions put to the author and the reader. Before I ask the questions, I like to hope that the author has become the reader. On first drafts we tend to defend a poem merely because it happened to us. First drafts often appear to be blood of our blood, bone of our bone. We are protective champions of ourselves. We concentrate on pleasant sounds and pretty phrases, on surprising discoveries and happy shocks, thinking in the flush of having made: "Dear

God, how can I be so talented?" We concentrate on gut, forgetting brain. When the loving author becomes the conscious reader he is ready to complete the poem, a product of heart, head, and hand.

My first question of a poem is, "When you shake the piece, what falls out?"

Honest shaking often leaves a mess on the desk: adjectives, adverbs, white spaces; often the very structure of the poem itself; oftener, the line you particularly fancied. Here is a phrase from somebody else's poem; there is a word which could not possibly be spoken by the poem's voice; over there are punctuation marks. And we need to shake again.

The second question I ask myself is more demanding. The second question is only impossible; but, hoping that the unit of a poem appears inevitable, I must ask it: Am I willing to carve this poem in granite?

The answer is almost always, "Not quite." I am lazy. Confronted with the labor of stone carving, I reconsider the words on a page.

Comparing a cumquat, a cantaloupe, and a kiwi is much simpler and more advisable than attempting to rank the poems "Tall Ship," "Cowtale," and "Sicilian Semaphore." The first is a lyric; the second, a dialogue; the third, a reflective narrative. Each poem displays particular virtues, presents particular problems.

Posing as a teacher in a classroom, I would give mimeographed copies of each poem to each class member. I would ask for written comments on the poems; the poets would be given the comments. At the next class meeting each poet would present his rebuttal. Very likely the poet will also present a rewritten version. Such is the virtue of a writing class. A class offers a wide variety of ears and eyes. If several readers disapprove of a word, a line, a concept, the writer is likely to reconsider that detail. Whether or not he changes his manuscript, he is strengthened in his approach to his own mind and artifact.

As a teacher I would want to engage in a word-by-word consideration of the poem with its author. My concern, I like to think, is finding the author's voice, not my own. I hope the meeting will result in our finding finally where the words live, and why.

Because I feel that these three poems represent early drafts of possible poems, I refrain from the item-picking customs of a classroom or a conference. Sensing that the next dish will be better, I refrain from sending deserved compliments to the chefs. I feel that the poems, as they stand now, are indulgent. The poets have not loved their poems enough.

While reading and rereading these three poems, I have added to the questioning of my willingness to shake and carve. Before commenting on small details of the poems, I list my new questions. They are conventional questions, perhaps, consciously and unconsciously asked by every writer. Often the mere asking will lead to specific answers. The good poem answers the questions fully.

What is the poemness of the poem?
What determines the language of the poem?
What is the norm of the language?
Does the language undergird the statement?
Does the sound of the poem match the statement?
Do the rhythms agree with the mood of the statement?
Are the white spaces working with the words?
What, really, is like what? Do the images cloud or clarify?
What determines a line?
Is the idea proved or merely stated?
Have I read these words, these phrases, this poem before?
Is this poem an experience for the reader as well as the writer?
Does the poem matter now?

I would advise the three poets, as I regularly try to advise myself, to brood on the answers to these questions in the presence of their poems.

Hoping I do not harm the poets or the poems, realizing the dangers of my sounding pretentious, I make a few specific comments on the works in progress. My comments are considerations, not edicts.

"Cowtale"

"Cowtale" presents a dialogue between a fella who wishes to trade a cow and a dolly who is determined to keep her blue beads. Since the man is given both the opening and the closing speeches, I assume he is our focus. But the girl wins the argument; there is No Sale.

I can imagine the real pleasure that the author experienced while making the poem. I can imagine his exuberantly reading it aloud. I can imagine an audience delighted with the little drama of the piece, its brash colloquial talk, its reality and surreality.

But what is the poemness of the poem? I am shy of asking the question, not really positive what the question means. Recently a first-year teacher in Michigan wrote me a special delivery letter, saying, "You forgot to tell me the difference between prose and poetry. Please call, collect." I called, of course, not collect, admitting that I had no proper answer. But I sense the difference between prose and poetry in the presence of prose and poetry. For me Whitman is sometimes prose; the King James version of the Bible is often poetry.

Once the conclusion of "Cowtale" is known, the show is over. With the punch line, the joke is done. After a half-dozen readings, the reader and the situation exhaust themselves. I feel that the vaudeville skit can be turned into a poem by a tightening of the piece, both verbally and rhythmically. A poem is shorthand. "Cowtale" strikes me as a tape recording. I am unwilling to carve the words. I hope the writer will consider the poemness of other dialogues, going back as far as the old ballads, "Edward" and "Lord Randal," through Browning and Hardy, forward to pieces which are, no doubt, appearing in current literary magazines.

"Tall Ship"

The writer of "Tall Ship" has a good sense of sound. My ear is pleased with *gallery, blank canvas, masts, lashes;* with *spars* and *yardarms* and *water*. I like the sounds of *abreast, masts, breath, chests* (although I am not sure that the word *abreast* agrees with the poem's norm of diction).

But what is like what?

A tall ship is like a floating art gallery. The canvases of the sails are like the canvases of paintings set on easels. I am delighted by the discovery of the first four lines. Breeze-blown salt water paints the canvases, I gather, as well as the rigging. Although I find the development of the image rather difficult to visualize (the paintings are pale? the sea-breeze painter, casual?) I accept the picture.

But my delight is lessened by:

<pre>
            A seascape
    where sails swell with breath
    like sailors' white chests.
</pre>

I shake the poem and eleven words fall out. Granted, sailors with white-covered chests do breathe in and out, as "sails swell with breath." I can imagine saving the image, even for this poem. But I was looking at "a floating gallery"; suddenly I am attending a seascape. What is like what? Both *whats* matter. The second *what* should clarify, not cloud, my seeing.

Of course a writer is quite justified in changing his image. I know that "my Love's like a red, red rose," and also "like the melodie / That's sweetly play'd in tune." But Burns does not set up the expectancy of a developed image. "Tall Ship" does.

"Sicilian Semaphore"

Of the three poems, I find "Sicilian Semaphore" the most ambitious, perhaps the poem that needs and deserves the most attention. Were we talking together, I would like for the poet to tell me first what he considers the point of the poem, what the poem is about. Certainly "Sicilian Semaphore" is more than a joke, more than merely "an interesting experience." Here the tidiness of a ship at sea, where "each man has his own purpose," is contrasted with the bedlam of a ship in port where "Strangers come aboard." The narrative begins in stanza 2, establishing the Sicilian Pilot; stanza 3 presents the septuagenarian Captain and the helmsman teller. Stanzas 4, 5, and 6 record the difficulties of the docking. The last stanza concludes the story. We are docked finally, "Not where we had expected," but safely; we are convinced, again, that "Communication is never easy." The story belongs to the teller, a likeable man, conscious of the ridiculous as well as two sea gulls "in full cry."

I hope that the maker of "Sicilian Semaphore" will become its caring reader, concerning himself with the whole poem.

I am not sure what determines the language of the piece. In a real conversation we are men and women on podiums, in confessional booths, at bars, behind desks; we exhort, confide, complain, advise, using a variety of languages. In the little world of a poem we dare not speak as hillbilly, sophisticate, comedian, and scholar without reason for our different words and intonations. I hope the writer of "Sicilian Semaphore" will consider the differences between the language of the first and last stanzas and the language of such lines as: "He broken-english ordered the engine"; "The bemused white hatted cooks"; "And I deadpanyessired them both" (and hardly incidentally: are the "both" the sea gulls or the Pilot and Captain?). The poem's various languages are acceptable; but do the languages belong in the same poem?

I do not know what determines all the lines of "Sicilian Semaphore" as lines. I am assuming that the writer considers the line, and not the stanza, as his basic unit. Almost all the lines work handsomely; the reader experiences a sense of inevitability about them. Because they work so well, some lines call unnecessary attention to themselves:

```
Triple expansion steam
That needs three minutes
For an order's relay, compliance
And the slow turning screw to show effect
Through an air scoop I could hear the Second
       Engineer swearing
```

I am bothered by the passive quality of an action story that seems to call for strong verbs. Stanza 1 gives us: *is, are, has, is, are*. Later we read, "Control was from the flying bridge," and "Those he gave were contrary to the Old Man's expectations," and "Was followed by an arm waving soliloquy."

In a conversation with the author I would be interested in hearing what determines the poem's punctuation (no end punctuation, but a few interior commas; capital letters for line beginnings); what determines the stanza lengths (from five to eight lines). I would like to hear the poet talk about his sense of sound in such lines as:

```
Mostly profane
The Pilot responded in kind
Made angry Sicilian sounds
And semaphored his opinion
Of the myopic Captain, his ship and Americans
       in general
```

I would urge the poet to choose what he considers his best lines in the poem, then concentrate on making the other lines live up to them. Such caring for the poem will result, I like to think, in some delighting discoveries.

The writing of a poem is an act of faith. We start with enthusiasms, envisioning the completed poem, the best poem we have ever written or read. Somewhere between the conception and the accomplishment dark times happen. I fancy that the poem is ultimately made in and from the dark times, searching light.

Blessedly, at some point in the shaking and questioning of a poem, the writer is able to say, "Finished." Perhaps no poet is ever totally satisfied with his composition, but at least he can say, "I have no more questions." Agreed, the poem might be a better poem if written last or next year; but at least the poem is finished. *Here* is the joy of making, the having made. And *there* is the next poem.

Hollis Summers, born in 1916, is Distinguished Professor of English at Ohio University, Athens, Ohio. He attended Georgetown College, the Bread Loaf School of English, and the State University of Iowa. His fiction includes the novels *City Limit, Brighten the Corner, The Weather of February, The Day After Sunday, The Garden,* and a book of short stories, *How They Chose the Dead.* His published books of poetry are: *The Walks Near Athens, Someone Else, Seven Occasions, The Peddler and Other Domestic Matters, Sit Opposite Each Other, Start From Home, Occupant Please Forward,* and *Dinosaurs.*

ROBERT WALLACE

"AND PRAXITELES WAS NOT FIRST"

Shaping a poem is a more ancient, possibly grander gesture than the student imagines it to be. All poets have been apprentices, and, more, apprentices of apprentices, in a direct line from those lost poets who first undertook to remake the world—make it new in their words. Robert Francis's "Aphrodite as History," although it is about another art, speaks eloquently to the point:

```
Though the marble is ancient
It is only an ancient
```

```
Copy and though the lost
Original was still more ancient
Still it was not Praxiteles
Only a follower of Praxiteles
And Praxiteles was not first.
```

We want to write poems because we have been moved by the poems of others. And those we admire determine the kinds of poems we try to write. The wider a student's reading, the greater variety of models (particularly among contemporary poems), the more likely will he be to have at hand sufficient tools for writing his poem. From others' poems, and when we are lucky directly from the poets, we all learn to practice the ancient craft in a new time, "in a spring still not written of."

It is at once a delicate and hardy business, this passing along of craft. The teacher's world is seldom the student's. The teacher will inevitably find himself balancing—on the one side, empathizing, trying to discover the new poem the student wants to write and help him do so; and on the other, passing on the authority of the craft and the language's immemorial ways. The too-adventurous student may need recalling, slowing, untangling; and the too-timid student, chivvying forward, tempting out of his rut. The only serious mistake a teacher may make, besides not telling the truth, is to expect the twenty fledglings to become his disciples.

There is one practical aspect of the student-teacher relationship which deserves comment before I go on to the three poems. The teaching focus should be on the student, not the poem—which isn't so much the emphasis in a literature class. In an actual teaching situation, my response to a poem would vary considerably with regard to the individual student as well as to a variety of other factors—whether a poem is offered early or late in the semester, whether it represents an improvement on or a decline from work the student has been doing, whether it is called forth by an assignment, whether I think the author should be emphasizing this or that aspect of the craft, whether he is a shy or confident student, and so on. Thus, with the exception of my student's poem, my comments here are necessarily arbitrary and, therefore, only approximate the teaching experience. In a class, the student's poem as initially submitted should be regarded as a draft, an imperfect realization of the "poem" the student wants to write. Finding that "poem," externalizing it fully, encouraging the student to find ways of continuing to mold it, is a more empathetic, Socratic process than is possible to demonstrate in an essay.

"Sicilian Semaphore"

"Sicilian Semaphore" presents an amusing scene. The verse is prosy, but appropriate. In general, the shorter a poem is, the tighter its verse should be; the longer, the more open. At some point during the semester, perhaps with another poem, I would want to raise with this student the formal slackness as a problem. The variation in line length, from "Mostly profane" to "Through an air scoop I could hear the Second Engineer swearing," seems arbitrary. And the piling up of lines which coincide with syntactical units, often sentences, seems inflexible—like stacking lumber. I would suggest the possibilities of more flexible, runover rhythms. Perhaps, for now, I might mention the matter and suggest that the rhythm of, say, these lines strikes me as stiff and "boxy":

```
Instant apoplexy
Was followed by an arm waving soliloquy
Mostly profane
The Pilot responded in kind
Made angry Sicilian sounds . . .
```

The passive "Was followed" also undermines the direct effect of the information.

In a similar manner, but for a different reason, stanza 3 seems flat, overly expository, fastened to weak structural formality. The job could be done more simply, less rhetorically—mindful of Pound's dictum that "verse should be at least as well-written as prose." Something like, in prose: "On the flying bridge, the Pilot gave orders in broken English while I manned the helm and the Captain, who had nothing to do, grew angrier and angrier."

However, my immediate concern with "Sicilian Semaphore" would be to point the student toward the problems in "focus"; I am being told, at the same time, too much and too little. As too much, I would mention the inclusion of irrelevant circumstances (like "in time for lunch /

Later"—a detail that should be either developed or dropped) or the repetitive reactions of the Second Engineer in stanzas 5 and 6.

As too little, I would mention the stereotyping of both the Pilot and the Captain. Given the poem's length, we are offered a very over-simplified and coarse picture of the Captain's reaction: "Instant apoplexy. . . ." There is no shading or nuance. No development of the anger, which appears attached to nothing specific. Similarly, the Pilot is presented as a stereotypically excited Italian; no shading, no development. In the quarrel, right seems to be on the Captain's side since we have in effect the supporting judgments of the speaker and the Second Engineer. Yet if so, the mention of the Captain's age and poor eyesight seems irrelevant and confusing—since it suggests some fault on the Captain's part in judging what's going on but doesn't clarify what.

Further, the title points one way, to the Pilot's anger only, but the poem's last line, "Communication is never easy," points another. The last line perhaps both oversummarizes (do we need such guidance?) and misses the mark. Unless there is something we are supposed to know and don't, communication isn't the central idea. What we are told points more to the Pilot's *incompetence* (and perhaps the Captain's, if his age and weak eyesight aren't irrelevant) than to any problem in communication. Each communicates his rage well enough; and whether there was anything else they might have communicated, the poem doesn't make clear. The labile quality of their anger makes it seem unlikely that either tried to communicate anything else? Also, we are given no details about the results of the Pilot's misconceived orders—although lines 1–4 of the last stanza suggest that were some funny or dangerous episodes. Note that it is difficult to take very seriously "or lose anybody overboard" when we have been shown no antecedent misadventures and are told, moreover, that the cooks were "bemused."

In sum, the poem very colorfully presents the peripheries of the central action, but leaves the center incompletely developed. Eight lines are used effectively for background in stanza 1; but hardly more than eight for the quarreling Captain and Pilot. I would encourage the student or the class to discuss the poem in this light, maybe to imagine how the incident might be told as a short story, rather than keeping to a mere tableau as the poet does here. I might suggest that the student read Robinson's "Isaac and Archibald" or Frost's "Home Burial" as models for a fuller sort of telling as well as Randall Jarrell's essay on

"Home Burial," for its beautiful precise account of how elegantly Frost presents the inwardness of a quarrel.

Several other details of "Sicilian Semaphore" are worth mentioning. The diction and syntax are occasionally awkward and flat. Phrases like "contrary to . . . expectations," "responded in kind," or "long as my arm" are clichés and therefore lack punch. Further, it is awkward to say "spoke no English / Except orders . . .," since the first part of the sentence creates an expectation that the rest of it denies. (Compare something like: "spoke only enough English / To give orders. . . .") In stanza 4, "He brokenenglishordered . . ." and, in stanza 5, "I deadpanyessired them both" strike me as odd as well as coy, and out of tone with the rest of the poem's language—interesting usages, but obtrusive and self-defeating in context.

In stanza 6, ". . . cooks / Spent the afternoon" overstates. Surely the redocking didn't require, as this implies, the whole of the afternoon?

I like the image of the Pilot's "semaphoring" his rage, although the Captain should be included in the image, instead of being given the rather vacuous and inaccurate "arm waving soliloquy." On the other hand, the poet intrudes in "my two sea gulls wheeled in full cry"—that "my" seems very condescending. And the sea gull image, suggestive in itself, feels to me merely decorative here, while the "semaphoring" is functional.

"Sicilian Semaphore" is a lively, likable poem, but it needs substantial shaping. The incident is amusing and, told more completely, might be more concretely affecting than the tacked-on moral suggests. All in all, I'd like to see the poem take more room to develop the center of the episode.

"Cowtale"

"Cowtale" is a sprightly shaggy dog story in which a young man tries unsuccessfully to trade a cow to a young woman for her beads. Someone in class might raise the question whether "Cowtale" is a poem at all, and that might be an occasion to discuss stichomythia. We might well conclude that the poem isn't verse. There is no detectable difference from a prose dialog, except that the usual descriptions and he-said, she-said tags are missing. Prose, then, but concentrated into a prose poem, a poem toward prose?

However, as a fantastical piece, "Cowtale" presents more interesting problems in criticism. The dialog is presumably not intended to represent a real encounter. Because we cannot take it literally, it must belong to the area of fantasy; and the poem seems an easy one to write. That is, given the formula of fantasy encounter, almost any material might be used to fill it, since the choice must be largely arbitrary. Why, for instance, "she gives yogurt" rather than "she gives chocolate milk" or ". . . ice cream"? For that matter, why not omit lines 4 and 5 in order to tighten the dialog—or are they important? Speech by speech, there is an arbitrariness of the kind inherent in fantasy in this poem. In this context, if a writer wants to say, "Jerome woke to find a Sherman tank in his bed," so it will be. But the power of fantasy is of itself thin and by itself cannot sustain a poem, nor is it fully satisfying unless there exists as well some psychological or mythical underpinning such as explains the universal attraction of (say) *Alice in Wonderland*. Because "Cowtale" presents an arbitrary fantasy alone, it resists criticism of its parts or details since we are given too little information to define the intention. It is the absence of intention which reduces it to a mere shaggy dog story.

   If some theme is intended, one must guess at it. The shape of the dialog suggests to me that its real content, aside from the cow and beads, may be flirtation. The manner, not the matter, of the dialog is effective. It is clear enough and enjoyable, since we are likely to perceive and share the pleasure of the young woman's having escaped the young man's effort to put something over on her. Both "miss" and "dolly" suggest the woman is young, and the shifts in the man's attitude are nicely expressed by the progression toward familiarity, from the polite "miss" to the disdainful "dolly," and finally to the rude "smart ass." Despite her initial lack of interest ("Listen fella, I've got to get home"), she gets involved enough to say where she lives and presumably is, albeit very briefly, somewhat tempted. Interpreting the dialog as flirtation also draws on the not very subtle sexual meanings of her "fuck off" and his "smart ass," as well as of other phrases in the poem.

   In any event, lines 11–13 seem to me to be a weak spot in the poem as it stands. Everything else fits the fantasy of the attempt at bartering cow for beads. But the young man's suppositions about what the young woman thinks (lines 11–13) seem arbitrary in a way that violates the literal level of the fantasy. He is surely guessing wildly, out of situational context, that she thinks this way about the beads ("if you plant

them they'll grow really high / and you can grab a golden egg").
Possibly the poet has struck a self-conscious note, or maybe he has some
definite symbolism in mind? A "golden egg" and "stairway to heaven
stuff" feel as if another level of meaning is being talked about. In that
case then the beads become symbolic, so is the cow, and so forth. But
if this is the intention, it doesn't quite work. The symbolism seems
tacked on, puzzling, and private.

Enjoying the poem's charm, we want to go beyond the simple,
fantastic situation, but the lack of development of theme prevents our
knowing exactly how to do so. A good discussion might be provoked
by bringing to the class a poem or two of Kenneth Koch's, perhaps
"You Were Wearing," or of Russell Edson's. In addition, in the actual
teaching situation one could ask the student about his aims and, there-
upon, define goals that the present isolated discussion of the poem really
does not permit.

"Tall Ship"

"Tall Ship," by a student of mine, illustrates the process of work-
ing out a poem. When Dave first submitted it, I was struck by the
originality of the idea—the likeness of sails to painter's canvases is a
true one, and the extension of that likeness to the idea of "a floating
gallery" makes a sharp, vivid impression. However, in developing the
idea, the poem goes astray from its initial impulse.

I niggled with Dave about whether a breeze is strong enough
either to lash or to splash; also, whether sailors have white chests.
"Abreast" is clumsy, probably trying too hard to prepare for the
"sailors' white chests." Primarily, however, I questioned having the sail-
painting completed by "salt water / colors" and, somewhat mysteriously,
"a seascape." The effect of salt spray on sails probably doesn't amount to
colors, and certainly not so suddenly as the shift from "blank canvas" to
"colors" makes it seem in the poem. Furthermore, he creates the colors
with splashes on the "rigging" (ropes), rather than on the sails? The
image of the sails swelling like sailor's chests is interesting on its own,
but here is an obstructive digression from the imagery the poem has
started.

Dave was trying to accomplish too much—going from the likeness
of sails to a gallery of blank canvases to having them (or the rigging)
painted. Rather than this elaborately false complication, I suggested

that he concentrate on the impression of a "gallery" and on the simpler
irony of sails/blank canvases contrasted with the colorful, real seascape
around them.

    Dave then submitted version 2:

SEASCAPE

```
Framing a floating
gallery of blank canvas
hanging on easel masts:

the sky—light, fluid
strokes of cream and grey
cloud the azure backdrop—
breathes like the down
breast of a blue heron;

the shore—sand painted—
with feet cool underwater
lies like a bather
tanning in the sun;

the sea—rows of green
and blue, almost black,
brushings curve, coil
agilely white—waves
stand
run
crouch
tuck
their white heads
somersault shoreward
like a watery
troupe of tumblers;
```

```
the horizon—air and water
colors run—miters
sea and sky.
```

The perils of advice! There are good aspects of the additions (particularly the painted sky of stanza 2 and the image of "a watery / troupe of tumblers"). But the stanza about the sand (stanza 3) "with feet . . . like a bather" seems awkward as an image, and the white-headed waves' somersaulting is forced. Overall, stanza 4 pushes too hard. Again, however, this version digresses from its initial impression, so that the sails/ blank canvases against real-seascape irony is lost. Even the elements of the scene—sky, sand, waves, as well as the metaphorical heron and sunbather—don't fit a single vantage point. The effort in the last stanza to recapture the initial comparison—"miters"—is inaccurate, or at least doesn't particularly call up the idea of framing.

Much as I liked the painterly description of stanza 2, pursuing this real versus painted idea strikes me as likely to become terribly self-conscious and literary (real landscape viewed as painting). Dave himself was unhappy with the poem's progress, and in version 3 tried to focus the initial idea directly so as not to bury it or overcomplicate it with description:

SAILING SHIP

```
A floating gallery—
blank canvases
on spars and yardarms
of tall easel-masts.

Around this exhibition,
sea, gulls, and sky
turn, a seascape
on permanent display.
```

I am pleased with this version. It focuses the irony, seems clean and relieved of irrelevancies and false images. Dave has worked the comparison deftly into nearly every line ("exhibition," "permanent display"); and the two equal stanzas reflect visually the balance of the poem's central idea. The two stanzas may also, properly, suggest the mounted, rectangular sails of a tall ship.

Dave subsequently added two further alterations which are distinct improvements. He replaced the slightly forced compression of line 4 with "of masts like tall easels." Also, he returned to the original title in the plural, "Tall Ships," adding an explanatory epigraph, "New York Harbor, July 1976." That is an especially good touch: giving the possibly too "poetic" subject a real-life context cuts the poem's patness.

"Tall Ships" is a modest poem, a verbal snapshot. It is also an accomplished poem. Probably it gives its idea as much weight as it will bear. And the poet's skill is evident in the precision of his choice of the verb "turn" in line 7. Dave struggled to find the word that would collect "sea, gulls, and sky" and pose, in its strong run-on, reality's action against art's stasis (in the verbless first stanza).

When I last heard from Dave, he still wasn't satisfied with the poem. "Actual color seems to be absent from the poem picture," he said, and mentioned the "coloring of a Monet." "Is the ocean represented? Is (are) the seagull(s) present? Is the Tall Ship really there?"

What can the teacher say? That maybe no poem is ever finished, only abandoned. That there may be another stanza, even another poem still to be written, lurking in the rubble of the workshop. That, possibly, being dissatisfied is being a poet.

"Sicilian Semaphore" and "Tall Ships," both sea poems, illustrate two of the ways of trying to revise a poem: expansion, inclusiveness, letting the material run and develop, *or* compression, exclusiveness, refining the material for a weighty nugget. Fortunately for poets, as not for painters or sculptors, the poet can always abandon a trial and return to an earlier, "truer" version and go on from there again. Working out the impulses, separating, untangling "a" poem from all the possible poems inherent in the material of experiences, feelings, and ideas may well be what writing is, in any case. The ultimate aim in teaching is that the student realize one of his possible poems. For the poet, as for the teacher, the recognition that he can be wrong is a necessary modesty.

Robert Wallace, born in 1932, is Professor of English at Case Western Reserve University. He was educated at Harvard College and Cambridge

University. His books of poems include *Views from a Ferris Wheel* (1965), *Ungainly Things* (1968), *Critters* (1978), and *Swimmer in the Rain* (1979).

JOHN HAINES

None of the three pieces of writing submitted to me for comment qualifies as a poem. One of them contains some interesting writing, and with a good deal of work might be made into something—not a poem, perhaps, but *something*, a story, a prose sketch. I am going to deal with these pieces in their ascending order of interest.

"Cowtale"

I find little to say about "Cowtale." As a comedy routine it might go over on TV, or in a café, but as writing it is nowhere at all. It is not even very funny. I think this person needs to decide what she wants to do, and it may turn out that her abilities do not lie in writing, but in some other direction entirely.

"Tall Ship"

"Tall Ship" has one strong image in the last two lines and a sort of general possibility in the rest of it. Probably the attempt to compare masts and sails to canvas on an easel, or to a gallery of paintings, is too farfetched to begin with, and would need a great deal of ingenuity to bring off. It needs an idea, a strong idea, or else great playfulness. And yet there is that possibility: canvas, a shifting surface on which the images pass, break and reform, like water itself.

The "poem" shows as much as anything else the lack of close observation of things. It is full of vague and easy word clusters: "easel-masts," "sea-breeze lashes," "salt-water colors," "seascape," none of which help us to see anything definite. Just on the off-chance, I might encourage this person to go down to a wharf, if he or she lives near water and can find a ship, and look at actual sails for a while. Or go to a museum and look hard at one of the sea paintings of J. M. W. Turner; or seek out a book of his paintings and study them.

There is a further problem in this poem, and that is that we are too far removed from ships with sails, and the kind of men who

sailed them, to relate to them easily, and any attempt to write about
them becomes a sort of reverie or picturebook fantasy, lacking in reality.
Which doesn't mean that it cannot be done, but that it would be very
difficult and not the sort of thing a beginning writer ought to attempt.

The piece is like a brief sketch for something that might be written.
The shorthand phrasing enforces this sketchiness. And this, I suppose,
is what many of us run into when we begin writing: a heap of related
or unrelated things, from which we may be able to rescue one or two
ideas that will make a poem. Here, I would point to the sudden clarity
that comes with those last two lines which I would rewrite as follows:

> sails that swell with breath
> like the white chests of sailors

It might be best to abandon everything but these lines, and see if from
them a new poem cannot be written. They have a fragrance and a for-
ward movement.

"Sicilian Semaphore"

The most interesting piece here is "Sicilian Semaphore." The first
stanza is striking for its oddness, a combination of exact knowledge and
the offhand yet ordered and rhythmic way the writer conveys this. Here
he has done what I expect a writer to do: told me something I had not
thought of, and in a way I had not expected.

It is prosy, if you want to say so, perhaps too prosy to succeed in
any great length as a poem. Yet it is saved by the tautness of phrasing
and by the variety in the rhythm. Just the first four lines illustrate this:

```
There is a tidiness about a ship at sea
The decks are clear
The watches come and go
And each man has his purpose
```

As statement it is clear, and if read carefully the pauses and surges in
the language fall in the right places. Moreover, the four lines that follow
these immediately set up a kind of opposition; the stanza gathers a
tension, the beginnings of what used to be called "argument," and I am

led on to read further. It is a dramatic quality, and although this is not a particularly strong instance of it, it is an element writing cannot do without.

Something of this quality returns in the fifth stanza with these lines:

```
And did not seem to understand
Triple expansion steam
That needs three minutes
For an order's delay, compliance
And the slow turning screw to show effect
```

Here again I see the authority that emerges when real knowledge comes upon the right words.

The rest of the poem, though, falls into a slackness and ordinariness that would be just as effective in a casual letter to a friend. The language is of an entirely different kind:

```
Somehow we got it to the dock
Not where we had expected
But we did not go aground
Or lose anybody overboard
```

It is as if the writer is not sure he really wants to write a poem; or he is afraid of, or embarrassed by, his own seriousness. In writing so close to prose as this, any falling off in the rhythm and precise choice of words, is fatal. I suspect the writer cannot tell the difference between the kinds of writing he has set down, or else he is being careless. I would try to help him see the difference and concentrate on bringing the rest of the poem up to the mark he has set for himself in his first stanza, and in those one or two other places where the writing begins to take on some energy.

As a further suggestion, I might steer this person toward a poem like Henry Reed's "Naming Of Parts," one example I can think of in which dry, matter-of-fact, technical terms are opposed to and fused with images from the natural world, so that the entire poem becomes a commentary of great power.

The best things we write can teach us a lot if we are willing to pay attention to them. Here, at any rate, is something that might become what I would hesitate to call very many things: a poem if the work were done.

I would expect to see in any promising young writer something compelling: a strong sense of rhythm, some original grasp of the language, an exceptional eye for details of the right kind. Some quality, a vividness, an excess, by which I know that a real talent is fumbling at the latches, hesitating and unsure, but alive and actual. There must be some mark by which we know a poem: a tone of voice, some natural force invading the language, demanding that we pay attention. Some hardness or difficulty, some intense joy, or there is no poem, at least none I can recognize. It is a thing we can sense only, whose existence cannot be proven. Nor can it be forced.

My impression from reading these three pieces is that their authors need to read a great deal more than they apparently have. In beginning classes one of the first things I try to discover is what the students are reading, and I frequently find that they don't read poetry at all, or very little. And so, the second thing I do is to make up a list of poets and books of poems, both past and contemporary, from which the students must choose someone and spend some time with their choice. I ask them to write me something—not a formal paper, but something that will let me know that they had read the poet and learned something from him. What I hope for in this is that the student will make a discovery, become influenced. Influences are great things, real influences, anyway, enthusiasms that mean we have swallowed a poet, taken a bath in the work of a great talent, and for a time confused our own imagination with that other. There's a danger in this, of course, but without it I do not think we can learn or grow. We are influenced all the time in our use of language, in any case, and a strong dose of a real writer might make all the difference. Better to take chances: timidity is a worse enemy of good writing than excess.

I don't believe in making things easy for people. Good writing is not easy, and I see no evidence that it will become any easier. If anything, it will become more difficult in a society whose aim is to turn everything into a cliché and to bend language to its own uses, mainly dishonest. We grow accustomed to the use of language to sell and to manipulate, to coerce. And it is a fact that writing, and its manifestation as print, has so often become an instrument of domination, persuasion to an immoral end. The effect of all this is to turn life and death into a cliché. The writing of a poem becomes an act of faith and courage, some force set in motion against the cliché. There is no room for dishonesty, and little to be gained from making things easy for people.

Nor do I believe very much in what is called "encouraging" people. Rather than encourage someone to write, I would try to lead the person to a place where he might be moved to ask himself the right questions. And one question he might ask is: "Do I need to write?" There is no shame in not being a writer, nothing to confess on finding that after all one is not a poet. There are many worthwhile pursuits in life, and writing is only one of them, but one presenting far more opportunities for failure than most.

A further impression I have gathered from my limited teaching experience is that people are not taught that what really matters in the end is *point of view*. I don't mean as a device for storytelling, but in the sense of having a point of view, some real and earned attitude toward life and death. Anyone of us might bring into a workshop a poem by Thomas Hardy, Edwin Muir, Robinson Jeffers, or D. H. Lawrence, and point to the frequent awkwardness, or old-fashionedness, places where the poet stumbled, and yet miss entirely the conviction of voice that carries all before it. And this is what really counts: *having something to say*. Of course it cannot be taught. But people *can* be taught to recognize it and respect it, and not be led to assume that any amount of talk or cleverness will ever make up for its absence.

The fashion these days seems to be all for a poem that does not ask too much of our attention, and whose meaning can be grasped at first reading and consumed on the spot. Rhythms, choice of words, use of images, and so forth, all seem chosen to this end. But my notion of a poem is of something that cannot be exhausted in several or in many readings, whose meaning grows with rereading and one's passage through the world.

I like Frost's remark that "poet" is a praise word, something a few of us stand some chance of becoming after many years of living and writing. It is not something to be handed around indiscriminately. Without assuming any special eminence for myself, I would like to uphold the dignity of that conception.

I'd like to end this brief excursion by quoting a few words once written to a young and aspiring poet by William Carlos Williams. They still seem like pretty good advice:

> "Read, read, read, all the examples of verse you admire, and some you do *not* admire. Concentrate all you can into your phrases, clauses, and sentences. But don't expect quick success. . . . The rest is up to you."

John Haines, born in 1924, has taught at the universities of Washington, Alaska and Montana. He did not study creative writing, but spent a number of years homesteading in Alaska. He has published seven books of poems, the best known being *Winter News* (1966) and the most recent, *Cicada* and *In a Dusty Light,* both published in 1977.

Group VI
MARVIN BELL
RICHARD SHELTON

These two poets worked independently on two poems from the Cleveland State University Poetry Center's public workshop and on the same poem by one of Sandra McPherson's students that Group III analyzed. Bell teaches in The University of Iowa writing program and Shelton in the University of Arizona program.

ALL UGLY SCARRED PEOPLE
Brenda Bochner

All ugly scarred people
see an angel inside of themselves.
Reaching for it,
feathersoft light,
they toss to stars and rocking fairy-boats
soft mirrored pieces of their souls.

I know because my mother told me,
when I was three or four.
I love my mother.
I used to pull her big, floppy strawberry beret
over my ears and my china-blond hair.

She took a picture of me in that hat.
I would sit lopsided on our steps.

When she was dying,
like all ugly scarred people,
she found her angel too
and screamed and screamed so everyone would know.

Brenda Bochner, born in 1947, has studied English with Wallace Pretzer at Bowling Green State University, Bowling Green, Ohio. She is currently a proofreader with a law firm in Cleveland, Ohio.

MY MOTHER DYES MY FATHER'S HAIR
Zena Krall

My mother dyes my father's hair, a crown
of thinning fringe, once white
turns red, dye like blood runs down
the blue sink at midnight.

He bathes like a fury-thrashing
in the sea of her hot rage.
Her nails fork his skull, gnashing
skin into ripples of white waves.

White feathers, blooming scarlet,
rim the mound of smooth skin,
a crest the sea sun once burnt bright,
the color of a rooster's comb.

This is a ritual, a sacrifice,
a witness to her lost womb,
for he shall strut a red plume,
a fruit plucked from her hands.

In impotence of age outraged:
the barren October maple
explodes the feeling in
a few perfect russet leaves.

Zena Krall was born in 1942 and has studied in the Cleveland State University Poetry Workshop for four years under Alberta Turner. She works as a freelance writer.

MOTHER'S SONG OF STRANGERS
*Paul Minx**

The mother like a fine-toothed comb,
the rich chocolate hair, the four steps
from her vanity to the bathroom mirror.
Mother plays her hair like a
violin. Children come to hear her.
Father plays her hair in lust.

Mother is a beautiful horse. No one
can ride her. She wears her hair
like a gown and gallops the village.
At night mother plays her hair
to sleep.

       Three bold men, like night
come and sleep with her.
Mother lies with the goats and the sheep.
Mother opens the door to her womb
that speaks no secrets, only sings

in a high, thin voice
like gold wire: her song of strangers,
her song of the gifts they bring,
of being wanted by all men,

of taking her own life away from them,
for herself.

* See biography p. 54.

MARVIN BELL

PERHAPS HERE

Let me make the necessary disclaimers, and then get on with it. Here are the disclaimers: (1) I teach writing in large measure by teaching reading; (2) When I discuss a student poem, it is partly in relation to other poems at hand and to the overall context of that student's writing, experience, and language; (3) In class, I teach as much as possible by example and descriptive praise, which requires good work for discussion; (4) Dialogue is required for getting straight the terms, and for finding out what the student did that was intentional and what was lucky, what was understood and what was merely accepted, what was programmed and what was intuitive.

Disclaimers aside (Don't anyone, please, take this essay to represent how I teach!), I'll do my best. Of course, none of these three poems about mothers is very good. They are full of attempts to write "poitry." No matter how much these writers have read or written, they are beginners. They do not write poetry so much as they imitate what they happen to think poetry is. Hence, harsh criticism is beside the point. But here's some of what could be said, poem by poem.

"My Mother Dyes My Father's Hair"

If the student can take some kidding, I'd suggest this poem be re-titled "The Blue Sink at Midnight," and directed by Alfred Hitchcock. (And if the student cannot take kidding, that's important to know too.) The new title is portentous and melodramatic, just like the poem. That is, once that dye in stanza one is likened to blood, we are long gone from conscious observation. It's no wonder that Father bathes in "the sea of her hot rage" in stanza 2, and that Mother has lost her womb by stanza 4. Anything can happen!

Enough kidding. Do you know why we like the ending of the poem, why we feel relief at the appearance of a maple tree in October?— Because it is the first piece of careful eyesight in the poem. Everything before has been "created" in the service of writing *poetry*, in the service of raising the event out of the ordinary—indeed, into the realm of ritual, sacrifice, myth! But it won't work. It takes a lot of narrative, circumstance and character to make a myth.

The error here is symptomatic of thinking of poetry as vision and universal art rather than as observation and personal expression. Stanza 1 is mostly descriptive but, even there, the poet is anxious to make things bigger, more important: the dye is "like blood." Thus, in stanza 2, a little liquid in the sink has become a sea of hot rage, Mother's dyeing of Father's hair has become mutilation, and everybody is furious. From there the metaphors of sea and feathers are given their head(s). The intention seems to be to deliver a large argument: that Mother is frustrated and angered by the loss of youth and sexuality (Is Father, like the maple in autumn, impotent?), and is taking revenge on poor Father's scalp even as she tries to make him (look) younger. That's an idea, I suppose, even a story. The language, however, overwhelms the possibility of believable narrative with unbelievable melodrama.

The best verb in the poem is "explodes" in the penultimate line. The best of the objects are that maple tree and its "few perfect russet leaves." The worst word is "fruit," five lines from the end, because its use means either that hair and feathers are fruit (not intended) or that Father is (definitely not intended).

If we are to learn something of Mother's motives in dyeing Father's hair, or of the relationship of Father and Mother to each other and to aging, let it come from fierce observation. The attempt here to give the event significance through metaphor is clearly willful and rhetorical, thus reminding us of Yeats's definition of rhetoric: the will doing the work of the imagination. I hasten to add that "imagination" means a special way of seeing, not of inventing.

As for the poet's erratic attempts at meter and rhyme, it's a fine sign that she is interested. However, she would best be taught about meter and rhyme by discussing it in relation to better examples.

Of course I could make this poem better—by re-wording, replacing, re-ordering. But what would be the point? I am very much opposed to teaching poetry writing by making bad student poems slightly better. That way lies a commitment to the mediocre, a goal of adequacy. In my own mind, I am interested only in the student's relationship to high standards. In other words, I am interested in how well the student will read and write ten or twenty years from now. To teach writing by "fixing up" student poems is a mistake: it lowers standards, creates a flood of miniatures, endorses the limits of adolescence, deprives the student of what genuine excitement there is in reading or writing first-rate poetry, and short-circuits true learning—which depends on the student's own efforts. If a poem is genuinely good, minor repairs are another matter but should still, I believe, be offered with some reluctance.

In this case, revision means writing the next poem. I might, depending on the student, suggest another way of looking at things. For example, I might wonder aloud in front of the student about which is the more bloodlike and suggestive: dye said to be "like blood," or red dye shown to be running seemingly out of the father's head into the sink. I might make a distinction between those things which exist in fact, can be shown and, if observed more closely, might be telling (hair, head, dye, Mother's nails) and those which are made up so as to force the meaning upon us (blood, the sea of Mother's rage). If I did that, it would not be in the service of improving this poem but in the expectation of a much better poem next time. I can already tell that this student is intelligent. *Next time,* therefore, I might discuss with her the relationship of things and language to ideas in poetry. *Next time,* not now.

"Mother's Song of Strangers"

This poem also sounds like *poetry,* which is too bad, although, unlike the previous poem, it is not lost to bad metaphors. No, it is lost to bad narrative. The melodrama that hurts this poem occurs in the form of Mother galloping, Mother sleeping with "three bold men," Mother lying with the goats and the sheep, Mother opening the door to her womb (Ladies and Gentlemen, the infant Jesus). See, I can kid this guy, too.

And he ought to be able to take such kidding, because there are two very nice passages in the poem, plus a few nice miscellaneous phrasings. The first of the good parts is lines 4 through 6. The comparison of Mother's hair to a violin is far better, obviously, than the earlier comparison of Mother to a fine-toothed comb. Moreover, the two sentences that follow derive from the comparison, and this, friends, is one of the secrets of poetry: things can follow. That is, we see in our time much poetry but few poems. Everyone, it seems, can write infinite numbers of lines of poetry, but few can write a poem. The way the three sentences which end the first stanza of this poem derive, one from the other, makes me feel that perhaps this student will be able to write a poem.

I don't want to linger on the middle of the poem. It would seem that Mother has become a horse (with a violin for a tail? or does the end of a stanza mean that what was said in one stanza does not have to be true in the next stanza?). Rather, I want to mention the other fine passage in this poem: the last four and a half lines. I think that, somewhere, there is a poem which begins with likening Mother's hair to a musical instrument and ends with the song she tries to keep for herself. The various "bold men" and animals in the middle of this poem are (to change them instantly the way the poem does Mom's hair) red herrings. And the first three lines of the poem are obsessive, interesting for the possibility of another poem but not germane to this one.

Like the previous poem, this poem has an argument to make. But, as in the previous poem, the argument yanks about the content, rather than deriving from it. But not in the two passages I have mentioned, which are beautiful.

"All Ugly Scarred People"

If the first poem under discussion imitated a half-understood notion of hard-working metaphor, and the second imitated a half-understood notion of symbolic narrative, this poem imitates (but just for a short while) a misunderstood notion of poetic language. I'm pointing to lines 3 through 6, which are false language in the service of a decent idea. It's a hell of a problem, in fact, because it's there in this poem that the poet must say something that means "soul" and something else that means something like a combination of "heaven" and "longing." But the language she chooses is too soft, too sentimental, too sweet.

The best part of this poem is its third stanza, which I like very much. It's a crude poem, this one, unimaginative in making sentences, a minimal report, a simple syllogism, not at all decorous. But it remains close to a genuine feeling, it is about something that matters, and it lets the details plus one trick of point-of-view speak for themselves. It is certainly true that the poem comes out sounding like that of a young person. It has neither adult grace nor a chance at profundity. But it is close to the bone, and its limitations should not be turned against it.

In that way, it is probably not a poem on which much teaching should be based. A little appreciation of its good parts will suffice. And on to the next poem. I wouldn't want to encourage the poet to adopt this childlike tone too often, or ever again. If she insisted on writing poems spoken by children, I would point her to poems spoken by children whose language knows more than they do: for example, Randall Jarrell's "The Truth." For now, let her be told that the language contributes little to this poem, but that it is a poem nonetheless.

In actual practice, I would never say all of these criticisms in this way to a student. It is always a question of what the student can hear. As for humor, it's true that, given some prior groundwork in the interest of mutual trust, I sometimes make light fun of a poem where it is nonsensical or pretentious. As an old ad used to argue, medicine doesn't have to taste bad to be good.

Still, medicine is medicine, and should be used with discretion. It is important to remind both student and teacher that there are no rules in the writing of poetry (except those that derive from the actual progress of the poem) and that the teacher can be wrong. I myself am often wrong. Perhaps here.

Marvin Bell, born in 1937, teaches for the University of Iowa. His available books are *Stars Which See, Stars Which Do Not See* (1977), *Residue of Song* (1974), *The Escape into You* (1971), and *A Probable Volume of Dreams* (1969). For his poetry he has received the Lamont Award of the Academy of American Poets, the Bess Hokin Award from *Poetry*, an Emily Clark Balch Prize from *The Virginia Quarterly Review*, and fellowships from the National Endowment for the Arts and the Guggenheim Foundation. For the past four years, he has written a column of informal essays on poetry for *The American Poetry Review*.

RICHARD SHELTON

"All Ugly Scarred People"
The first and last stanzas have a good emotional thrust, although they need some cutting and rewriting. The middle stanza is doing nothing at all for the poem except distracting the reader from the poem's focus on the mother. It is not sufficiently interesting within itself nor a very good transition from stanzas 1 to 3. If the poem needs a middle stanza, and I'm not sure it does since "my mother" could be substituted for "she" in the first line of the last stanza, it should develop the mother in some interesting and human way and not pull away from her to focus on the child.

Also I would suggest that the diction of the last three lines of stanza 1 is soft and fuzzy. Especially "feathersoft," "rocking fairy-boats," and "souls." These lines should be rewritten. Then I would suggest slight changes in stanza 3 so that it would read this way:

```
When my mother was dying,
ugly and scarred,
she found her angel too
and screamed and screamed so everyone would
    know.
```

"My Mother Dyes My Father's Hair"

I'm not sure the poem is salvageable. On the one hand, it lacks clarity to such an extent that I don't know whether the mother is actually dyeing the father's hair or mutilating his scalp. On the other hand, the language of the poem is so loud and uncontrolled that it constitutes a bad case of overwriting.

The language and associations are mostly stock and expected—clichés of language or ideas. Such language as "thinning fringe," "ripples of white waves," "fruit plucked," "impotence of age," and "barren . . . maple" is worn out and uninteresting. And while the writer undoubtedly wanted to suggest violence, this might have been better accomplished by suggestion and understatement than by such loud, uncontrolled language as "blood runs down," "fury-thrashing," "hot rage," "nails fork his skull, gnashing / skin," and "explodes the feeling." There is also an overdependence on abstraction. The writer often abandons the attempt to show or translate her emotional values into concrete terms, and begins to tell—as in "This is a ritual, a sacrifice, / a witness to her lost womb" and "impotence of age," and "feeling" in the last stanza.

There is a relatively sophisticated attempt to include and sustain certain figures of speech, but they turn into mixed metaphors and get in one another's way. And I believe that no matter how sophisticated or clever the devices of a poem, if its basic language is not good, it will fail. I would suggest that this writer work very hard to improve her basic diction; by that I mean her taste in diction. She lacks a certain sensitivity to diction, a level of sensitivity, without which her work will not improve except superficially. The best way I have found to improve one's diction is to do a great deal of reading of the very best contemporary poetry available. Also, of course, the very best modern prose.

The writer's confusion registers itself in the rhythms of the poem as well as its language. She begins in iambic pentameter, slides into shorter lines which are basically iambic, falls into anapests in the second stanza and then seems to abandon the whole thing and settle for free verse, although she returns to her original meter in the first line of the fourth stanza. This suggests to me that she is allowing herself to be led along by certain rhythms she has heard but does not fully recognize nor understand. The entire poem suggests to me that she needs a great deal of reading and technical study in poetry, prosody, and basic principles of language.

"Mother's Song of Strangers"

First, I would commend this poet for his ability and willingness to handle intricate and interesting sound patterns—assonance, consonance, off-rhyme, and internal rhyme. Then, for his ability to handle a most difficult subject without slipping into any of the traditional pits.

Then I would suggest that he rethink the rhythmic structure of the poem as it reflects itself in some of the line breaks, especially in line 4 where he violates normal syntactical rhythms. He is capable of creating fine music, but sometimes I think he doesn't listen to it.

Then I would suggest that he reconsider some of the language in the fourth stanza: "high, thin voice" and "gold wire" are worn-out expressions. They stand out in a poem in which the language is usually simple and fresh.

Then I would suggest that the last line is a disaster, possibly the entire last stanza. The idea is important and a good way to end the poem, but it is stated so badly, so flatly, that the poem doesn't come to an end, it disintegrates. Possibly the last line could be part of stanza 4 and it could be "of taking her life away from them." But I feel that this is a bad compromise. The emotional energy ran out before the poem was finished. I suggest an entirely new last stanza which contains the same basic idea.

Richard Shelton, born in 1933, teaches at the University of Arizona. He had no formal training in creative writing. His books include *The Tat-*

tooed Desert, Of All the Dirty Words, You Can't Have Everything, The Bus to Veracruz, Journal of Return, Chosen Place and *The Heroes of Our Time.* His honors include the United States Award from the International Poetry Forum (1970), two Borestone Mountain Poetry Awards (1972, 1973), a National Endowment for the Arts Writer's Fellowship (1976), and a nomination for the Pulitzer Prize (1978).

Group VII

ALBERT GOLDBARTH
STANLEY PLUMLY

This group worked independently on a poem by one of Goldbarth's students, a poem by a member of the Cleveland State University Poetry Center's public workshop, and a poem by a student of Lewis Turco, at the State University of New York, Oswego. Plumly was teaching in the writing program at Princeton, and Goldbarth in the program at Syracuse University.

FEAR AND A ROSE
Daniel Van Riper

When the Fearful One found an elegant Rose
Looking at him with her petals open
Sprouting precise, counted words,
He saw a small figure throw a line
But it was only this woman's hand
Displaying an ancient signal.

Love was the essence of her signal
Encased in mental rhythms that rose
With each minute motion of her hand;
Upward finger petals were spread open,

A flaming boat that cast filament lines
Through the murky litter of her words.

She arranged some ideas into words
To supplement her simple signal
With unique conversational lines
While he fought the image of the rose.
The point of their dialogue was open,
The meaning rested with her hand.

They discussed the motion of the hand,
How it seemed to fashion dancing words
As it turns on the wrist, opening
And closing with pulsing mental signals;
In that moment he mentioned the rose
And now she struggled with her lines.

Although she wanted to strengthen the lines,
She checked the motion of her hand
Breaking the accidental rose,
Abandoning the realm of the word,
And holding the force of the signal,
She closed, and left the matter open.

While the palm of her mind lay open
For him, to inspect the strength of her lines,
She felt a need to protect her signal.
Still, rising from the pits of her hand,
Wrapped around the essence of her words,
He imagined the scent of the rose.

Between the open depth of her hand
And lines composed of picked words
Fear was the signal of the rose.

Daniel Van Riper was born in 1956. He has studied writing with Lewis
Turco and Dan Masterson.

IN THE TERMINAL
Linda Monacelli

in cold rush-hour underground
we stood or sat to wait

a tall girl in a long open coat
and corduroy jeans danced

a cop watched   we all tried not to

she romped and reeled in the dim light
a car jumping its track

shivered and slowed to a walk on the moon
eyes going blank   holes where headlights had been

then stiffened into a tap routine
we prayed for a train

an old black guy chuckled from his seat
"you're gettin' that policeman all upset"

she answered with a pirouette
"so ask him to dance"

Linda Monacelli, born in 1949, studied creative writing with Harry
Isbell at St. Mary's College, with Alberta Turner and Leonard Trawick
at Cleveland State University. She has published two poetry collections:
Wild Leisure and *Lacing the Moon* and is currently promotion writer
and assistant to the director for the Santa Fe Festival of the Arts.

GRANDFATHER'S FUNERAL
Nancy Ring

I seek the white sky to blanket my passion.
Standing out against the marshmallow of
winter day, from nearby,

something shining.
No shadows were thrown on the sparkle.

I bow like a shell hunter and peer wondrously
into eyes,
eyes not unlike my own, dangerous,
dipped in the sepia of ancient photographs,
a still and doll like vision contained in a two
by three,
of a grandfather you and a grandmother me,
drawing in their minds forever a connection
between themselves,
humming in three parts the song of themselves,
the cookie,
the wine,
and the fruit.

If I am with you,
I will build a bridge of spectrum wealth into the
uncertainty of your winter age,
like the bleak landscapes admit bluntly their lie
when they show color surprises, sometimes,
in sunsets.
It is a strong bridge, and you can walk upon it.

Numbing cold teases to bite feelings,
by slapping faces until they curse and forget.
The years are coming,
as the snow before me,
smooth and without prints,
not even the wipe of lost lowflying wings
make a mark there.

Some cry, running head on into the ice,
trying to crack the future with useless hammers
of salt and juice.
Some shine,
but most are magnets, hungry for the pure metal
in the human core.

Nancy Ring, born in 1956, attended Syracuse University where she studied writing with Albert Goldbarth and worked on the school literary magazine. She received her B.F.A. in studio art and is currently working at home and seeking employment in the art field.

ALBERT GOLDBARTH

CONFUSING BUT NEVER CONFUSED

"Grandfather's Funeral"

Nancy's poems were always long and lavish. Her specialty seemed to be weaving permutations of two or three initiating images through the body of a sixty-line poem, feeling free, with this understructure in mind, to indulge herself along the way in any number of rich, seemingly free-associative, verbal felicities. This made for dense going. When the density was at its most supportive of the understructure's tone, and at its most skyrockety brilliant, the proper critical response was: *largesse.* At its worst, of course, this dense verbal thicket lost the reader, sometimes even infuriated: he suspected a path, but had to spend time beating in circles through the gaudiest swirls of flora.

This latter response was the class members' most typical. Their own attempts at writing were for the most part brief finely drawn portraits or short tamely surreal sketches that tried for *le image juste* and then knew when to clear off the page. Often these were promising examples of craft in some of the obvious virtues: compression, clarity. Class members at times seemed to feel they were working toward, and out of, a shared aesthetic. And their poems normally provided easy access to constructive critical commentary, and solid ground for ensuing discussion: one could zero in on line 4 of X's sixteen-line portrait of Aunt Matilda with all the assurance of Aunt M. herself retouching a faulty line in her makeup.

My own response to these tight poems, *if* they were already strong, might be in suggestions for future expansion. Full criticism, I'd remind a class, can continue from a word-by-word, idea-by-idea, vivisection of the dittoed poem on hand, to include ways of using a fine-finished poem as a first step: can other pieces extend from it in linear fashion? (Here I might bring in examples from a good poetry sequence—say Norman Dubie's "Alehouse Sonnets." Or can it become one of a number of segments that circle about, and so by implication define, some central concern, as the hole, the real focus, in a donut takes shape only from its chewy surrounding? (And to help make lucid that confectionary analogy I might bring in, say, one of Jim Harrison's suites, maybe "War Suite" from his *Locations*.) Or, natch', should the author leave well enough alone? Does the poem, despite its technical ease, really sound earned and urgent—the *necessary* drive behind Blake's cosmos or Sexton's early self-psychohelp—or does it have that ground-out-for-a-grade feel? how? why? huh? And so we'd go on, sharpening.

But Nancy's work created different and, for this group, special, problems—not a wordsmith's version of shaping one topiary tree but of giving direction to the entire garden. Often the class grumbled and often it was correct: too much helter-skelter, too little tension over vast spaces. Sometimes, though, that grumbling seemed unwarranted, infrequently even strangely hostile. I came to believe the class had little experience in approaching Nancy's inclusive kind of writing; that her work upset some of my students' too-inflexible beliefs about the well-written workshop poem; and even that there existed a subconscious jealousy of the bounty in Nancy's uneven output.

My job sometimes came to be a defending of her work, likely through a demonstration of Nancy's aesthetics as realized in the writing of "professional poets"—so few young classroom poets begin with an intense personal vision and voice, at least in a standard undergraduate class, and I believe strongly in providing outside examples (have, despite the classification "creative workshop," in many situations asked for formal critical papers). Whitman could show the class the power of cataloguing, of sweep, yet still exhibit to Nancy the power of control; or Wakoski's darting certain figures in and out of the serpentine length of one poem, or Koch's cornucopiac yet careful outreachings. . . . Here were two poems on the *same* theme, but *how* did Yehuda Amichai's exquisitely pared-down image differ from Jarrell's more leisurely treatment? . . .

So things went. Sometimes I'd "win," sometimes "lose." The chemistry of the writing workshop makes—need I say it?—for a volatile alembic. What may be necessary advice for one poem or one student

can be intrusive, even negative, for the whole group. The most bizarre
isotopes form. I'd repeat the ground rules (read the work ahead of time
and make notes; be excruciatingly honest—but in a constructive way—
and always exemplify generalizations with specific reference to the text),
then sit back to guide discussion as unobtrusively as possible. And of
course I'd obtrude. The class usually continued to turn thumbs down
and noses up; I continued to be half-impressed. Nancy was, after all,
very young, younger than most in this junior-senior class, and it was, I
believe, her first university workshop. All in all I enjoyed her flawed
rococo murals more than some students' near-perfect miniatures, and I
trusted their self-knowledge. They seemed confusing but never confused.

If the group and I continued to be so at odds, it might make for a
difficult rendering of an objective amalgam of opinion at Nancy's end-of-
semester conference with me. And so I was glad when the class re-
sponded to the early draft reproduced at the start of this section.

Nancy read it aloud. The class followed on their worksheets. I re-
quested an initial gut-level response, some *ooh* or *nyaah* presumably free
of academic finesse. And the class appeared pleased with this new effort.
Despite its too many marks of the novice, "Grandfather's Funeral" indi-
cated to us, in the context of her earlier work, Nancy's willingness to
provide a clearer-cut set of rungs by which to travel down the page.
While not in response to a specific assignment (which I will occasion-
ally make in a lower-level class if students' muses seem blind to certain
options in language), Nancy had (perhaps) kept class opinion in mind.
Now the room began with honest interest to answer my questions on the
poem—before I asked them!

Let's start big: What's the poem's strategy? Well, maybe something
like attracting the reader's conscious attention with a few images that
disappear and then reappear in various modulations (like the vision of
hidden metal/color) while slowly, under all that, an emotional base
(the grandfather-grandmother relationship) begins to clarify and speak
to the reader's subliminal attention. (Then someone might disagree, or
say yes, I agree, but doesn't the blatant title work against such a plan
. . . and we'd be off.)

*Let's get smaller: Which specific sections stick in your head long
after you put down the page?* Well, the places where description is most
physical, like those low wings marking snow; or where the language takes
on a crazy music ("the cookie, / the wine, / and the fruit"). (Then all

of the corollary questions: which of those highlights, even if strongly
done, are just surface beguilement, and not integral to the argument and
emotional cohesion? Which sections are the weakest, too lax, too trite—
and come on, why do I think "the marshmallow of / winter day" hits a
tone that jangles wrong? And so on.)

*Finally, let's get smallest: Which words are just an atom too far off?
Where in the lineation, the rhythms, the punctuation, do we need to do
fine-tuning?* Pick, pick, pick . . . I say *x*, someone disagrees with *x*,
someone else dusts off *y* and *z* . . .

Plus all those other minute discussions touched off by Nancy's poem:
Does it always skirt sentimentality? What *is* sentimentality? Is the lush
onrush too self-indulgent? What's wrong with self-indulgence, though?
Does the tone ever slip from sincerity? If parts *should* be excised, is
there another context that can save them? blah blah . . .

I will generally encourage a discussion to begin with the poem's
strengths, and only later zero fiercely in on its weaknesses. And there
were weaknesses aplenty here: hackneyed phrasing, wordy gushes, ideas
expressed through correlatives that seemed far too tangential to the
poem's main flow to make sense. But below the poem's awkward faces,
something in its muscle, in that muscle's curious moves, encouraged my
faith—yes, the small assured litany of "the cookie, / the wine, / and the
fruit." The introductory music just above that, rhyming *three* and *me*,
then interlineally repeating *three* while *themselves* ends two successive
lines. The way the overlong, overripe, overselfconscious first sentence
of stanza 3 gives way to a single, simple, sincere line of prose sensibility
—a knowing and convincing slam shut of that stanza. Touches like
those, through the whole piece, touched me.

For the most part the room, including myself, was in agreement. We
saw some promise, but wanted a pithier piece, with *fewer* of the poem's
strong visual moments bearing *more* of the poem's thematic weight. I
probably reminded Nancy to attempt a balance between openminded-
ness to community response and her own full-speed-ahead conviction in
her writing. Perhaps she could treat the poem in front of us as rough
notes for a future project—a kind of artist's sketchbook. A few weeks
later the class received a fifth version:

GRANDFATHER'S FUNERAL

Walking the beach for shells,
I bent down to smooth the lightly drawn
    stripes
that black feathers had wiped in the sand.

I found a piece of fruit there,
that wine had stained and dried into a face.
Not unlike the way I think of my grandfather's
    face,
when all the arms were bearing him.

They carried him.
They carried the weight of his rest.
Black wings, the arms lowered him.
They rolled a soft print on me with the back
of his heavy head.

I find much to like here, especially the ease with which the poet-grandfather relationship extends from the image of stanza 1 and is then enriched (truly *supported*, as the corpse is borne) by a return of that imagery in stanza 3. That ordering brings a canny intelligence and a clarity to an emotional fullness that might otherwise have slopped over into *schmaltz*. There's something right in the physical vividness and implicative quality of that wine-dried face on the fruit; in the grammatic incompleteness of "Not unlike . . .," making it compelling for the ear; in the heavy, mimetic repetition of the *carried* lines—yes, mimetic of so much in both the heart and the narrative; in the way that *carried* sound is itself carried over from *bearing* in the stanza above; in the resonance of "the weight of his rest"; in the increasing line count of the stanzas as they approach that final idea of weightiness; in the light touch (remember "the lightly drawn stripes") that blends the funeral scene with the earlier shell hunt. I could go on . . .

The suggestions I have are to let the muscle work even more cleanly, don't let us in on the joints' every creak. In line 3, strike *that;* in line 4, *I found; that* again, in line 5. The poem seems to want that unclutter. I would point out interesting speculation in the poem's first draft that is missing from its last (I think the first version was, inside its plethora of verbal zip, more meditative) and suggest it appear in some future poem. And I would simply make sure the poet was *intending* all the connotation of her *becoming* the beach's sand, or at least some form of the ground, in the poem's last sentence (the two are separate in stanza 1), and not merely contriving that association for a neat tying-together of strands.

But the poem works. I think its doors click shut surely, and its windows give us the view that takes breath.

"In the Terminal"

"Terminal" reads to me like a beginning. The writer sounds untried, and the piece itself like a rough draft. This can mean lack of accomplishment—but can also, I'd remind a class, imply promise. If I were nudging a group into discussion, I'd probably begin with obvious questions like these:

Form. Why the lower-case and lack of punctuation? Do these seem outgrowths of the spirit of the poem, or arbitrary? Does the breakup into couplets seem right? (I like it: the lone units, their own dance down the page . . .) and again: Does it feel planned, or accidental? Why is the fifth line the only one-line unit? *Should* it call so much attention to itself? What about the rhyme the poem eases into (from partial-rhyme to full-rhyme): *moon/been, routine/train, seat/upset/pirouette.* Is this supportive of the tall girl's dancing, is it a pattern the poem earns and knowledgeably uses, or is teacher reading in more than the poet intended?

Language. There's some fairly nice description of the dance in lines 7-9, and the vivid imagination at work there is supported by a musical prosey rhythm—but doesn't this only call attention to sections of weaker description? Though *cold rush-hour* sets the scene clearly and immediately, doesn't it do so the way McDonald's architecture, or a Walgreen's, or an airport lounge does: in overfamiliar, too easily recognizable terms? Given the information implicit in line 1, and certain information that quickly follows, do we need the mundane description in line 2? Does line 6 compare favorably in quality with lines 7-9? Don't you like the *l*'s in line 3: their sound, their own visual length on the

page describing *her* length? And for any number of good reasons, can't
we trim line 14 down to the only necessary word, *pirouette?* I'd be
adamant in defending this last suggestion.

Perception. This subway scene is a typical one, and none of the
props is given much substance, none of the characters given much depth
—to what extent does this reinforce the feeling of big-city standardiza-
tion, big-city isolation, big-city lack of care? To what extent does it
weaken the poem's ability to compel our interest? Why single out the *old
. . . guy* for racial distinction? Does it make any difference that he's
black (as opposed to "white cop" or "tall white girl")? Does the easy
bland phrasing *old black guy chuckled* say anything about his own
easily being categorized? What does this imply about the speaker of
the poem? If "the speaker" equals "the poet," do these implications help
move the poem forward, or do they intrude from some other, tangen-
tial, sphere of concern? And finally, how do you respond to this state-
ment: This poet obviously has an urge to write, an urge arising from
high emotional pitch and sensitivity, but it seems a free-floating urgency
and attached to this subway scene by pure chance.

Discussion might spark if this effort were paired with an Edward
Hopper painting or with Pound's "In a Station of the Metro."

"Fear and a Rose"

"Fear and a Rose" reminds me of a Robert Francis statement on the
sestina—that if a dancer weighs himself down with thirty-nine chains, the
whole point will be to make the dance appear effortless. This poem is
ambitious, and each of its six-line blocks displays care—but I'd be quick
to ask a class at which points we can see, too clearly, this dancer's
sweats.

And something here reminds me, too, of the potential difference
between what's good for *the poem* and what's good for *the poet.* I'd ap-
plaud this beginner's diligent attempt at formal structure, I'd encourage
his continued playing of that old great game; it's exercise that can
muscle a writer. And yet I'd also have to suggest that this poem, at times
so overcompacted, at times so overdiluted, in its effort to fit the sestina's
strictures, might best pour its thematic contents into a very different
container—I'd say this even realizing that, yes, much of the poem's
sensibility (*lines,* for example—how clearly one of its connotations is
"lines of a poem") *wants* a traditional, self-conscious form. This is the

confusing responsibility of advising not a writer on his poem, but a
student on his development.

Because I like the polishing here, I'd want especially to begin with
a list of the strong moments—those most perceptive, most memorably
phrased. Maybe the magical transformation of noun to verb at the end
of line 8, or the way the hand is equated with a rose in stanza 4—gently,
with nothing so blatant as a simile's glaring *like*.

That cleverness often goes awry. The rich associations link up
quicker in the poet's mind (now! line-of-poem-as-lifeline-so-as-hand-sig-
nal-from-a-boat-then-as-rose-like-a-hand-leading-to-lines-on-the-palm . . .)
than his verbalized, exterior play can keep pace with. So we lose that
boat early in the poem, and eventually come to feel that in the thrust
of the organic (*hand-rose-palm-petals-fingers*) and the aesthetic (*words-
conversation-dancing–mental rhythms*), a *boat* wasn't really needed at
all, save for some initial punning. We can see how that punning, in the
rapid domino-downfall of connotation I've already tried to chronicle,
would at first have seemed to the poet to be another layer of association
with which to enrich the body of the poem. But we can also see by
poem's end how questionable is its inclusion in a final version.

Still, this rapidity and wide embrace of the poet's thought will
likely pay off well one day. In contributor's copies, if nothing else.

I'd bring in contemporary examples of the sestina I thought were
particularly smooth—Hacker's "Untoward Occurence at Embassy Poetry
Reading," from *Presentation Piece* comes to mind. And I might try to
use a poem like this to encourage class exploration of the seemingly
"artless poem" versus the "art-for-art's-sake" variety. In this corner, Bu-
kowski; in this, Wilbur. Watch 'em go.

Albert Goldbarth was born in Chicago in 1948. He received an M.F.A.
in poetry at the University of Iowa and has since lived in Utah, upstate
New York, and Austin, Texas, where he currently conducts workshops
for the University of Texas. His published work includes *Comings Back*
and *Jan. 31*, which was nominated for the National Book Award.

STANLEY PLUMLY

READING & WRITING

The three poems in front of me are, I assume, undergraduate. The point is not meant as a judgment so much as it is meant as a determination of what we can and should expect—both of ourselves as readers and of students as writers. We would expect, obviously, more mature work from graduate students; we *suspect* that "In the Terminal," "Grandfather's Funeral," and "Fear and a Rose" represent beginning, undergraduate efforts.

Students, like their teachers, do not operate in a vacuum—there is tradition, as Eliot has told us, as well as individual talent. And even sons and daughters of the swan can share something of every paddler's heritage. Beginning student writers, no less than the rest of us, live inside the history of poetry, within the anxiety of many influences. The thing is, especially at the beginning, to allow those influences, to be informed by them. I would like to think, for example, that the author of "in the terminal" is aware of Pound's famous "In a Station of the Metro," if only for its single-stroke visual authority; that she has at least read Theodore Roethke's "My Papa's Waltz," if only for its beautifully balanced connection between dancing and romping. I would like to think that the author of "Grandfather's Funeral" has read and ruminated over a whole range of elegies in English, has come to a little understanding of how the elegiac occasion itself implies a certain ceremony, a clear need for control of the potentially sentimental—has some sense of how the occasion *indicts* formality. I would like to believe that the writer of "Fear and a Rose" has looked up the fact that as an established form the sestina began with the troubadours as an intellectual complication of more ordinary musical values; that he has read enough sestinas—especially modern and contemporary, especially Auden and Donald Justice—to realize that as an elaborate, interweaving form it favors reason over rhyme, a pattern more primarily of sense than of sound; that he has played enough with the form to know that form itself can be an enemy as well as an ally.

Teaching, like many other arts, is the art of love, of telling the truth with affection, and, if needs be, with appropriate anger. These three poems, as writing, are not very good; as feeling, as examples of a particular emotion being worked through—as opposed to worked over—they feel false. The problem for teacher and student, whether in workshop or con-

ference, is how to negotiate such news—the basic news that one writes
badly for a reason, that whatever the terms for writing well, writing
badly is no accident. Admitting other people's poems into the discussion,
both the consolations of the contemporary and the relevant past, is one
way to begin. Surrounding the student poem with an actual context lets
everybody know that poetry is the issue, not personality. Reading ought
to be another form of writing; the student should be encouraged to lose
him- or herself to that process, that testing of one's own experience with
the language against someone else's. Roethke was literal-minded about
this process. He literally "rewrote" other people's poems in his notebooks
—rewrote by copying by hand, and re-copying Yeats and others. I am try-
ing to say that when a student and a teacher sit down to talk about a
poem there ought to be witnesses, there ought to be poetry in the room
as well. *The ABC of Reading* is a good place to start, if not with poems
themselves.

Finally, of course, every writer must become his own best reader—
the ultimate arbiter between what works and what he or she wants. The
writing workshop or conference is a means to that end, in which all the
roles—writer and reader, teacher and student—are reversed. Every poet
who teaches and every student who learns, therefore, is in school.
Teaching and learning proceed from the shared love of the art itself. The
individual personalities involved are secondary.

Once an atmosphere of trust is established, once it is understood that
the authority lies in the art and not with the poet, then full attention can
be turned to the single poem at hand.

"In the Terminal"

None of these poems deals directly enough with its sources. "In the
Terminal," however, is more cleanly written and felt out—it at least speaks
in the language of its experience, though "romped and reeled" is not
quite the music, to my ear, for the kind of dancing implied in "pirou-
ette." (And with "tap routine" most of the dancing bases are covered.)
But that is only one of the inconsistencies here. I have trouble connecting
the "cold rush-hour underground" with a place where old black men
"chuckle" and young girls turn figures of speech. Not that it is not pos-
sible: with so little information, visual and actual, the sweeping generali-
zation of the first instance exaggerates, melodramatizes the possibilities
of the second. I have even more trouble with the imaginative convictions

of the poem—how tall girls dancing can get converted, at the convenience
of author and setting, into "a car jumping its track," and how that trans-
fer can jump ahead to a slowmotion "walk on the moon," and how that
leap can replay back to a headlight hyperbole about a girl's "eyes going
blank." This is more than footwork; it is manipulation; it is arbitrary
rather than discretionary imagining. Rimbaud may have been the first
poet to teach us that there is real energy in the fragmentary, discrete
imagination; he and the French surrealists carried dissonance to a logical
conclusion. But underneath the broken surfaces—and this is perhaps the
most important lesson to come out of the whole Symbolist/Modernist
movement—there had to be a coherency of tone, of feeling, of attitude, of
point of view.

"In the Terminal" is too small a poem to tease with such a big bone
of contention. Still, it misreads its own internal music, the music in a
line like "shivered and slowed to a walk on the moon" in which we can
see, in time, what we have been told to feel. Most of the other lines are
concise, short-cut readings of the full event. Two vital needs are not
being met in this poem. First, as readers we are not assured of why we
are being asked to watch this tall girl; secondly, we are not clear who,
throughout, is doing the asking, the watching-narrating. We do not need
names so much as we need identities—a more local, limited sense of our
speaker, the one who is speaking for others. The answer to *why* is nec-
essarily tied to *who*. The point of view in the poem is blurred, if not
anonymous. The poet seems to be speaking for a fairly large audience
of commuters, whose chief characteristic is embarrassment ("we all tried
not to watch"). There is also a cop and an "old black guy," between
whom the girl, the heroine of the story, is suspended. For fifteen lines,
even as spaced as the seven couplets are, this is a lot of traffic. Too much.
Poetry, like fiction, begins in point of view. Why we are asked to watch,
to share this experience, is dependent on who is asking. If the present
speaker is merely going to perform an act of journalism, the reporting of
the event, she should not expect much response—if she is intending social
satire, social comment ("we prayed for a train"), she should write an
essay. When a writer is not clear about his emotional resources he tries
to "write" his way out. The high-stakes metaphor-making in this poem
is an attempt to impose an emotional solution not inherent in the
material.

This poem is really about the speaker's attitude toward the raw material of the girl, the cop, and the old black guy. With that much population it deserves a longer, fuller reading—the kind of reading Williams would give it or, more recently, Louis Simpson. Experience has its spokesman as well as its syntax. By purging the poem of certain cause-and-effect information—further clues about the place and the girl, for instance, that might more completely suggest atmosphere and texture and that might more fully dramatize a reason for dancing—the poet-speaker has all too willingly surrendered her authority, and her "consistency." More to the point, she has called into question the moral position of "we all." By keeping her virtuous distance from the event she has invited us to make a judgment. And if we are to judge the observers here they should be better identified as to situation or stereotype.

Is the poem supposed to be satiric of its "speaker"? I would rather not think so. I would rather think of the poem's potential for lyricism; I would rather think of the dancing as a celebration, the girl not drugged but the "happy genius" of her body. But my sympathies are closed off by the apparently patronizing speaker, a speaker who has pluralized her position. How much more effective if just two people were watching this scene unfold—lovers perhaps, though not necessarily stated as such. How much better if the girl were inventing her dance in front of us. How much better technique if the cop were mentioned only in the report of the old black guy (a possible hoofer himself). How much more evocative if it were not the rush-hour, but instead an empty time of the day, inside the echo chamber of the "underground." And how much richer an imaginative experience if the poet had stuck to walking on the moon, the terms of the real dance, and stayed away from the obligatory train.

"In the Terminal" is not living up to its own promises—the dance as discovered from within the event. Its short-cut rhythms are too abrupt for the continuity of motion the content is proposing. The grammar of the experience is asking for completer yet more varied sentences—sentences that are themselves questions rather than conclusions. Sentences spoken in sympathy and honesty. Rhythm is the expressed reading of an emotion, but that emotion must belong to someone. The one saying it.

"Grandfather's Funeral"

"Grandfather's Funeral" is cluttered with actual clichés and invented clichés—the blanket of snow above, the "marshmallow of/winter day" below. It wanders from place to imaginative place as if in search of a center of gravity. Almost every line is understood as a kind of free-floating verbal "skill"—an assumption that poetry is something made up. Creative writing, I think it is called. The poem's lack of focus, its apparent inability to deal directly with the stated source of its concern (the grandfather's funeral) forces this young writer into strategies of repeated "discovery." The poem begins and ends as if the poet were speaking to anyone, us. In fact, though, it is addressed to the dead, the grandfather. The poem seems filled with images when in fact they are abstractions. The poem talks about "feelings" without actually demonstrating them. It tells us almost everything we did not need to know; it starves us. It chooses to describe rather than evoke; to be discursive rather than directed.

The "conceit" of the sepia photographs (there is no such article as an "ancient" photograph), it seems to me, is the true center of things here. "A still and doll-like vision contained in a two by three/of a grandfather you and a grandmother me" pretty well accounts for the genealogical and ontological connections, to the extent of a nursery rhyme rhythm. The frame of a photograph would have been the natural way to limit, to draw in, to concentrate the assemblage, emotional and visual, detailed and landscaped. A literal focusing event, such as looking into the fixed past in order to transcend the present grief, would have also "released" the poet from the indictment of invention. Some of the writing in this poem is good—

> The years are coming
> as the snow before me,
> smooth and without prints,
> not even the wipe of lost lowflying wings
> make a mark there.

—but most of it suffers from its failure to find and hold on to the one thing. At one moment the speaker is a shell hunter, at another she is building bridges of "spectrum wealth"; other moments have no attachment to anyone in particular—"Numbing cold teases to bite feelings/by slapping faces until they curse and forget." The last stanza is nearly silly in its admixture of metaphor.

We write badly for good reasons. The poet in this case has allowed the language to lie for her because she is either unwilling or unable to deal with the emotionally complicated headline of her title. The poem is supposed to be an elegy, an elegy in which the writer is looking for a way out of her "passion" by looking into the eyes of the dead. Yet contrivance continually gets in the way of the content, which is that the years are coming as the snow before me. The grandfather is the antagonist in this piece: the protagonist is the speaker. The snow is coming to get me. Forget "the cookie,/the wine,/the fruit." Remember those sunsets that sometimes show color surprises. Forget the "useless hammers/of salt and juice." Remember the snow without shadows.

If language is our chief moral commitment to reality, then this poet has avoided the initiating and advertised issue of her poem. These may be bells for John Whiteside himself, and we may be bending over the casket, and we may be looking into that face, those imagined eyes, and seeing a photograph of the man and grandchild together in winter, where outside, right now, it is snowing—but as readers we cannot be sure, because the poet labors under no obligation to discriminate the living from the dead, photography from pretty pictures. With the "subject" unfocused, the emotion spreads thin, and we are left with announcements rather than acts. Grief is the subject—"It is a strong bridge, and you can walk upon it."

"Fear and a Rose"

"Fear and a Rose" has the smell of an assignment. If true, I hope the assignment was made with the expressed written consent of at least a dozen other sestinas, particularly contemporary. Sestinas are difficult enough without the extra burdens of the allegory. This one weighs in heavy with not only the "murky litter" of its words, but the goldplate of symbology. It has too little alternative to coming off archaic—archaic in language, archly abstract in conception. It reads like an exercise, as lines being filled according to formula. I simply cannot see the point in allowing a student to play such games, unless everyone involved is agreed that poetry is a party favor.

If this effort is a love poem rather than the rape of a lock, it should be allowed its struggle in a form consistent with its ambition. If it is only a form disguised as a "love poem" it should be mailed as a valentine. The idea of the sestina, of repetition and return over a territory of some size, in a timing of some dimension, is the most wonderfully obsessive notion in poetry. In no other poetic moment does form so surely assume content—whether the form is only being appealed to, as in Henry Reed's "Naming of Parts," or whether it is being slavishly exploited, as when Swinburne *rhymes* the pattern of the six end-words. Assignment or not, "Fear and a Rose" reminds me of the container concept of teaching "creative writing." Give the student some empty bottles, let's say some sonnet bottles, a shapely villanelle, a long-necked sestina, a squat little rondeau, and a Baedeker's knowledge of French or Italian, and let him fill up.

Stanley Plumly was born in 1939. He has taught at several universities, including The Iowa Writers' Workshop, Princeton University, and Columbia University. His books include *In the Outer Dark,* for which he received the Delmore Schwartz Award, *Giraffe,* and *Out-of-the-Body-Travel,* which was nominated for the National Book Critics' Circle Award. He has received an NEA award and held a Guggenheim fellowship in poetry for 1973–74.

Group VIII
DONALD JUSTICE
JUDITH HEMSCHEMEYER
JOHN WOODS

The poets in Group VIII all worked independently on three poems by members of the Cleveland State University Poetry Center's public workshop. Woods teaches in the writing program at Western Michigan University, Justice in the program at the University of Iowa, and Hemschemeyer (now at Douglass College, New Jersey) was then teaching in the writing program of the University of Utah, Salt Lake City.

HER DAUGHTER
Bob Vance

sometimes has the same displeased wrinkle
silenced across her brow;
can be the child wishing
for small sparkling things
to be put on shelves and dusted.

Her daughter has dark skin too,
olive and mediteranean.
I read her stories of wizards

flying in huge sailed schooners
and she thinks
I must be one: "where's your mooned hat?"

But it is only this chair I say,
you could feel kingly too,
the captain of some fleet
of water-wavered angelfish.

No, she would much rather
rollerskate or take long walks
for ice-cream when leaves
pull down in night-heat
and I find speech hard

because of rhodedendrons,
bits of glass on the walk,
a cooling breeze, yes
her daughter

knows about earthen hands, thinks
I am tall enough to touch
another sky and I shake my head
rolling the cigarette between
my fingers thinking about

her daughter
watching waves from some light-craft
her sails blushing orange,
billowed with wind.

Bob Vance was born in 1954, studied creative writing with Alberta Turner at the Cleveland State University, and is currently completing his studies with John Ruhlman at Thomas Jefferson College in Grand Rapids, Michigan.

PROGENY
A Poem from David
Anonymous

The last time I saw my grandmother was in a rest home.
"Mother, you remember David, and this is his wife Daun."
She didn't understand that or anything all that visit,
would point to us and ask, "Who's that?"
"Now Mother, you remember David, and this is his wife Daun."

Finally I answered.
"Grandma, I'm David. This is my wife Daun.
I got married."

She blinked, asked blankly,
"Well, do you feel better?"

It was the perfect non sequitur.
"Yes," I said, "yes, I do."

ASTRONOMY I: THE VOID
Rosalind Neroni

I am the blackhole in space
            a ferocious suck.
        even as he hurtles to me
    I rip him in half
    tear him front from back
            nose liver testicles
        drawn to the wound in
        the void.

    (I am hung here, damned,
    but I am merely the hole.
    He comes, foul-smiling fake
    bearing empty boxes,
    crying "fill me, hide me
    cover my fear.")

He hurtles to beginnings
littered with other livers,
re-assembles
where he starts.

The void is only for me
I hang in the place between
here and here, a hole to
nowhere:

like the eye of a needle,
I separate nothing.
A fly passes, a camel
no matter.

Rosalind Neroni was born in 1946 and has studied in the Cleveland State University Poetry Workshop under Alberta Turner. She writes fiction and poetry and works as a house painter in California.

DONALD JUSTICE

"Progeny"

Of the three poems, this one comes closest, I think, to saying itself. It's very prosy, which is probably a part of its somewhat primitive charm, and the prosiness seems appropriate to its anecdotal character. It disdains decoration and even effort (except for "blinked . . . blankly," which perhaps sticks out a little). Even the near repetition of line 2, which might appear moderately artful, seems forced on the writer by the anecdote itself, and therefore properly artless. Best of all, the poem ends at the right place, and when it does end, the writer has tact enough to stop at once, a knack not everybody acquires.

He also shows himself alert to catching the sort of point experience itself sometimes makes—almost as though he had caught a found poem in the act of happening. The very shape and extent of this piece—I hardly want to use the word *form* in this connection, so little worked up is it— are determined by the anecdotal matter, and the writer is wise enough to leave that almost alone, once having noticed it in the first place, which was the main thing.

I would have preferred that he leave the anecdote entirely alone. I feel mildly condescended to when told that the grandmother's inquiry was a *non sequitur* and not only that but *perfect* as well. Such commentary, such nudging might be spared. A pure exchange of dialogue here would go better, I'm pretty sure. In fact, the whole poem might, in its purest imaginable state, consist only of dialogue. Try that. If any exposition at all proved necessary, it could be put into a title: "In the Rest Home." I'm usually in favor of shoving the exposition up into the title anyhow, at least with many short poems having so definite and pointed a character as this one. (By analogy with epigrams, say.) In any case, the title and its subscript here strike a somewhat false note, if titles are to count for much, sounding just a little pretentious in comparison to what follows.

No need, I suppose, to go into the wit and pathos of the grandmother's last question nor the agreeable appositeness of the poet's reply, which constitutes, really, a kind of recognition. That was what made the whole thing worth noticing in the first place, and worth recording.

"Her Daughter"

This one is more literarily ambitious, and it is not without its pleasures and marks of talent. What I object to, however, is just that it does seem so "written" or "written up." It is as if certain handbook prescriptions for literary excellence, familiar ones at that, had been handed out and followed. For instance, an injunction to use plenty of sense detail ("bits of glass on the walk"). I like sense detail almost as well as my friends seem to, and I even like the bits of glass all right, in themselves. What troubles me here is some suspicion that the sense details count for less in themselves than as examples of something required by imagined rules. Even admirers of the poem will have to concede the sentimentality of a good deal of the writing ("small sparkling things") and of the general attitude. There is a softness overall and a lingeringness and a slight overemphaticalness, like a sort of drawl of feeling. In rhyme and meter this might have ended up seeming like society verse.

I think the literary and the sentimental may be connected in this poem and, if so, come probably from the same source, a partial and prescriptive notion of poetry. Is poetry supposed to be full of the fanciful—wizards, mooned hats, angelfish? Is poetry the better for including mostly pleasant things—ice cream, long walks, rhododendrons, angelfish again?

Is it meant to encourage certain attitudes—roughly those shared by a selection of UNICEF cards? (Gottfried Benn, where are you?) I exaggerate, of course. But the poem does make me think of what one of Kenneth Koch's bright and gifted grade-schoolers, grown up, might have written, developing his formulas.

One last, smaller objection. What is a *light-craft?* Is a light (i.e., not heavy) boat intended? Or a vessel that gives off light? Or what? Is the craft, as convention would have it, female—unhappily confusing the reference of the pronoun *her* in the next-to-last line, which I find hard to disentangle from the little girl of the poem? Such confusions are not helpful, nor are all ambiguities enriching. Probably this is mostly unintentional and ought to be, in any case, easy enough to clear up, if the will to do so is there.

What I like best about the poem is the continuity of voice in it, an effect clearly related to the rhetoric and syntax, which keep going on and on and making connections as they go. ("But . . . No . . . yes") The poem comes close to possessing a sort of paragraph rhythm, if that's possible, in the very unwinding of the argument, in its simply not stopping. I wish the writer might have taken less pleasure in dwelling on things along the way, while the poem itself, it seems to me, wants to keep moving, moving.

"Astronomy I: The Void"

This looks to me like a rather early draft, in that the parts don't seem to follow from one another, though all deal with the same thing, more or less. It's like notes on a topic, notes in the form of images mostly. But organization is not the real problem.

The violence of the language quickly proves more than a match for the subject. I don't at all mind the subject; in fact, I like it, abstractly. I am put in mind of a handful of images in Baudelaire or of Rochester's poem on Nothing. But it isn't this text which calls the others to mind so much as its declared subject, and no amount of grandeur in a subject will make up for what is lacking in conception or treatment. Some sort of undigested rage seems to be boiling up here, and from the content of several of the images I suppose it to be sexual, however unacknowledged. I would prefer the explicit in this case: then it would have to be acknowledged and dealt with, instead of remaining in hiding.

The most salvageable clause, one with a dignity equal to the subject, is "I hang in the place between / here and here," and of course this contains a perception of some interest, not only contains it but expresses it with wit and in a plain, effective style. Other perceptions may be findable here but I don't find them expressed. "Beginnings / littered with other livers"? A sound effect has been got up here, featuring numerous short *i*'s, but I am left with too dense an impression of the kind of beginnings these must be to care. Insofar as I can *see* them, they seem to belong to an abbatoir. As for the allusion in "like the eye of a needle, / I separate nothing," I think the *camel* which follows only adds to the muddle, if one is supposed to be recalling the biblical point. Part of the problem seems to lie in the verb *separate*—is it accurate? How much does it matter that nothing is separated by this needle's eye?

Similarly, can we have a "hole *to*" anywhere? A door to, yes, but this seems strained.

I think violence has been mistaken here for expressiveness.

Donald Justice was born in 1925. He studied at Stanford and at the University of Iowa, where he now teaches. His books of poetry include *The Summer Anniversaries, Night Light,* and *Departures.* His first book received the Lamont prize, and he has held several fellowships since, including a Guggenheim.

JUDITH HEMSCHEMEYER

"Her Daughter"

This poem has great potential. The writer sees the child as an extension of the wife, a very powerful concept. As I read it, the poem is written by the father to the reader and it is written "through" the child and the wife. This device provides layer on layer of emotion, a technique that I find just right for a "family secrets" poem. The writer has very good control of the material, that is, he or she is able to write about love and a child dramatically but without sentimentality.

If the student who wrote this poem brought it to me for advice, I would start by emphasizing these positive aspects of the poem, since I have observed that the first thing a poet develops is an ego. Having praised, *not* flattered, I would proceed with the nit-picking.

I find the description of the child in the first two lines so delightful that I want more. I feel a bit let down when, in stanza 3, the father is made to say, "you could feel kingly too, / the captain of some fleet / of water-wavered angelfish." As *The New Yorker* would say, "Lines we doubt a father ever said." They are too obviously "poetic" and draw attention away from the child and toward a grown-up trying too hard. I would ask the student to read the lines over and over, aloud, hoping that a few readings would make it obvious that eliminating "water-wavered" would make the whole stanza work more effectively.

Stanzas 4, 5, and 6 are strong except for the self-dramatization of the lines "and I find speech hard / because of rhododendrons, / bits of glass on the walk, / a cooling breeze, yes." This again draws attention to the grown-up ostensibly trying to understate his emotion by implying it is *caused by* rhododendrons, bits of glass, and so on. It isn't. It is caused by much more than that, by years of living and loving, years both before and since the child's birth. Why diminish this? Why not just itemize the rhododendrons, the glass, and so on, and then, at the end of stanza 5, use the line "and I find speech hard"? In this way understatement would work to open up the poem, implying that every-thing noticed and anything that happens in the presence of a loved one contributes to the mysterious moment of perfect love. In fact, the writer *might* be able to recreate the shared experiences of the "long walks" so intensely that the line "and I find speech hard" becomes unnecessary. Conveying emotion by successfully manipulating and jux-taposing physical objects and sensations is one of the oldest devices—think of the Chinese poets—and still one of the best.

Moving on to stanza 6, I would ask the student about the first line, "knows about earthen hands." Is it supposed to imply the child's aware-ness of mortality? If so, I feel that the use of the poetic word "earthen" is too precocious for what we know about this child. It is the grown-up's diction obscuring the child's direct pragmatism. Or does "earthen hands" mean that she likes to make mudpies? If so, why not say so? The rest of stanza 6 works very effectively, suggesting emotion by a close reporting of observable events.

Stanza 7 is marvelous, I think. Here the child is transformed into a sailboat in the father's imagination. Implicit are the grace and strength of a sailboat, the inevitable "sailing away" of the child from the parents, adolescence ("blushing orange"), and even pregnancy ("billowed with wind")—her own *and*, of course, the wife's.

This is the best possible ending, I think, one that satisfies the emotional and aesthetic expectations set up at the beginning of the poem and yet takes off on its own.

Because the substance and the structure of this poem are so sound, I would assume that this student is ready for some criticism on craftsmanship—line breaks, for instance. The lines of the first three stanzas are arranged in phrases that "make sense" separately. This sets up a pattern of expectation that breaks down in stanza 4 ("for ice-cream when leaves"), and so on, and then is reestablished. Now, the line "for ice-cream when leaves" is perfectly acceptable if it is part of a pattern, if there is a reason for it, and I find that getting students to talk about line breaks is one of the best ways to introduce them to prosody. Why, in this instance, does the writer want the reader to pause after the word "leaves"?

My final word of advice to this student would be to get an O.E.D. or gain access to one somehow. The words misspelled are *mediterranean* and *rhododendrons.* By spelling *mediterranean* with one *r* the writer indicates his or her ignorance of the etymology of this splendid word. And *rhododendrons,* tree of Rhodos . . . Words, after all, are all we poets have.

"Progeny"

This is an accomplished poem, psychologically sound, yet startling. The grandmother, who "didn't understand that or anything all that visit," manages to ask exactly the right question with the candor of old age. It cuts right through the social niceties of polite discourse and evokes a swift and honest response from her grandson. The student cleverly ends the poem right there, with the response "Yes, yes, I do," the same response he gave to the minister, priest, or J.P. awhile before and the response he may someday regret.

The poem is so well done, so pared down—as spare, in fact, as a thin old woman about to die—that I would ask the writer how he or she would pare it down further, what lines might be omitted. Hopefully, he or she would realize that line 1 is unnecessary, or could be if the title were something like "Rest Home." The people in the poem, David, Daun, David's mother, and his grandmother are perfectly delineated in the dialog, so the flat expository line is superfluous. If I am reading the poem correctly, the line "It was the perfect non sequitur" is also superfluous. The grandmother's question, "Well, do you feel better?" is a perfect sequitur, in fact, as his response indicates. Surely the writer is aware of this and by saying "perfect non sequitur" means sequitur. But I think he should trust the reader to make the jump from the grandmother's question to the grandson's response without any comment, ironic or otherwise.

The reader, almost any reader, has "been there," has participated in some similarly stark, hopelessly affecting rest-home scene.

"Astronomy I: The Void"

I will admit that my heart sank when I read the title of this poem. Like most "teachers" of poetry, I dread the words *cosmos, chaos,* and *void* or any combination thereof.

But this poem, somehow, has the potential to transcend its *verboten* celestial imagery. I would begin a discussion of it by pointing out the powerful rhythms set up in stanza 1. This student instinctively knows how to slow down and speed up the reader and does it in the first five lines with alternating dactyls and trochees, a terrific spondee (*nose*), another trochee (*liver*) and then, with *testicles,* a return to dactyls.

The strong stress meter and the skillful use of alliteration, the Anglo-Saxon poetic devices, are well suited to the primitive subject matter of the poem: sex. Of course, the student might have done all this unconsciously, and only by talking with him or her could one ascertain how much of the "technical stuff" she or he is ready to absorb. (I remember being very depressed when a helpful German student analyzed my first published poem. It meant I had to *learn* what I had been doing naturally.)

Having pointed out to this student that she or he has a natural gift for putting words together in a dramatic and pleasing way, I would point out some problems. First: starting with such a strong image—the female as the "blackhole in space"—means that everything else in the poem must be downhill. That's all right if the writer is content to go from a bang to a whimper, and I think it works here, with the casual, prosaic ending: "no matter."

Second problem: overexplaining. The second stanza tells the reader, or tries to tell, what is wrong in the relationship. I don't think it works because it is such a letdown imagistically—from a dismembered male to a "foul-smiling fake"—and because what is wrong turns out to be just the cliché male-female thing—he is scared and needs to use her.

Also, having him "bearing empty boxes" adds a note of confusion, since she is the blackhole, the empty one. I think the word "wound" in stanza 1 is sufficient; it tells the reader that she is suffering and the reader can take it from there. Stanza 2, then, could be omitted.

Stanza 3 moves to the idea that the male hurtles through the female and reassembles, more or less unchanged. I would ask the student to read it through aloud a few times, hoping he or she would sense the ridiculous literal image of the line "littered with other livers" and the weakness of the word "beginnings." The stanza needs more than paring; it needs rewriting, and often the impetus for the rewrite will come when the student tries to answer my naive question: "What were you trying to say?"

The last two stanzas are strangely wistful—the "ferocious suck" has become "the eye of a needle"—and very effective, especially that throw-away last line, "no matter."

Very well done, I would say. Then I would give my short lecture on line breaks and punctuation. If you start by using a pattern of line breaks and standard capitalization and punctuation in a poem, use it consistently throughout the poem or violate the pattern only for a reason. In this poem, line 1 in stanza 4 is end-stopped and lines 2 and 3 are run-ons, but the reader must deduce this. And surely there must be a longer pause than is indicated between "camel" and "no matter." This pause could be indicated by punctuation (one of those infamous colons) or spacing. Asking the student to read the poem aloud will usually make these technical problems obvious.

Judith Hemschemeyer, born in 1935, teaches at Douglass College, New Brunswick, New Jersey. She has published fiction and two poetry collections: *I Remember the Room Was Filled with Light* (1973) and *Very Close and Very Slow* (1975). Her poem "Penelope" was the winner of the 1976 Anne Sexton Memorial Poetry Contest. She and Anne Wilkinson are now translating the poetry of Anna Akhmatova.

JOHN WOODS

The problem with this exercise is that it does not provide the continuum one enjoys in a writing class. In class, one can comment on work in light of reasonable expectations one has for the poet, based on his or her age, point in the semester, level of the course, and career expectations.

There are always those who think it would be enjoyable to write and read poems. They enjoy the communion of the workshop, but they have no plans to be perched in the anthologies by thirty. They usually provide the future audience for those few who feel they have the calling. For the majority, especially in beginning classes, one does not bring the full moral weight of criticism to bear on their amiability.

Two other problems. The poet's development does not always coincide with a semester: many have not even read poetry. Secondly, for those who develop career itch: how many more MFA's will the market absorb?

"Astronomy I: The Void"

For Neroni's "Astronomy I: the Void," I would note that the poem has a lot of energy, but that the energy is exerted in space. I am constantly insisting that poems be located in the senses. I am ministerial about the advantages of imagery, compressed narrative, evidence of human experience, the face behind the voice. I do not like voices that yell at me out of a cloud. My heart sinks when I run my eyes down the page and see nothing but *truth, silence, despair*. Not one *tongue-depressor* or *coasterbrake* to rest on. Neroni claims prodigious emotion, then prodigious futility. The poem has not earned them.

Who is the speaker? Who "he"? Is the black hole the vagina? Why is "he" a fake? Why is the void only for her? *Is* the speaker a woman? Not only are these characteristically nosy questions unanswered, they are unanswerable. We lapse into guessing games.

In a class, I might suggest that the poet return to whatever experience(s) led to this condition. I am cautious to keep autobiographical concerns in perspective. My concern is to constantly focus on the words, not the writer—male, female, white, black, gay, attractive, young —who is so obviously present. By the semester's end, I will have rung every change on the distinction between the poet and the speaker of the poem.

Often, the poet's description of the occasion of the poem is more interesting, more promising, than the poem. All happenings are sensual or are abundantly accompanied by the senses. I ask the writer to con-

sider reconstituting the poem, restoring the abstractions to the world
in which we all live.

"Progeny"

"Progeny: A poem from David" is very plain, indeed. The language
is not interesting. After "rest home," it is all radio: no liver spots, beige
walls, elevators, trembling hands.

There is a problem of speaker. Since this poet got the poem from
David, the "I" would seem to be a writer persona. Not until line 6 is it
clear that David speaks. Let David say it all, I recommend.

Finally, there is a problem with "perfect non sequitur." It is not
wise to introduce anything as *perfect*. Besides, all non sequiturs are
equally perfect, that is, equally nonsequiturious.

I would recommend some establishing imagery, a sense of the cir-
cumstances. I would drop the "non sequitur" line.

"Her Daughter"

Bob Vance's "Her Daughter" has a sense of authority. His voice is
confident enough to be playful.

The poem is haunted by the woman who is the mother. The poem,
subtly, is to the woman. Nice.

I call attention to the language: the "wrinkle / silenced across her
brow"; "water-wavered angelfish"; "when leaves / pull down in night-
heat"; "earthen hands"; "sails blushing orange." I find these very effective.

This poem sounds good, too. Most students approach the sound of
a poem with either indifference or Tennysonian regularity. The poem
has no overt regularity, but it does have a very attractive pattern of
stresses.

I do not quite understand the beginning of the third stanza. The
"chair" is not firmly enough established as a wizard's throne.

Is "rhodedendrons" a lucky accident?

John Woods was born in 1926 and since 1955 he has been teaching at
Western Michigan University in Kalamazoo. He has written six books of
poetry, the most recent of which are *Striking the Earth* (1976), *Turning
to Look Back: Poems 1955–1970*, and a chapbook, *Thirty Years on the
Force* (1977).

Group IX

JON ANDERSON
MARK HALPERIN
STEVE ORLEN

Because so much of our teaching is done in workshops, three of us
—Jon Anderson, Mark Halperin, and Steve Orlen—decided for the pur-
poses of this article to tape-record informal discussions of poems by
three of our former students. The three young poets were Bruce Cohen,
Michael Collier, and Boyer Rickel, all of whom were invited to partici-
pate in the discussions.

We've chosen to reproduce this particular workshop as much for its
digressions on matters of poetic process and strategy as for the typical
workshop "doctoring" of a poem. It may be that each of us reached the
unspoken realization that re-ordering, editing, and cutting weren't
enough to save what was interesting, imaginative material; so the con-
versation moved into the problems of the poem and what they indicated
about its process, strategy (or lack of it), and human necessity. We all
had some familiarity with Bruce's previous work, so there developed a
focus on the poet-in-process—more than most workshop discussions,
this was about the *next* poem.

Jon Anderson teaches in the writing program at the University of
Arizona, Mark Halperin at Central Washington University, and Steve
Orlen at the University of Arizona.

AN AUTUMN DROWNING
Bruce Cohen

The ocean collapses into itself, swelling like a blowfish,
or how the breeze behind the bathhouses
might be a genetic means of becoming human.

Most things bounce off themselves in different directions:
the first chill from Canada speaks in soft French
and your hands release a yellow box-kite on the breakers.

Maybe you just got too human too fast
and it tightened round your finger like your father's ring.
Maybe you lost it. What you mistook for a flaw

was illusive charm: you could have been handsome,
but your profile swims like your ancestors,
back to the ocean, half evolved . . .

The shirt and pants you left on the beach
scampered in the breeze,
giving your body new shapes, as if to tease.

It's annoying how the afternoon dissolves
separating each grain of sunlight,
but not related to the way people live.

It never occurred to anyone
that people would have to live separately:
why you spent your childhood here,

opening clams under the hallucination of pearls.
The rain's become a hairline pleasure,
the dream that returns where rust is favorable.

But your father's ring is not lost after all.
It taps your shoulder and says thanks for coming.
But you've already drowned, and are coming into a new life.

This time your own.

Bruce Cohen was born in 1955 and received his B.A. in creative writing from the University of Arizona where he studied with Steve Orlen. He presently lives in Tucson and works in a residential treatment center for emotionally disturbed children.

(*Bruce reads the poem in the original.*)

STEVE: I don't know where to start, but I could begin somewhere off the poem. Given Bruce's imaginative style where almost every line becomes a surprise—one of the things he's worked on the last year—the voice is natural, controlled. Almost every third or fourth line Bruce could have spoken aloud. And you stay high with it when you realize it's stuff that comes right out of his mouth.

(*Laughter.*)

MARK: There're two kinds of surprises in the poem: The kind that sets you back on your heels because it hits you somewhere that hurts; then the kind of surprise that's arbitrary, anything could happen at any point, and *this* is what happened at *this* point. My tendency is to cut back on the arbitrary, and shuffle the poem toward its deeper surprises. For example, I'm not enamored of the first two stanzas. The only thing I'm interested in is the last line of the second.

STEVE: What holds Bruce's poems together, aside from that tone of voice, is location. Sometimes it's shifty and arbitrary, but here he makes use of ocean and beach, and the first two stanzas set us up for that. Now if there's anything disturbing about that—and this is a matter of taste and control—it's "the ocean collapses into itself, swelling like a blowfish, or how . . ."

BOYER: It's at the point of "or how." I have the same tendency Mark does. I would have chosen other details that were plainer, setting up the place. The second two lines of the first stanza make a crazy, arbitrary leap—not the imagination that runs deep later on.

MARK: There're possible ways of reordering the material so that you have some of that set up; I mean, there are other places in the poem that have the same function, and they're much more interesting.

STEVE: So what we're saying is, it's a matter of realizing what is just charmingly interesting, and what goes deeper.

MARK: To take Steve's point, how much of the setting is functional, and how much of it is to give us some kind of body into which we can incorporate the other more resonant lines.

STEVE: Also, the statements are so large, that if they don't start off in their largeness—"genetic means of becoming human"—if you don't start off with the real big ones, you might be able to progress towards them. When we're saying this, what are we telling Bruce about the next poem he'll write? How do you generalize about a different kind of progression in the poem?

BRUCE: You're talking about a sort of inverted pyramid?

STEVE: Yea, start more tentatively, by whispering—unless you start out with something large then go on to a series of other, completely different, large statements. You're not doing that in this poem because it is under control: It approaches this sense of evolution, both large and small—the personal evolution, the evolution of the race from the ocean and back into the ocean.

MARK: Those first two stanzas are generative material, but when the poem is really going, cut them.

STEVE: Yea, but I want Bruce to see what that means for the next poem he writes, because he's a generator of material.

JON: I think things like cutting that beginning can be done after the fact. It shouldn't be thought of in the process of writing.

STEVE: Oh no, I think you're right. But still, in the future, he's gotta know what the difference is. Because he could have fifty just like this. One after another of alarmingly surprising, charming, baroque poems.

MARK: It's a kind of alarm that will go off *in* him eventually—when he's gone past the materials. I mean, that's what we're after. Not just what comes out of Bruce's mouth normally, but how when they come together in the poem they become something extra that makes them larger than just chance sayings. What Steve's saying is something he could learn; he has so much, he can really afford to clamp back, not when he's writing the poem, but when he's looking at it the second or third or fifth go-round. There's never a question of not being able to fill the thing up. It's a question of paring.

STEVE: I worry about it because I've seen poets who are imagination machines, and their poems finally lose meaning.

MARK: But Bruce is a meaning machine; it's almost a tic. I'll show you some places where I'm not so enamored of it. The next to the last stanza, for example. "You open the clams under the hallucination of pearls"—that "hallucination of pearls" throws me. And then, "the dream that returns where rust is favorable." Both of the endings of those two lines are attempts to enlarge. Here they do it in terms of fancy words like "hallucination" and "favorable," and I don't think they're necessary. Whereas when he does something like "what you mistake for a flaw was illusive charm," it comes off nicely. It's an insight, not an enlargement.

BOYER: He carries it further there, too: "You could have been handsome, your profile swims like your ancestors." He takes what could have been just a lovely imaginative turn, and makes it dive into the life of the character. Whereas the other two examples are just end-ringers.

STEVE: Well, what you've got in those three lines in the second-to-last stanza are three entirely different things. "Clams" and "pearls," one thing; "rain" and "pleasure," another thing; and "dream" and "rust" and "favorable." I don't know yet how to tie them together. There might be an easy way to make those already generated statement-images into something that's part of one whole. Do you have a sense of what's going on in that stanza, Bruce?

BRUCE: Only in the first line did I really have an idea of what was going on.

JON: I like the first line a lot. I didn't have any problems with it.

BRUCE: But I think what Mark said about the last line is 100% true.

STEVE: It's like, why is it "rain becomes a hairline pleasure?" Why not something to do with "clams," childhood, "hallucination"—becoming a hairline pleasure?

BRUCE: I think unconsciously I had to get myself under water.

STEVE: So rain may be the wrong thing, maybe something that's already in the poem. Because you've already got sunlight in the poem. I don't see that it's been raining anywhere; it seems, again, arbitrary.

What I like to do when I've got all sorts of crazy material is to force some weather sense, place sense, on it—an easy magician's/editor's trick towards a logic. Does that make sense to you, Jon?

JON: Yea, uhm . . . this is an odd poem. In reading and re-reading, I'm in and out of the poem all the time. I'm a believer in process, and the process being on the page, but this is simply a case of my not believing the poem enough. The images generate statements, and the statements are at loose ends. They're large and they're pleasing, and they're put forth gently, so that they're not pretentious; but they don't seem earned. I guess it's as simple as that.

STEVE: How do you do that? What could he do with *this* poem? or another poem like it? Because most of his poems are similar to this.

JON: Well, you can play content off content, instead of off image. I'm thinking of content in terms of statement. As far as the writing process is concerned, it's being aware of building one thing on top of another. I don't have the words for it yet.

STEVE: What you're saying is the most difficult thing to say, and I think you're close to it.

JON: It may simply be a question, in the process of writing, of trying not to be elusive about the content of the poem. Once the poem has found its emotional home, to follow through very strongly and directly toward that.

STEVE: But you had already said not to worry about that when writing the poem.

JON: Not to worry about it until the poem is really generated. There comes a point in the poem where you understand at least partially what it is you're talking about, and you have some emotional sense of where the poem is going. And then to really follow through.

MARK: What would happen if this stopped being "you"? And was particularized in some way so that it was "he"? So that its gesture was more circumscribed, a particular person finding himself.

JON: I think that can be done with an epigraph or a dedication, assuming that this *is* a real person.

BOYER: If it were someone directly related to the speaker, you could begin to become responsible to the complexities you arrive at in direct statements. I'm trying to get back to what Jon was saying, the fact the large statements are beautiful, but the speaker isn't quite responsible for them. If you make a closer relation between a speaker and subject—it could be a little brother, a mother, anything—you're forced to go after some of those emotional complexities.

STEVE: Yea, because there *is* an actual situation. Bruce was close to his father; his father has died. Bruce is close to his mother; his parents were close. There's a family situation that *could* be worked out. That would force you to go back into the content and make it bend toward the mother, or whoever.

JON: One problem is, the poem keeps on inventing itself, after the point where it becomes real. There is, however, an ebb and flow, a rising and falling, that I do like. But as is often the case, a strength in the poem is also a weakness. That ebb and flow, that moving in and out between invention and statement, keeps throwing me off just when I start to become located emotionally.

MARK: You know where one of those places is, it's the comment— there are several comments like it—that comes from way outside. "It's annoying how the afternoon dissolves." I like the little piece of language there, but it comes out of no place. I don't know who says it's annoying, why that person finds it annoying. It's a different kind of comment than, say, "You could have been handsome."

JON: You mean because there's no one specifically participating in the "It's annoying how . . ."

MARK: It's a judgment that isn't located.

JON: It reminds me of something very strange. A teacher I had when I was an undergraduate told us a story about when he was a kid. Swimming in Boston Harbor he had dived off a raft, and when he came up for air and was almost out of air, he came up underneath the raft, and he realized he was gonna die. He had two thoughts: One was how badly he felt for his parents, and the other was the beauty of the sunlight coming through the spaces between the logs of the raft. He managed to breathe between the logs where there was air, so he survived.

But that stanza reminds me of that. There is something right about it. There's a weird separation on the part of the perceiver. I have a feeling there are a number of moments like that in the poem, but because they need a little more sense of sequence, they only occasionally ring in the ways they might.

MARK: Too much has been filtered out, and we only have these evocative pieces of description and large statements. Maybe it needs to be more cluttered.

JON: I don't think so, it's not that kind of poem. It *is* an evocative poem, and I think it's gotta remain so, almost a tone-poem with occasional large statements.

STEVE: What's your writing process, Bruce? either in this poem or in general?

BRUCE: I sat down with two lines that I liked—something a friend said in a conversation—because I thought there was a poem in them: "Maybe you just got too human too fast . . ." And it must have hit other things. Actually, I always hated poems about the sea, and I figured I lived right by the sea all the time and that I'd write a poem—well, that's how it came out. But what you were saying about the poem being arbitrary —when I first wrote it, it was twice as long and that's what it was. And I started cutting stuff out. The reason the dream came into the poem was because I kept having dreams about losing my father's ring, and it was always such a weird anxiety. Kind of like I realized I couldn't lose it after a while.

STEVE: What makes you cut one thing and not another?

BRUCE: Anything that didn't touch on more than one level I tried to get rid of.

JON: Again, another strength and weakness of the poem is that it lacks a center. The poem floats in some way, sounds like a pun, it . . .

STEVE: Well, it has no dramatic action. There's a mention of the importance of the father's ring, but what you've just said, you know, a dream, or reality of losing your father's ring—that suspense and drama and action really is not in there. It's a stand-still, floating, just above the ground . . . I wasn't sure that was a problem. Was that what you meant, Jon? Whatever arrivals there are in the poem are of content. There's no actual dramatic motion.

JON: I'm not sure. What I mean may well be it would ring more if there was an especially telling line or sentence for the others to generate around. Something that rises above the rest of the poem.

BRUCE: That's interesting, because when I write a poem I try to make it so that doesn't happen. I thought that might be bad because it would call attention to itself.

MARK: I can sympathize with that feeling. And I can also sympathize with Bruce's not wanting to have any kind of narrative to it, you know every moment generates the next.

JON: Could be. Since it's as passive and delicate as it is, maybe the poem would be destroyed if the center were brought about in the way I suggested.

STEVE: Very often when Bruce has a large statement, it's surrounded by charming, casual, conversational devices: "It never occurred to anyone that people would have to live separately." People having to live separately, you know, that's a large statement, but it gets diminished—not necessarily wrongly—by "It never occurred to anyone."

BRUCE: It seems like you should *want* to tone down those statements.

STEVE: Well, often that's true. But if Jon's suggestion is right about a central line, if somewhere in the poem there were some statements other things could ring off of, you might find out which one it is and strip it of its rhetoric, of its conversational surrounding. You know, "*Maybe* you just got too human too fast"; "*Most* things bounce off themselves"; "*It might* be a genetic movement . . ."; "*It's annoying how* . . ." —those kinds of devices.

MARK: I had another idea. Sometimes when you have big statements like that, what I like to do is throw them into a question form, so that they're not being stated directly, they're just being raised as possibilities. For example, "Why did it never occur to anyone that people . . .?" Then when the poem becomes declarative—"Your father's ring is not lost after all, it taps your shoulder and says thanks for coming"

—there would be a difference in the quality of statement, a greater weight.

STEVE: Well, if we knew that the father was dead, and it was happening to a survivor, the son or wife-mother, and she asked that question, then living separately would become a dramatically important problem.

JON: Yea, it moves then from passivity to a kind of helplessness, which could be really poignant.

MARK: I think the statements in the last stanza, those two lines about your father's ring and "taps your shoulder saying thanks for coming" are potentially the real heavies, without seeming heavy in the language. They don't partake of that same kind of general statement that other parts in the poem partake of to get their weight. And so I like them enormously.

BOYER: Another tactic which pushes that sometimes is to suddenly introduce an "I." You've got a vague speaker, and suddenly the speaker asks a question and brings in something very personal that appears to be outside the poem, but which gives some of the other more vague statements about life a ground. Do you know what I mean? Tate does that to a certain extent in the poem "The Boy," where he starts so large, so distantly, something about the boy "shoving his frail boat out into eternity." It's in the third person, and then it shifts right into the "I." That shift suddenly gives those large statements a ground. And it gives the story a ground—in the case of this poem—that is, why it became important to the speaker.

MARK: As long as it doesn't happen right at the very beginning, as though you're trying to crack the whip.

BRUCE: That's one of my problems, trying to get all the pronouns right. In the two poems I'm working on now, I realized that you *can* switch, there are ways you can say "I" and then "you" and "he," and have it work. Maybe I could do it with this poem. Because it seems like the poem is not personal, and it *is* personal. I think I know ways I can do that now.

MARK: It's strange, because things are falling between the cracks in the boards all the time, is what we're saying about the poem, and yet the boards are really there. They're firm, there's no kind of goozh writing going on, and yet . . .

(*Laughter.*)

BOYER: Glob was your word for the last session, now goozh for this one.

MARK: I learn to speak from my son. But there's something missing, and it's really hard to locate. Jon's coming at it really from a "way back" sort of position, how did the poem get to this place, and Steve's doing that too. And I'm coming at it in a more surfacy way. But both positions keep coming to this notion of something absent.

STEVE: It's not just arriving at a pronoun, but arriving at a pronoun that counts. What I do when I have imaginative material on the page, if I'm just generating material and filling a notebook, is that in order for it to go to the next stage, I've gotta ask myself: How could this material be important to my life, even if I'm writing about somebody else.

JON: How consciously do you do that, Steve?

STEVE: I do it very consciously. It's the second stage of going at a poem if I've got a lot of material. I say, where in this material is there something of possible importance to me. Not, where's the necessity, but where's *my* necessity. Then all of a sudden some part of my life becomes at stake in my statements. I don't have any moral stances about poetry; I don't mind lying. But I try to get close to something that gives me a pain in the heart.

BRUCE: But it seems like the most dangerous thing to do, and in some way you've got to hide it, undercutting as much as you can.

MIKE: You have to do that, because otherwise if it's just *you* all the time you might not ever include anybody else.

STEVE: No, when I make that suggestion, it could be about another character, but it's always a character you're related to. I mean even if it's a poem about Bonaparte, you know, what's your relation to Bonaparte, what do you feel about him, why are you bothering to write about him.

MIKE: Still, it could be such that your relation to Bonaparte has nothing to do with a more general . . .

STEVE: No, I mean my relation to ideas that would surround Bonaparte, that have come out of some life-thing about him. Do you understand what I mean?

MIKE: I'm thinking of what Auden would say, and Auden would say Well, my position compared to Bonaparte's is very important. But still, there's another position that's more important—*every*body else's relation to Bonaparte.

STEVE: The problem is now to make that "everybody else's relationship" important enough.

BRUCE: Shouldn't that emerge out of the personal relationship?

MIKE: You hope it does. You hope your personal relationship is important and profound enough that it does include everything else.

STEVE: Auden works at a public, historical level at times. And just personally, it rarely matters to me. It's when he takes it and turns it back into my inner, nonideal life, like in that Sigmund Freud poem—he's talking publicly, he's talking about a public figure, but somehow he makes it filter into my private life. And that's a beautiful trick if you can do it.

MARK: I think there's a place in between what both Jon and Steve are saying. Jon's talking about getting that process working so that you're aware, at some deep level, of yourself, of what's going on.

JON: And trying to get closer to more difficult emotional content.

MARK: Yea, and Steve is talking about taking the material and then searching it in a very conscious way. One way I would phrase Jon's approach: When do I feel in danger? You have a sense the poem is going OK if all of a sudden you're afraid to write the next line, because there's something actually at stake and you're not sure you really want to face it. And Steve was talking about *looking:* OK, I have all this stuff, now what do I do to make it more personal? I think there's a place in between that might correspond to mine. Try this. You take what you've got, but also you're throwing things into questions, into the third person whatever—and at the point where all of a sudden it flares a little bit or you get a little tight about what's going on, *then* you become aware of something, but you don't have to follow it consciously. Trust that feeling of danger, but the conscious thing is still just to move things around, to rattle the surface.

BRUCE: I think that's one of my processes, how I get the stuff. But once I get it, I try to organize it. Probably the way I wrote this poem, like I write many of my poems, is that I'll write a lot, and then I'll circle whatever seem to be the good lines. Then I look for two lines that could go next to each other, that would make good couplets. I do that first. And then, from that, I usually get one or two *new* lines. So eventually, even though the order is originally arbitrary, I get some kind of order, I have to have that order.

MARK: Is there a time when you stop moving the lines together and you start letting the poem just take off?

BRUCE: Usually, by that time, I have enough material. I just have to cut down.

MARK: You see, I want there to be something else. Not the construction of the poem. The poem has found itself now . . .

JON: You've found the center, you're putting it together now and discovering how it adds up, but there isn't a *generative* process anymore, so it doesn't go far enough.

MARK: You get to that stage, and then you let go of it entirely. It's no longer a question of assembling a poem, it's a question of finding out what's going on. By now the poem should really have struck fire, and now all you gotta do is feed it the fuel. I'm not saying it right, but there's a way where you stop crafting the damn thing and you just let it fly.

MIKE: I think what Mark means is, when you're working on a poem in the beginning, at least when I'm working on a poem, there's an incredible amount of anxiety that you're not going to get enough of this rough material down. But once you calm the anxiety, then everything seems to be there, and you can let it fly. Even when I get the first draft done, when I reach that final line, the anxiety to get the poem out is gone. And then I don't have to worry about the material so much. It's just finding out the correct combination, the correct placement.

JON: Boy, that's accurate. That's what I dislike most about writing, that anxiety that remains with you for such a long time while you're waiting for something to get going.

MIKE: Because you know you're going to do it an injustice. You know the poem is there, but you're the one that's going to fuck it up.

JON: My only anxiety is that I'm not gonna generate anything *real*.

STEVE: Something, but not something real?

JON: Yea, so I have to fool myself, I have to play around with language for a long time without investing too much of myself in it until that anxiety is overridden and I get into the heart of something. And by then I can write fairly automatically, because by playing with the language it's become accessible to me.

MARK: I think there's a slight difference with Bruce. He doesn't have to worry about getting that first draft out. When it happens for him is when he starts putting lines together in funny ways, and then suddenly something will take flight, so it comes at a later stage. And if we were going to say a big thing, we could say, OK, once you get the lines together, let the poem build itself. You know we all do the editing at the end again anyway. But you're working too carefully at a certain point.

JON: I think that once a poem has started happening and there are occasional connections being made, then you can use your process, putting those connections together. But the poem will still be in process then. Because you want to run with the poem, but in a certain willed way at that point. And I don't quite have the words for this, but when you realize that the poem is finally starting to come, live up to that poem *in the process* of writing it. That's the willed aspect. You don't go on in the poem until what you've said, you've got down right.

STEVE: I think Jon's saying the opposite of what we often say in workshop, which is, *don't* worry about what you've written, just keep writing more. He's saying, Go back to what you've written, tinker with it, find out what it's about, get a handle on it, then go further from there. I mean, that's dangerous, but that's the suggestion.

JON: I think the danger that we feel is that we've put ourselves on the line in writing a poem, we've said something pretty direct, pretty transparent, and now we've gotta follow through.

MARK: This is the "earning" business again. I hate to use the moral term, but at this point, where there's something actually going on, to be responsible now. You've put it out, and now you have to play it through.

STEVE: What you're suggesting is exactly what stopped me from writing many poems for about ten years, so I'd think about it. It *is* a way of working, but it sure didn't work for my temperament. It made me too self-conscious.

MIKE: It's not like you have to put a perfect line down when you go back like that, but it does exclude a hundred other things.

BRUCE: I'm afraid if I read what's come before so many times, I probably will realize what I think I want to say, and the poem will end for me.

JON: The problem with this poem, Bruce, and this is given the fact I like most of it a lot, is that it lacks a sense of commitment, a commitment to an emotional state, an attitude, a pure intelligence, whatever it might be. The poem keeps beginning again, rather than following through.

STEVE: It's a commitment to imagination now, rather than to your life.

MARK: I think we've left the particulars of this poem so far behind, our orbit has gone so wide. This is really a lovely poem, and I wanna know more about the things we like about it.

STEVE: I like the way Bruce gets something that sounds like an eccentric conversational voice going. I like the delicacy, which at times goes passive. I mean, that passivity might be a flaw. It might be interesting to see the opposite sometime, say anger . . .

JON: Use a poem as an act of aggression.

MARK: Not totally, please.

STEVE: Oh no, these are experiments, to get at something different.

MARK: How do you feel about the very end of the poem?

BRUCE: It's weird, when I was writing, all the time I had this tension because I didn't know how it was going to end. I didn't realize it was because I'd lost, or thought I'd lost, my father's ring. The images were in the poem, but I didn't know they were important.

MARK: It's interesting that it comes down to the father. But if it could become clearer that the father is dead, that would help the poem enormously.

STEVE: That would give it the center Jon was talking about.

JON: One thing you can do, for rewriting this particular poem at least, is to compose a poem, or something like a poem, made up of just the statements. Get the order of their progression right, and then plug in the images that seem right. I think in just dealing with the statements, you'll see where the heart of the poem is, and what images without question belong and allude to those statements or shape them.

Jon Anderson was born in 1940. He is currently teaching at the University of Arizona, having taught previously at the universities of Iowa, Pittsburgh, Ohio and Portland (Oregon). He has published three books, *In Sepia* (1974), *Death & Friends* (1970) and *Looking For Jonathan* (1968). He was the recipient of a Guggenheim Foundation grant in 1976, and a nominee for the National Book Award in 1972.

Mark Halperin was born in 1940 and teaches at Central Washington University in Ellensburg. He has also taught at the University of Arizona during which time the discussion above took place. He was educated at Bard College (B.A. physics) and the University of Iowa (M.F.A. poetry). A book of his poetry, *Backroads*, was published in 1976 as the winning entry for the U.S. Award of the International Poetry Forum.

Steve Orlen, born in 1942, studied at the University of Iowa and now teaches at the University of Arizona in Tucson. He was the Transatlantic Review Fellow in Poetry at the Bread Loaf Writers' Conference in 1978 and is currently a staff assistant at Bread Loaf. Among his publications are two chapbooks, *Sleeping on Doors* and *Separate Creatures*, and his most recent book, *Permission to Speak*. He has received the George Dillon Memorial Award from *Poetry* and a National Endowment for the Arts award.

Michael Collier was born in 1953 and studied with William Meredith, Steve Orlen, and Jon Anderson at Connecticut College and the University of Arizona. He is finishing his M.F.A. in creative writing at the University of Arizona.

Boyer Rickel, born in 1951, received a B.A. in English from Oberlin College where he studied with Stuart Friebert and David Young, and an M.F.A. in Creative Writing from the University of Arizona where he worked closely with Steve Orlen. His poems have appeared in *Agenda, Field, Gramercy Review, Ironwood,* and *Mississippi Review.*

Group X

DAVE SMITH
HEATHER McHUGH
CYNTHIA MACDONALD

Group X worked independently on one poem by a student of Cynthia Macdonald in the writing program at the University of Texas, Austin, one by a student of Kathleen Fraser at San Francisco State University, and one by a student of Sandra McPherson at the University of Iowa.

BY HIS STRIPES
Helen Williams

"And by His stripes we are healed,"
we sing at Christmas time.
I know the tiger is not meant
but still I see him padding back yards
on the other side of the railroad tracks,
among the smallish trees, the carports,
and the air-conditioning towers, his tail swishing.
The railroad tracks run parallel to infinity,
and I have yearned unstoppably for tigers.
I caught a streetcar once, in another town,
and muffed a chance to look him in the face:

a woman picked my pocket; fear hung
in the air like lead; I turned my back
and let her go unchallenged. Still I dream.
The railroad tracks run to the depths
of central Asia, home of tigers.
Things split open in the living room
last week, and the tiger stepped in through the crack,
shining like aluminum foil,
me up against the wall and holding,
and the tiger filling the room.
I learned a thing. I will tell you.
The tiger is love.

Helen Williams was born in 1926 and studied creative writing with How-
ard Moss at Vassar College, and Cynthia Macdonald at the University
of Houston. She is a member of the poetry workshop at Houston led by
Terrence Doody.

WALKING OVER ROCHFORD BURN
Dave Cole

It is our day of hot rasberries.
One of our last
of this summer.
They are deep sweet.

They are small. We have travelled far
and now we bend low for them.
And though there are few, at least
here we are alone.

We walk separate;
the ground, plowed years ago
to take trees in,
spreads uneven.

But we stop when we can,
and as a sort of love

to each other
we offer what we have in our hands.

We find, as the heat
pries odor from the pines,
that our teeth find seeds
as quick as our tongues, taste.

❋   ❋   ❋

This place was once fire.
Acres enough to earn it a name
were laid black.
A few hopeful trees were planted.

Since then have crept
the scavengers of burnt ground:
rasberry, burdock. They tangle
around our ankles.

They bury seeds in our socks.
We could carry some
like this
for years.

We cross Rochford Burn not holding hands.
The incidental result
of a fire years ago
scratches towards our knees.

Dave Cole was born in 1953 and attended The University of Iowa where
he studied with Marvin Bell and Sandra McPherson.

LOOKING FOR WINTER: A SEASONAL CHANGE
Doreen Schmid

Back in San Francisco, on my balcony—how I gloat over these gray days.
When the fog rolls in I am thrown into relief, tho it makes me want to
deckself in colors of the rare October sunset composing maroon and purple

dragon scales, putty mushrooms, cauliflower and pumpkin huddling in
  groves . . .
wanting to be/the first red bough/of the tree/turning . . . already. I
  miss the
confetti of Vermont autumn: a mosaic of the loneliness of each/when we
  can't
strip any further to the bone.

I am loose in my new bark though, and wondering if I'm really changing
seasons and shades, not wanting to lose the cathartic itching in my bones—
the first small breaking of the bud into twig, first painful crack, to forego
again, all the well-learned lessons in survival.

How real was the newness in old friends, love & the Atlantic; how to lend
character to perpetual change with energy
that doesn't stiffen.   How to
harness the transfusions riffling through the brain—the billboards of
  change,
and not miss the ones that rise quiet like mushrooms. Like the way our
lives jell and un-jell, solidify and melt; the actual fabric of the moment
changing substance. To be capable of uncertainties in the face of
multiplicities—what words can I trust.
When chance *is* myself. And everything necessary.

I used to want to want, but now I'm not oxbowing—I'm fleeting, dedicated
to learning to fall off cliffs with grace—now I'm a firecracker lighting
its own fuse.   But not forgetting what is loose-limbed and finely
  tuned—
the deep seed/of this hunger, the slow pulse, the point of reference
for undoing the self.

The pacing of the dancer on the floor, the offering to myself of
my self. Nothing more perfect than this: motionless, raw, stunning.
Yet I cannot stay still here for long
    the clear greenness pulling at me harder and harder (in my dreams
    I am flying, surrendering, rising like the song of balloons).
I want to elope with what is myself.   I am
birthing, stitching   up my knees before it's time to go

into winter, straining   to hold my heart still on the edge
    and slowly breaking with the field into   (flower of frost)
         dying for what is new

Doreen Schmid was born in 1955 and received her M.A. from San Francisco State University in 1978. She studied with Kathleen Fraser, Nanos Valaoritis, and Stan Rice. After a year of working, dancing, and writing in Europe and Africa, she plans to relocate to the East Coast to work in publishing or return to graduate studies.

DAVE SMITH

PASSION, POSSIBILITY, AND POETRY

Poetry is, I presume to think, passion and possibility. Naked, it is more passion; intricately clothed, it is more possibility. At its finest, it is both. We speak of how poetry is all language, the beautiful contrivance, but I am not one who cares much for form without content, or even content serving form. But the poem whose language is indivisible from its content—and how few of those excellencies there are—is the balance we must honor, for it is the dynamic body of passion which both celebrates and is possibility. This dualism, like anything that matters, is complex and scarcely permits the easy resolution of flat statement. James Wright tells us that all he can do is speak in a flat voice, but who among his admirers (and I am one) finds Wright truly flat? Wright is a singer whose primary characteristic is complexity, a sense of the multiplicity of thing and meaning which he trusts to reveal itself in the plainest of words. If the world and our lives were simple, if flat and honest statement were easily possible, there would be no need for many poets and less need for our feeble attempts to discriminate toward excellence.

The fact is that poems of real passion and credible possibility are ideals we do not often achieve. That we fail our poems does not, however, mean we should abandon either the task or those monuments of our poetic heritage which show us what is always possible. Those poems are our first and primary teachers of what I believe is still an art, not a sociotherapy. Those of us who set up to evaluate poems are secondary teachers, and it is our function, or ought to be, to insist on standards of excellence and to do what we can to suggest how such standards have been and may be attained.

Like many of us, I grew up throwing one sort of ball or another. I did it for pleasure, without thought of excellence. It is impossible to do anything without learning to do it with increased efficiency, accuracy, and understanding. But it is also possible to learn wrongly, to impede growth and skill, which is what coaches hope to prevent. And, I think, teachers of writing. It is equally possible that one's inherent abilities, in spite of the American vision of equal opportunity and common-manism, are so limited as to preclude the highest achievements. There is no shame in this, though some would have it so. Time and experience taught me that my ball-throwing abilities were limited. I wasn't going to pitch for the New York Yankees or even the Norfolk Tars. At fifteen, no one had to tell me. So I dedicated myself to football and basketball. I learned that I hadn't the speed, the size, or the reflexes to continue beyond high-school competition. Nevertheless, I loved sports and watched so closely that I gained a good knowledge of athletic mechanics. I was for a time a high-school coach and a good one. If I couldn't personally measure up to the standards of excellent athletes, I could and did make them available to players with greater ability. I know what makes ex-cellent basketball, what it looks like, why it happens, and how it may be encouraged. Gaining that knowledge took a long time and was, in various ways, earned.

Poetry takes a long time and must also be earned. Before I go too far, I will say that I recognize the dangers of comparing basketball and poetry. I'm aware that basketball, and all games, have a clear, ordained intention, which is for one team to score more than another and to win. Games are competition in ways that poetry is not. But only the reader entirely disinclined to consider similarities will insist the two activities have nothing in common. My point is merely to suggest some principles important to me in playing, learning, and coaching are also integral to my teaching of poetry writing.

I begin with the notion that everyone has inherent limits and has a right to discover those limits with and without me. It would be criminal to say to a student, "You haven't the ability to succeed." When I was an undergraduate at the University of Virginia, a professor did tell me that. But it isn't criminal to help a student discover, through one's own experience and knowledge as well as the student's explorations, what his limits and possibilities might be. To recognize a student who is either unable to write even competently or is woefully ill prepared and to slick that over with untempered praise seems to me equally criminal. Which is to say, I have little patience with anything less than the judicious and gentle pursuit of excellence. I have no time for poetry as therapy and only contempt for touchy-feely teaching. Let me add here that I am speaking only of the teaching of poetry in colleges and universities, for I believe that if such institutions do not devote themselves to the pursuit of excellence, then whatever else goes on in our society will not much matter. Standards of excellence, then, are not going to be met by all students. I was not an excellent athlete. We are all not excellent at something. I try to give my students patience, attention, intensity, honesty, and the lessons of my own experience. I try to help them avoid the mistakes I have made and seen, to recognize the benchmarks of excellence. I encourage them to believe in possibility and to love knowledge, for I believe that knowledge is love. Teaching for me, then, is largely a matter of developing an attitude toward experience. I cannot teach them passion, that thing which the true poet is never without, as that is a product of some mysterious conjunction of genes and desire we must take as a given.

If I begin with a notion of limits, that is not to say I stand watch for weaknesses to triumph. Indeed, I do stand a constant watch over the poems of my students and it is always a readiness to clap my hands with delight and ask, "How in the world did you do that?" All of us know that it happens and though we may carp a little to keep our own pride intact, what is more wonderful than the surprise of that moment we discover the poem that could not have been predicted and cannot be explained? This is the moment when passion and possibility are so fused that I stand in the presence of a poem humanly beautiful and original. It didn't occur because of me, but in spite of me and, with luck, somehow beyond me. But such poems do not occur in voids. They occur because of preparation, knowledge, hard work, and the lonely commitment of the writer to push to his limits. In the presence of such an achievement, there is little use to cant of structure, vision, and so on, all those lesser activities submerged in the process. The thing exists. It testifies that the process also exists.

The process of writing, and of teaching writing, as I know it, is my subject here. With all of us, this process is more intuitive than rational. If it were not so, if we had a formula, what results we could expect from every student! All I can do is try to say how I conduct each student as far as he or she can go toward that moment of delightful handclapping, and to say it with the knowledge that my own informing attitudes may be revealed if unspoken.

Doesn't it seem a bit unnatural to begin a workshop of college students by immediately throwing their poems into a public glare and asking for a response? We might say, well, they are people after all and have the required emotions. At least, I will agree, they have an emotional investment which they have, on assignment, tried to shape as a poem. They have this much whether or not they have any idea what constitutes excellence in a poem. Likely, however, they are strangers to each other, and likely they haven't either standards or a vocabulary to respond; or if they do, likely they are uncomfortable in articulating before strangers. Most of the workshops I have been in, and they are mostly workshops I have taught, began just as I have described above. For this reason a student says, tentatively, the poem is, well, it's well written. But what does that mean? According to what standard? Or someone says, kindly, that she likes the poem. Is this response the same as she might have to a fresh salad? Ask why and the response may well be that there is a line, a phrase, an image which is in some nebulous way attractive. For some teachers of writing I have known, the rule of thumb has been let us like and dislike and leave enough time for a quick beer. I think a more properly prepared instructor, one who really means to take his students seriously *as writers,* will plan and organize his workshop so that it builds rather than fumbles.

A good workshop might begin with a couple of sessions spent examining poems not written by class members but by previous students, the instructor, or published poets. I am not personally skittish about criticizing the poems of "name" writers, but students are. In order to avoid the weight of those names, I usually offer poems from good little magazines and do not provide the poet's name. I ask the class to make marginal notes, then to discuss the good and bad points as they see them. Initially, I make no attempt to guide their discussion and only listen. I learn what and how the students think because, not having to confront an as-yet-unknown peer, they are not cowed. They know the poems in question are neutral game; they respond. Importantly, this process introduces them to each other. They begin to test each other not on the level of ego but in the act of criticism, in the application of intelligent and justified response. This first step builds trust in the group, and I think no workshop goes very far in helping its members without trust. I don't, of course, mean back-patting and hand-holding empathy, nor even the solidarity-against-the-leader that Lee Marvin creates in *The Dirty Dozen*. I mean the recognition by each person that his colleagues are capable of useful and provocative criticism that he can modify with impunity and respect. Of course, the poems I choose and employ in this way are selected to represent degrees of quality. If I haven't the experience to know a good poem from a bad poem, according to standards I am willing to articulate, I am being paid by my university for the wrong reasons.

Some of the students, quite naturally, will praise the bad poems and attack the good ones. Some will know intuitively which are bad and which are good but will have difficulty saying why. Some will be openly puzzled. When the class has scoured each poem and the discussion has begun to decline, I take over the class. I've been making notes from their comments, and I begin to address the salient points, both good and bad. I take care not to undercut anyone's enthusiasm or seriousness and go to whatever length necessary to demonstrate my respect for his or her act of the mind. Neither am I loath to point out what I believe to be the rightness or wrongness of that act. That everyone's response is equally right, however divergent and pluralistic, is a heresy I will not accept. I will encourage disagreement and even heat, but only where the student can bring to bear an argument, an evidence, a standard as sufficiently convincing as my own. Among the splendid benefits of such a class is the making of friends, the encouraging of citizenship, the progress each makes toward full humanity—but we are not here for such benefits. We are here to learn what excellent poetry is, what it might be, what various and fundamental ways people have made that poetry. This process begins, in a classroom, with the generation of a modest commonality: with establishing some critical zones in which to work, a language, a mutuality of respect and integrity, a sense of standards, a sense that the product of our labors is always going to lie before a reader, inert and vulnerable and in need of the best efforts we can muster toward helping it live and bloom.

Clearly, all that I have said and will say is a code of partial expressions, all intentions as often as not honored in the breech. But a vague sense of direction is better than either a rigid direction or no direction. Totalitarian instruction is no more desirable than touchy-feely. I once heard a football coach from the University of Michigan tell an assembled group of high school coaches that his success with burly defensive linemen was due to a simple formula. He taught them to read offensive pressure (for poetry, think of tension). When a tackle, for example, felt himself being blocked from his outside shoulder he was to shout, "Sweep!" If he felt blocked on his inside shoulder, he was to shout, "Dive!" In this way, his teammates knew instantly where to respond. This coach had his players practice shouting such instructions, with roommates, long before the first practice, ingraining the process. Once, he said, he took his wife to a movie and she, seeing one of the players, leaned forward to say hello and tapped his shoulder, whereupon he screamed "Sweep!" Pavlovian discipline is not only funny, it may be insidious in a free society. But discipline, even if it must be breeched by any artist worthy of the term, is yet necessary and fundamental.

When I enter my class's discussion of those first, anonymous poems, I am introducing my code and my discipline. I tell them that the rules, the standards which inform my responses and theirs will be, for us, a framework that each, in his own way, will transcend at the moment he or she begins to do important work, at the moment those inherent limits become pushed. But I also tell them the framework will create in each what Auden once called the censor in the self. It is a kind of fog detector and we have, individually, enough fog to need whatever help we can get. I tell them that the best and truest help will always come from inside, from the censor.

But the discipline needs initial tending, so I employ a code. It is really a three-part formula, and I am aware of the nasty implications of that word. Haven't we all noticed in our composition apprenticeships how Directors of Compositions cling to their formulas? First, I ask, what is the poem about? What is its subject, its object of focus, its plot (if it has one)? There is no poem which, in its literal dimension, is not about something. I want that laid out in paraphrase as clearly as we can do it. Generally, my students give me interpretation. The poem about the used car salesman is actually about cosmic injustice. I disallow this kind of comment initially. I want the salesman, his cars, his place of business, his emotions, the weather, the conflict, the point of view—whatever the elements are—to be specifically and without judgment or interpretation identified for all present.

Secondly, how well does the language present these elements? In Part Two, knowing the landscape and objects, we must consider how well or ill they seem to coexist. This means, of course, we have to consider what the writer intended to do, as best we can discover that. We must try to place ourselves in the writer's passion, to understand what complexities he approached, to see what design underlay this committed action. The writer is not allowed to tell us, only the poem on the page. The instruction is clear: meaning, expression, coherence, clear sense, possibility, passion, beauty are all in the language employed and shaped or they do not exist. But how could we talk of these ineluctable qualities so necessary to poetry if we had not previously determined the elements out of which they must rise and in which they can only be found? Part One of this formula was nonjudgmental. Part Two must move toward judgment but must also attempt to restrain emotional effusion while encouraging hard-headed attention.

Part Three, however, inevitably causes shivers in my students and among those colleagues to whom I have mentioned it. The students generally come to see the value of this part, if not to be truly passionate about it. I have little knowledge of its effect on my colleagues. Some, in their relativistic sophistication, sneer. Part Three asks, Was the thing attempted by the poet worth doing in the first place? I am one of those people who believes there is nothing in this world which is not available to poetry, but even poetry may be demeaned by triviality, by an adolescent act, by a refusal to be ambitious for art. If a poem is something done solely for assignment or fame, something done with no deep personal investment, something that denies the valuable balance of passion and possibility, something that is repudiated by its creator as a sham, then the creator is at fault and should be told so. We are certainly playing in our writing, but we should always be playing for the highest limits. Even more significantly, I believe that a poem is a moral act. Not a moralistic canard, not a pious statement, not a simplistic or sentimental lip-pursing, but an act of healthy celebration. Even the darkest poems are celebrations. Who is darker than James Wright, the most moral among us? Yet there are poems, and books, which are mean-spirited, evil, life-defeating, and the hugger-mugger sophisticate who denies it is the same one who will complain students have nothing to

say and say it badly. I think it is up to the keepers of poetry to defeat
such work. If life is not beautiful—and for many it is scarcely that—
the most faithfully accurate and heart-rending poem may be. Auden's
elegy for Yeats says poetry makes nothing happen, but the poem which
says this makes Auden's words a lie. That poem makes something hap-
pen to anyone who reads it, unless the reader happens to have wooden
ears. I suppose, then, my code also tries to establish three standards:
clarity, beauty, and value. Clearly the best poets haven't a need for
this code, but those poets haven't a need for a writing class. In the
absence of those poets, my approach has proved capable of creating at
minimum the illusion of confidence in students who despair of saying
anything that matters and has sometimes even provided a good base for
the intelligent and critical exchange of responses which is somehow at
the heart of the educational act.

"Walking Over Rochford Burn"

"Walking Over Rochford Burn" presents a speaker who describes a
leisurely walk by himself and another person over ground that, in
some indeterminate past, has been burned. Both people eat raspberries
which have grown from the scorched ground. This place is, apparently,
familiar to the walkers, but they do not live on it and have come here
from some distance. It is an interesting and archetypal situation, with
the wounded earth suggesting other wounds. There are, however, no
linear plot events. The writer's "walk" is an act of interior drama, a
concentration of subtle gestures seeking a shaped resolution. The poem
is built of tensions, not events. What seems most important is that
the two walkers are estranged and that the speaker offers "a sort of
love" which precipitates a resolution best described as understanding.

This poem intends to explore one of life's most crucial and complex
moments: that moment, dramatized, when love is more pain than plea-
sure, the sadness of a necessary ending. What is important and well done
is that the moment is not compromised by glibness or easiness. The poet,
here, intends to realize the experience, not to speak about it.

Such moments exist in connection, in process. The initial stanza be-
gins with identity: time and place, season and thing. "It is our day of
hot raspberries" is a personal statement which indicates a legacy of
previous experience. The line is uncomfortably close to echoes of "our
song" and "our special place," thus to the sentimentality of pop songs.

But there is a surprise in "hot" since we expect raspberries straight from the earth to be cool and refreshing. And these raspberries signal an ending, for they are the "last / of this summer." That they are also "deep sweet" is arguably easy modification. Does the writer mean to suggest their sweetness proceeds from their *lastness,* their source in this deadened ground, or only that they are especially tasty?

The information given in stanza 2 seems equally puzzling. What is the relationship between size and the distance traveled by the speaker? What has prevented the two people from being alone elsewhere that, apparently absent now, aids their aloneness? The poem appears to want to imply that this place will allow love to flourish as raspberries have. But the poem later denies this direction, telling us, "We walk separate" over ground that "spreads uneven." If there is a rationale for the ungrammatical phrasing, it is not obvious. But the poem begins to make clear its exploration of division between the walkers. Stanza 4 begins to suggest a certain force driving this division with "But we stop when we can. . . ." Yet there is still, I think, unclear information. What exactly is this force? They are walking after all, not running, trotting, or sprinting. At this point, the virtual center of the poem as well as its experience, the speaker returns his attention to the raspberries. Each offers this gleaned fruit to the other in a quasi-ritual and "as a sort of love. . . ."

"As a sort of love" is actually no love at all because of the vague language, language too characteristic of the poem's first five stanzas. However, the gesture rightly introduces the tension of love's existence and dissolution. The poet doesn't say the fruit is rejected, or bitter; he doesn't qualify the act of the offering by melodramatic or editorial comment. But in the following stanza it seems important to do some qualifying, so he tells us they discover the seeds of the fruit and, moreover, that this process is as natural as that of heat drawing "odor from the pines. . . ." We note the poet's verb, *pries,* is a mechanical one, and it reveals the mechanistic quality of his metaphor. What is the point of discovering seeds just now? We must suppose that seeds should somehow correspond to the early heat of love, which even in diminishment is, through memory, still discoverable.

With stanza 6, the poet breaks the poem's flow by asterisks and shifts our attention from raspberries and love to the field itself. It is a retreat from immediate action to reflection. The first, dramatic line is

taut and evocative of a kind of history. Yet its strength is compromised
by the passive constructions which follow and the poor pathetic fallacy
of "hopeful trees." We are in the presence of lulling concentration.
Stanza 7, by contrast, regains mystery and activity. Why are "scavengers"
attacking these walkers? All the poet goes on to tell us is that somehow
these scavengers leave the seeds of stanza 5 on the walkers' socks. We
are aware that seeds grow, that the suggestion working is one of con-
tinuity. But a continuity of what? Lines 3, 4, and 5 of stanza 8 might have
told us, but they are wholly undistinguished. They merely repeat the
image of continuity. The final stanza adds the interesting notion that all
this is "the incidental result" of that original fire. The result "scratches
toward our knees," we are told. The effect of the verb *scratches* is not
to clarify but to confuse the implications of *scavengers*. Do scavengers
beg or are they aggressive? The poet wants only to suggest incremental
force, but for true accuracy he must be responsible for all the nuances
of his words, not simply those working in his favor.

At this point, I begin to suspect that the poem doesn't need two
sections, that it needs more attention to the employed imagery of fruit
and place, that the quality of love, the poem's real subject, needs in-
tensification. The poem's language, its plain diction and tight cadence,
is generally right to control an understated but necessary pathos. The
poet, to my way of thinking, is not far from a finished poem if he will
only discover a degree more of clarity which can make his experience
more available to his reader. The speaker, it might be said, has come
through to his own understanding, but the oblique and terse language
of his poem leaves us yet on the edge, unable to say yes or no with
conviction.

"By His Stripes"

If raspberries and burned ground can make so much of a poem,
then a poem about a tiger chasing someone ought to be, as gamblers
say, a *lock*. "By His Stripes" proves nothing is certain.

"By His Stripes" presents what I believe is a common difficulty for
many students of poetry. Without attempting to say why or how it hap-
pens, people come to poetry with a sense that a poem's function is to say
something in disguise, to hide what is meant under a kind of verbal
puzzle. If this were so, complication, diffusion, and willfull obscurity
would be poetic virtues. We would ask of a poem not clarity and

powerful expression, but fog. Even good poets sometime fail to see what is crucial in this misunderstanding, that we must not prize novelty but originality. Novelty is a hula hoop, is 3-D vision. Originality is Picasso.

The poet in "By His Stripes" is straining to be novel, to find a stunning way to express what is thought to be a simple matter: love. One can almost see the wheels in the poet's head grinding. What figure can I muster for love? A tiger, of course. No one will expect that. In consequence, the tiger, naturally aggressive, dangerous, and passionate, follows its victim—the role chosen by the poet—through various unexpected domestic and urban zones. The chase is interrupted on occasion for the speaker to inform us that she has "yearned unstoppably" for such a creature, that she has been frightened by a pickpocket, and that she is dreaming.

Nothing which happens in this poem really matters to the speaker. Hers is a dream poem not because it allows her to explore those important zones of the psyche, or even zones on the other side of the tracks, but because a dream, she feels, suspends any rules we might bring to poetic discourse. The dream allows anything and everything, however substantial or artificial, to happen. Of course, the poet's instinct tells her we must be made to understand her allegorical fable, and so she concludes by telling us, "The tiger is love." Once we have read the entire piece, we are able to read it once more with this clue and to see the speaker all along wanted to say that to be without love is to be wounded but that she is no longer without it. If we had not had this interpretation, we might have thought the tiger a symbol of hate, guilt, Christianity, Vietnam, or a psychic double. Anything, in fact. How, then, is an attentive reader to respond to this poem? Does it engender that inevitably true sense of a particular human experience which is the characteristic of all superior art?

"By His Stripes" is not yet art but is formula trying to find a language which will support a message. Through novelty and fancy it dismisses the rules which govern clarity, precision, resonance, and expectation. It fails at what it most wants, universality, because it abandons common referential communication. It does not imagine a reader with a shared interest, language, or desire for meaning. This poet hasn't yet learned that the single human experience is inevitably and inherently universal and that the task isn't to heap mechanical complexity onto experience, but instead is to try to be simple, to be direct. The poet doesn't allow her experience with love, whatever that may have been, to evolve. She imposes a tissue of rhetorical and social exaggeration and loses credibility. Her poem is arbitrary, though it is not without an energetic mystery.

Ultimately, this poet must face the problem of form. What form is appropriate for her subject? She has conceived it to be a kind of leaping imagery couched in a dream narrative. Fair enough. But she must create images of such power, such clarity, and such credibility that they will speak for themselves. Such images must extend, qualify, and reveal each other. They must operate by rules contracted between poet and reader, whatever the rules may be. And above all, the language of such a poem must be capable of containing the complexity and depth of mature experience. The poet who writes a dream poem in the belief that these needs are abrogated by hinting this is all divorced from any factual reality is self-deceiving. The poet of "By His Stripes" needs to understand clearly what there is about a dream vision and a tiger which might cogently work in a metaphor seeking to reveal the joy of love. She needs to justify her decisions and to be certain what stays in the poem is not caprice. When she does so, she will surely see there is no need to conclude with an editorial swooping down like Groucho's duck.

That is to say, this poet must learn it is the poem's function to earn that conclusion and to make it implicitly. An *earned* poem is not a poem which has been pushed through many revisions, though that is certainly one kind of earning. I mean here that the vision, the operative ambience of the dramatic construct, has been somehow submitted to the testing and tempering fires of rational, skeptical disbelief. All poems, like good magical tricks, are illusions, but when the illusions are transparent, crude, or wholly beyond credible possibility, they are unearned. The difference between an earned and an unearned poem is what the conscious and sympathetic reader will accept on faith and what he will reject because it cannot be imaginatively swallowed. Since, here, the subject and the poem's attitude toward its subject is foregone, all that can achieve our genuine interest is the quality of the language and the angle of vision. Even a commitment to unconventionality has its limits. This poet ought to be directed to reading poets who have accomplished work in the modes of allegory, fable, and surrealism. I would suggest, as a start, Blake, Smart, Ted Hughes, Charles Simic, Neruda, and Borges. As Roethke tells us, imitation is a primary way of learning, and though I would not send the student to such masters for imitation, imitation would surely be the initial result. The poet would learn what has been done well and, with luck and perseverance, might well discover a way to bring her own poem into control, if not to press beyond imitation into originality.

"Looking for Winter"

"Looking for Winter," like the previous poem, operates according to the notion that the good poem is a fortune cookie: hide the message under layers of obscure language. But there is a significant difference, too. This poet loves language more, loves possibility and resonance more, loves the saying of things to the point of intoxication. That is a good sign of talent, but it does not mean we are necessarily in a poem's presence. Indeed, "Looking for Winter" is a poem only in the sense of minimal definitions: it has certain basic qualities which name it a poem—lineation, a few interesting phrases, white space, occasional nonprose rhythms. It fails most standards of craft, clarity, durability, wisdom, or emotional impact.

Yet there is something more attractive in this spaghetti of words than in "By His Stripes." When this poet writes, "To be capable of uncertainties in the face of / multiplicities—what words can I trust . . . ," I feel the presence of an active and interesting, perhaps even poetic intelligence. I look for the dramatic body which might sustain this rhetoric, however, and I find only words. I do not find charged phrases or words in their best order, not human eloquence or even simplicity. I find verbal leftovers. If energy is, as I think, a requisite of true poetry, it must nevertheless be controlled energy, a shaping and shaped power. The poet here cannot even control his impressive metamorphoses which willfully lead him to become a tree, a patient, a jello, a fabric, a firecracker, a seed, a dancer, a balloon song, a lover, and a mother. Can anyone find such indulgence credible?

This poet seems immune to the act of selection. The first line is slack and down-homey anecdotal. San Francisco does not function in the poem and is only a label. The poet's love for "gray days" has no passion and only sets up a convenient pose which is presumably *poetic*. It wants to justify a composition of rapturous gush, which is exactly what stanza 1 (if those seven lines merit the term) is. Notice how many bookish tricks surround the indulgent language of these lines: "deckself" and "thrown into relief," the "rare October sunset," and the typographical slashes which are only visual instead of functional line indicators. Consider how the glib metaphor of "confetti" reduces the archetypal autumn foliage of Vermont. How could this speaker sincerely "miss" that? He wants to tell us how sad and beautiful he is when "stripped to the bone," but his glibness disabuses us of his integrity.

In stanza 2 he asks us to see him as a tree "loose in [his] new bark," and a tree which *wonders* at the same time as it feels "the cathartic itching in [his] bones. . . ." The point of this stanza is that the speaker wants to go on budding, to avoid growth that is death. But how seriously can we take such a speaking tree?

From such an entrapped position, the poet does not transition to stanza 3. He merely leaps to a large, fuzzy, and near-ontological questioning. He asks: "How to / harness the transfusions riffling through the brain—the billboards of change, / and not miss the ones that rise quiet like mushrooms." Not really a question, but a statement. We might answer, since neither our speaker nor his poem attempts an answer, that one doesn't "harness the transfusions"; that transfusions don't "riffle" the brain; that the referent of "ones" is nowhere to be found; that those "billboards" might be encountered on the highways of somebody's mind, but the drivers who can see them are rare indeed. How transfusions become billboards is a question we must beg altogether.

If the poet's language so far seems a gibberish filtered through a computer (I can no longer characterize it as food, since that implies a sustenance the poem doesn't have), stanza 4 is a nonreferential drone. The poet says he "used to want to want" and that seems almost clear, a longing, except its synonym is "oxbowing"—which he is not doing anymore. Presumably, the poet means he's made some decision which prevents a continued vacillation. The closest I can come to deciphering what is said is that the speaker abandons something like self-scrutiny, desire, even consciousness. In consequence he becomes a firecracker—apparently forgetting a firecracker is all noise and little effect. He doesn't, however, forget the hunger for "undoing the self" which was romantically imposed in stanza 1 and rejected in those buds of stanza 2.

Through four stanzas we are not yet clear about the poem's subject, but we do know there is some kind of running argument with the self. In the fourth stanza the poet offers self to self and says: "Nothing more perfect than this: motionless, raw, stunning." The act or the self? we might ask. He doesn't wait to tell us, pulled forward by the pitch of emotion to say, "I want to elope with what is myself." Immediately, then, he writes that he is "birthing, stitching up my knees"—which seems an odd place for the violence of motherhood. The poem concludes with the speaker "dying for what is new."

It is easy enough to dismiss this piece of work as a confused version of the "I fall on the thorns of life / I bleed" theme. The poem as it is is not *about* anything; it has no subject, no events, few clear images. Yet the poem wants to be about love, and that is no small thing. I mean the unsullied love of being. It wants to celebrate the self's recognition of inevitable connection to the process of life, the tears of things, and to mourn mutability. The love which lies behind this poem is deep and complex, but the poem's language is not yet capable of handling such an ambitious revelation. Instead of force and pathos, the poem gives us bubblegum and bathos. The love revealed in this language is solipsism, for the poet is essentially narcissistic. In effect, this language demeans what it would celebrate. The natural human exploration of the nature of reality becomes, through inattentive language and nonselective disorder, a monologue of trivia.

Trivia, however, is something that all writers experience, and I would not dismiss the student-poet in dismissing this particular poem. Such a poem offers the opportunity to make the poet aware of his gifts and his possibility as well as his immaturity with words. But with such a piece as this, a piece I would gently explain is not much of a poem, it may be that our best criticism is unnecessary. I have a sense that the writer here is quite young and may well be one of those talents who needs time rather than our concerned push. We sometimes fail to recognize, I think, that not all of our students have lived enough to write well. They may be extraordinarily articulate, sensitive, and even educated and still lack experience. I have recently heard a famous poet and author of books about how to teach poetry to children and the elderly say that any seventeen-year-old can write better than any forty-year-old. I could not disagree more. Such an argument denies historical experience. It denies Whitman, Yeats, and Robert Penn Warren, among others. The woman traumatized by divorce or the young Vietnam footsoldier may well be better prepared to make important poems than the insulated children of suburbs whose life has been primarily that of classrooms. We must be willing to accommodate ourselves and our methods of helping to the needs of each student, not by refusing to stand for standards of excellence or abandoning our literary heritage for relevance, but by determining what to emphasize and what to leave in abeyance for each individual we serve. There may be some facts of nature with which, perhaps, we ought not to meddle.

It is true, however, that with the poets who write poems of varying quality, we are often obliged to meddle since they are our students. They lay their poems before us, and we owe them our best, most honest responses. That is why we hold faculty ranks and take our salaries. Therefore, I would tell the writer of "Looking for Winter" everything I have written about his poem. I would buy him coffee and suggest that he put those lines about uncertainties and complexities in a notebook, that he leave them for a while and try to discover what interested him about his poem, that he ask what was important in the whole business. I would say, quietly, begin again. I would tell him to seek the simplest possible language and to remember that each word must fit well with each other, that the poem must not only try to see the world but also through the world. I would say he must trust himself enough to go off alone into the room of the examined life where, alone, he might undertake the required work of creating one true line and then another.

This is not, ultimately, an essay about the three student-poems I have discussed, but a statement of pedagogy. Therefore, one last comment seems in order. Implicit in all considerations about the pedagogy of creative writing is a continuing quarrel between writers and teachers. Both vehemently advance certain aesthetic positions when they meet, often opposed positions. Again, I recently heard a famous novelist harangue an audience to the effect that a writer writes, a teacher teaches. Some are so passionate about the division that they might, I suppose, insist on separate but equal toilet facilities. The fact is, we ought not be surprised at such passionate partisans. They exist in one body, in our individual bodies. The writer in us wants, like a jealous lover, all of our attention. The teacher wants no less. The student makes a third, equal claim. Most of us simply don't know how to divide our service to obligation, responsibility, and function. As teachers and as writers we sometimes don't know what to say to our students, and the confusion, the anxiety backs us into corners within ourselves. We fall into and out of strident pedagogical positions. Though it may be heresy to some, I believe this unresolved split of energy and affection is often a good and desirable situation: it means we are concerned about what we are doing, concerned for our students. Of course, some of us can never serve two, much less three, masters, and these ought to make the hard choice not to serve what destroys them. In any case, we must all make choices, for that is what it means to live maturely.

I have chosen to teach creative writing with a realization that what I do will not show full, visible results in the short range. With many students, my instruction may lead to nothing. This is equally true of instruction in biology, psychology, calculus, and basketball. I do not believe, and am disturbed by, the contention that instruction in creative writing accomplishes nothing. At best it enhances knowledge and provides a vital community among a society of Philistines. Theodore Roethke helped make writers of Richard Hugo, Carolyn Kizer, David Wagoner, John Haislip, Kenneth Hanson, Tess Gallagher, and others. At worst, creative writing breeds good, close readers. Some of my colleagues in the field refer to our teachers of literature as academics or scholars, and sneer. It is true that scholars often condescend to us and let us know, for example, that neither Faulkner nor Hemingway needed workshops, that neither Eliot nor Stevens was a teacher. Their memories are short, just as are ours. They forget the teaching of contemporary literature is an historically recent innovation, however well entrenched now. And of their examples, our best response is that those writers made a free choice as to what they would do with their lives. Their examples are neither generic nor particularly enlightening. Saul Bellow, Elizabeth Bishop, John Gardner, and Denise Levertov are teachers.

What is more disturbing, however, is the teacher of creative writing who feels (1) that teachers of literature are the enemy and (2) that creative writing instruction is merely something necessary to keep food on the table while we write. Of teachers of literature, we might say they have kept alive writing itself. They have taught us all to love and respect what many of us would not otherwise have known. As Milton says, they also serve—and not a few of them serve immeasurably well. If they are our enemies, who are our friends?

The creative writer who believes he need expect nothing from his class is, whatever else he may be, not our friend. He is the teacher who approves or disapproves indiscriminately whatever appears. He refuses discrimination and standards. What's the use? he says. He fails to demand ambition in students, the ambition for art and excellence. This reflects an essential disinterest in the student or an ignorance in the instructor. Either is unforgivable. Within the past six months I heard a young poet preface a reading by ridiculing all professors of English and by saying that he was glad to be among people who, like himself, distrusted all ideas unconditionally. We cannot hold anyone specifically responsible for a contemporary collusion of stupidity, democracy, and poetry, but ignorance should not be tolerated. Ideas are part of life, part of poetry. The young poet was also a teacher of creative writing, and I have sympathy for his students who, I suspect, are being cheated out of a rightful heritage. The kind of teacher, his kind, who refuses to encourage their ideas *in* poems and *in* class implicitly stumps for constricted experience. He quite simply condescends to his students by not taking them seriously. He does not, as the true creative writing teacher must, teach art or teach artfully.

The instruction of creative writing, perhaps more than literary instruction, does teach art—the process, not the product. It is and can be a respectable, important segment of a young writer's education. It ought not be the primary part of that education. We must understand and be tolerant of the limits of our instruction. And we must not overrate ourselves, because what we do is so little available to objective quantification. Neither should we belittle our own knowledge, experience, and commitment to excellent writing. We must try to be what we would have our students emulate and surpass. In every art, in every craft the world has ever known, there have been masters. Those masters and their works have provided models for students. These masters have been willing, as teachers, to say a loud *no* to inadequate accomplishment. They have been singular in their demand that students comprehend the heritage of particular and general art. We are obliged to do no less. This afternoon I watched a televised report about a man considered to be the finest kite maker in America. Many of us would consider that an irrelevant pursuit at best. But this man was so devoted to his passion that he apprenticed himself for three years to Europe's finest kite maker. He said that he *hoped* this would prepare him to accomplish something in his future. Unlike him, many of our students and colleagues appear to believe that successful completion of a specified number of hours in creative writing will certify them as masters of poetry, the Queen of the Arts. Many writing programs graduate such masters in only two years! Perhaps some of these students have acquired all the experience and all the training of long years of patient study. Perhaps some understand that creative writing courses can only form an appropriate portion of a necessarily larger study.

We will be able to take ourselves seriously, and be taken seriously, only when we recognize the need for integration with literature and other disciplines. We cannot insist on isolation and simultaneously reduce the suspicion of what we are and what we do. We cannot be everything to everybody. If we set up as masters, we must be willing to say no to work that is inadequate, unpromising, clearly unexcellent. We must demonstrate allegiance to standards which will liberate the imaginations we would nurture, remembering always that the true master of an art exercises mastery and responsibility in equal measure: he masters in order to achieve and accepts the responsibility for the keeping of the art he has undertaken, not for the keeping of the lives of his students. His function, and his students' in turn, is to tell the truth and to seek excellence. We are not meant to be the social workers of verse, but witnesses to civilization's highest values. If we manage to sustain a continuing excellence in our work and our students, we will perform a most valuable social service indeed. We will, in demanding the best of ourselves and our students, be doing what writing has always done—teaching the inarticulate to comprehend, express, and shape human experience. That is not only a very human act, but the exactly divine function meant by the name *poet*.

Dave Smith was born in 1942 and is director of creative writing at the University of Utah. He studied at the University of Virginia, Southern Illinois University, and Ohio University. He held an NEA fellowship in poetry for 1976–77 and is a board member of the Associated Writers Programs. His books of poetry include *The Fisherman's Whore, Cumberland Station,* and *Goshawk, Antelope.*

HEATHER McHUGH

"By His Stripes"

Often the process of writing a poem is one of discovery: however firm and artful your designs on it, the poem, as it happens, is no servitude; whatever you intend, it tends to itself. Often the resistance is of

feeling over format, presence over prescience. In revision we must pay it
our respects.

"By His Stripes" is framed by the Christian occasion of the first
and last two lines, but its most convincing moments come despite that
packaging, in the weird potent juxtaposing of imagination's tiger exotic
against the backyards and carports and living rooms of daily suburbia.
The poem never makes use of the juxtapositions: unenhanced by paral-
lel placement, a clearly ironic tone, or other formal evidences of in-
tent, relations among parts (Christmas and air-conditioning, tiger and
carport, up-against-the-wall and love) appear accidental, and the poem's
wishing is washed out, finally, when the conventions prevail and the poet
falls back into her former faithfulness, poetic and religious. The yearning
was, for a moment, ecstatic. The last lines cannot work because in the
world of the poem they are untrue: the tiger here is something rather
more adulterated than the poet decides to acknowledge, a kind of sexual
power partly, partly the unnameable power of the imagination, but no
bland healing hymnal love. After the most evocative passage of the
poem, when the poet and power confront each other ("things split open
in the living room . . . me up against the wall and holding, / and the
tiger filling the room"), we are fed a neat little triplet of tenses subjugat-
ing primeval energy to a pale morality.

It is the poet's paradoxical responsibility during revision to recognize
and honor the poem's essential independence and give up his precon-
ceptions for it. Perhaps what happened in the process of this poem was:
out of its wrappings of piety stepped the untamed figure of the poet's
own unlegislated desire: no matter how much framework of singing and
meaning and learning and telling is made to tame that figure, its liberated
image (that pacing beyond the squares and keepers of an L.A. landscape,
its taking of living rooms by force) is what touches us. I mean the poet
must herself face the threat of the tiger, not domesticate it. The dread-
fulness in reverence, the power behind praise, the brute behind beatitude
are the truths revealed in the course of the poem. Just when the tiger in
all its awesomeness and violation has her up against the wall and starts
its terrible expansion beyond the physical, she wags her finger didac-
tically at it and snaps a flea collar around its neck. Such a resolution, in a
poem straining to bear witness to a wilder, more carnal Christianity, is
too simple, too neat a naming for the poem's own terms, too much a re-
fusal to be ravaged.

In workshops I consider the poet's intentions irrelevant. The poem must be defensible in itself, must need no spokesman. The *power* at the heart of this one lies in lines 4–9 and 15–21; the *potential* lies in relations among parts (the local infinities of perspective; juxtaposition of "home of tigers" and "Living room," and all that contrast afforded by parallel design); but the impotency lies in attempted conversion, really, of raw into civilized feeling.

The middle section of the poem (lines 10–14) seems like historical fact or associative accident (tracks to streetcar), and poetic failure. I mean it does not operate illustratively or logically in the design of the poem (to challenge the pickpocket would have been to face the tiger of love?). And the kind of explaining we find in lines like "I know the tiger is not meant but still . . ." and "still I dream" and "I will tell you" is a common enough symptom of the failure of poetic faith; the poet does not trust the objects and events to explain themselves. Artfully selected and arranged, they will, beyond all telling.

"Walking Over Rochford Burn"

The art of selection and arrangement is precisely what is needed in revision here. This poet does not make the mistake of overexplanation, or of translating experience, with a plodding omniscience, into abstraction. In fact, there is a fine poem to be had in his own words, right here on the page. They only remain to be selected and arranged in such a way as most potently to suggest the delicate relations at the heart of the poem.

For me the great virtues of this one are its spare articulation, its sharp metaphorical sensibility, its constant reconciliation of history with immediacy, and the subtlety of design under the pressure of feeling. I think the poem can take advantage of its natural tendency toward simplicity and become much sparer, without losing any of its power and suggestiveness. Consider the following reorganization:

WALKING OVER ROCHFORD BURN

```
This place was once fire, acres
enough to earn it a name.
Since then have crept the scavengers
of burnt ground: raspberry, burdock.
```

They tangle around our ankles.
They bury seeds in our socks.

It is our day of hot raspberries,
one of our last. The heat
pries odor from the pines.
We've travelled far and now
bend low. As a sort of love
we offer each other what we have:
not much, but sweet.
We cross

Rochford Burn not holding hands.
A fire years ago
scratches toward our knees.

What is only suggested in the original, but actualized in this sample revision, is the centrality of words like "burn" and "heat" and "fire" to the metaphorical designs of the poem. By the end we know there is some historical pressure, not just at that place but in those people; that is why the landscape offers so fine an accommodation of their uneasy relations. This is no uncomplicated love poem; good; there are no uncomplicated loves. What we suspect about the people gathers power from (and is reiterated in) their *grounds* for travel together: the tangle and seeds, the heat and pitch, the meager harvest. Here is sexuality and subtlety both: the poet does not broadcast his pain; he modifies his love ("a sort of"); it's a winsome modesty, an accomplished understatement, a kind of wisdom.

What I miss in his poem is a consolidation of effect, the architecture of detail that would make his sense inescapable at last. The formal design of a poem takes place at all levels, word and line, the whole surge of the poem on the page. This poet wanders, emotionally, because he wanders formally. Early drafts often serve the purpose of discovering what we mean; in later drafts the *how* of meaning must accommodate that *what*. This poem is divided against itself; the form reveals it. My feeling, as a reader, was that the essential gesture of the poem was the single movement (literal and metaphorical) across a landscape, into insight; I felt that the organization of the poem muddied its intelligence by trying to tell the truth in more than one way; that the form's division and repetitions signaled the critical defect of the poem. If you believe, as I do, that a defining power of poetry is the play of line against sentence, affording cadence in speech and accumulation in effect, then you work to get rid of the flaccid lines, the ones which don't pull their own weight, don't merit their allocation of space. The unit is significant and powerful; you don't squander a full line on mechanical adjustments or prosaic exposition. Such lines as "of this summer" and "to each other" and "like this" and "for years" do not deserve the formal distinction. A sense of the form of accomplishment in a poem is no mere formality; it is the motive and force, revelation's method.

"Looking for Winter"

Here is a poem demonstrating many of the weaknesses I've described. First, its formal insecurity is almost visually evident: the page a quixotic strewing of suspended periods, dashes, slashes, indentation, exdentation, parenthesis, hot and cold running stage effects. The poem affects a looseness of style which serves no purpose (unlike Cummings's celebrated lower-case choices and visual anomalies). I can imagine a poem in which the spelling "tho," for example, would corroborate some spareness or catchiness or colloquial intent in the poem; but this poem, for all its love of fashion, all its trendy self-preoccupation, cannot be so defended; elsewhere it forgets its own poetic contract (as with the ampersand) and reverts to conventional spelling. A reader faced with such oversight and indifference is likely similarly to respond; we are not moved, even to celebration of sloppiness. An experienced printer would wonder how to render this poem, as prose or in lines; the only generous reading of the first stanza suggests it's meant to be printed as prose (otherwise, how justify the line break on "I miss the"); yet the third stanza's line break after "How to," for example, seems deliberate. Such inattentiveness to materials bespeaks the poem's own ill-definition as a formal construction.

Then there is no consistency in the figurative texture: transfusions are harnessed, are like billboards, mushrooms. Lives jell and melt and solidify in a "fabric" of moments. We are asked to accept "a firecracker . . . not forgetting what is loose-limbed." That the self appears in so many guises (tree, cliff-diver, firecracker, dancer, song of a balloon, woman in labor) is confusing. Because I believe anything is possible, I assume a poem *could* be constructed to take advantage of such a series of transformations. But this one does not. Its churning interiority is more like indigestion than anything else. Even a poem about confusion cannot afford to imitate it.

Conceptually, the poem is flawed in being about, not of, emotion. It attaches emblems for feeling to abstractions for feeling, and goes, despite its concrete fixtures, uninstructed by the world. Its habit is metaphorical; the uses to which it puts a flurry of different things are reductively similar; its very substance is presumptive, its objects ornamental, not generative. It is a poem limited by and to the self, yet not communicative of it; its narcissism seems, finally, self-indulgent (any reader who has suffered four long paragraphs of teething of this sort is not likely to want to keep nursing when he hears "the offering of myself to my self. Nothing more perfect than this").

The poem constitutes a failure of feeling, a kind of self-fixation, feedback. It is not a transmission of energy but an exhaustion of it. In general, I would want to urge this poet to listen more and make less noise; to sit in the world literally transcribing things and events that do not enchant her, things she never imagined, real people speaking, the unconverted music of counter-to-kitchen bellowing in diners, announcements at bus terminals, laundromat conversations. I would ask her to forget herself, to spurn her pet romances, discover herself to be a part of the world, and not the other way around. By way of encouragement, I would select a few fragments from the poem for praise (the visual texture of the sunset passage, perhaps, with its "cauliflower and pumpkin huddling in groves"; the simple nearly paradoxical delicacy of "to be capable / of uncertainties"; the insight in "I used to want to want"). But the single compelling moment in the poem for me, the one point at which I was caught up, persuaded, *engaged*, was the sudden "what words can I trust. / When chance *is* myself. And everything necessary." That is so relatively powerful and plain a statement of quandary, so potentially complicated and honest a vision of the poet's dilemma, that I would argue for its ending the poem, a whole new poem, in which every thing precedent was relative to that declaration, supporting without spilling it. It must be an insight we suspect or feel all along, but only find articulable at the very moment it's articulated in the poem. Once again we see the poem's power is to reveal *itself*, even to the poet: the relation of chance to necessity, of the self to the everything-else, of language to trust, is just what this poet needs to ponder. In that one moment of stress, it is the poem itself which says so.

Heather McHugh was born in 1948 and teaches in Goddard College's MFA program. She studied at Radcliffe. Her book, *Dangers* was the New Poetry Series winner in 1977.

CYNTHIA MACDONALD

Several times a year I have the pleasure of sharing a workshop with another teaching poet—someone visits my class or I visit theirs, or we both are guests at a third institution—and I'm always eager to discover how that poet will deal with poems-in-the-making. Alberta Turner's plan for this book sounded like an expansion of those pleasures.

But when the student poems arrived I became aware of something I must have known but had never verbalized: to respond to a poem as a teacher certain information about the student must be obtained. Is "Looking for Winter: A Seasonal Change" the first effort of a fifteen-year-old or was it written by a participant in a graduate writing program? I must know the answer to this kind of question before I can respond fairly and appropriately to work-in-process as opposed to work-as-artifact. Editors usually deal with a poem as an artifact, asking whether it is suitable for a junior high literary magazine, an anthology of poems by American women, a Poetry in Public Places bus placard, *The New Yorker*. But teachers deal with the writing process.

"Walking Over Rochford Burn" and *"Looking for Winter"*

Even if I imagine "Walking over Rochford Burn" and "Looking for Winter" as poems presented during the first workshop of a term, or during a class at a university where I've gone to give a reading, or during the workshop of a fellow poet while she's in a coma and unable to give information about her class, I would still find out what I needed to know about level and intention during the course of the session. But the only poet about whom I have such information is Helen Williams, the author of "By His Stripes"; she was my student. Because I can look at her poem in a different way, I shall do so only at the end of this essay.

There is a third way to respond to any poem, not as editor or teacher but simply as reader. What if I came across either the Schmid or Cole poem in a magazine? "Walking Over Rochford Burn" is neat and well made but too one-level nostalgic to interest me in reading it more than once. I want a poem to engage me more deeply than it does. The raspberry (interesting that Cole's spelling of the word leaves out the *rasp*) picking and the once-burned ground which yields fruit are meant to be a metaphor for the relationship between the two people. But what we know about them (lovers? friends? siblings? parent/child?) isn't specific enough to generate that strange combination of tension and clarity between the subject and the elucidating comparison which is the essence of metaphor. Therefore, although the poem is pleasing (a praising word almost as suspect as "interesting"), it does not engage me. Only the title sticks—I believe readers pick up burrs just the way Robert Frost said writers do—because of its use of Burn as both location and fiery instrument.

"Looking for Winter" is the opposite of neat and well made. I can see that even before I read a word, just by its look on the page. The first two stanzas are awkward in places and lumpily unmusical most of the time, but as long as Schmid stays with the tree metaphor I'm willing to stay with the poem. But the questions (without question marks) at the beginning of the third stanza make me want to turn away, and the phrase "Harness the transfusions riffling through the brain—the billboards of change, / and not miss the ones that rise quiet like mushrooms" would make me stop.

My irritation with this poem is evident and, I believe, justifiable if I'm a reader, but if I'm a teacher, it would only be justifiable if the student has had a chance to learn certain things and hasn't done so. As a teacher, I want to criticize honestly but in terms which are useful for the student. Wordsworth said, "We murder to dissect," but I don't dissect to murder.

Perhaps it would be useful to imagine that the two poems are being presented at the first meeting of a workshop where I had not selected the participants and where Ms. Schmid and Mr. Cole had each brought only a single poem. I would have asked each participant to share something of her or his history as writers and readers and thus would have this information about Schmid and Cole.

In Schmid's case I would probably say only one or two sentences about "Looking for Winter"—something like, "This poem shows a lot of energy and shows that you get pleasure from using words, seeing what they can do. But there isn't enough control. And there is excess." Then I'd move on to giving her a reading and writing assignment for next week. The best way to avoid murder by dissection is to get the student to write something much better. That's what the assignment would be calculated to do.

The reading assignment might be to read the following poems by William Carlos Williams: "Young Sycamore," "To Daphne and Virginia," "To Waken an Old Lady," "The Widows Lament in Springtime," "By the road to the contagious hospital," "Danse Russe," "Burning the Christmas Greens," "The Yachts." I intentionally selected a limited number of poems by a single poet in order to begin the process of focusing which Schmid urgently needs. The choice of Williams is deliberately ancestral; I want her to trace the lineage of her work. Williams is one of her progenitors, but does she know him? Pound would have been an alternative choice, but my experience is that a poet of glut, like Schmid, would take from Pound exactly what she does not need.

A writing assignment might be to read the Daphne myth, then to write a poem dealing, in the most precise language she could summon, with the physical transformation of woman to tree. Or I might leave the subject open and ask Schmid to write a strict form—a villanelle, perhaps. Whatever the assignment, she would be told to reread and proofread!

In Mr. Cole's case, "Walking Over Rochford Burn" would be discussed in class with the suggestion from me that he could either try to revise the poem, dealing with the metaphor more actively, or could decide to leave it as is and go on to new work. In either case, I would also give him a reading and writing assignment. Read one of the following: Merwin's *Writings to an Unfinished Accompaniment,* Pastan's *The Five Stages of Grief,* Rich's *Diving into the Wreck,* Valentine's *Pilgrims,* Simic's *Dismantling the Silence,* Strand's *Reasons for Moving,* Levine's *They Feed the Lion.* This is a sample list; there are many possibilities; they all contain poems about specific experience, but they go beyond that to the element which cannot be explained: what is discovered when you *dive* or *dismantle* or *move.*

As with the reading assignment, the writing assignment for Cole would be broader than for Schmid. One possible assignment would be to take an emotional situation like the one which generated "Rochford

Burn" but to use it in an entirely different context. For example, Cole
might go to the *Biographical Dictionary*, find a person whose life engages
him, and invent the circumstances for the poem, using his own emo-
tion and the biographical detail suggested by the dictionary entry. He
could even keep the berry picking. How about "Napoleon and Josephine
Pick *Fraises des Bois* before He Leaves for Egypt"? No. In a class such
specific suggestion must be resisted as overintervention in another's
work. Though I hate to abandon the little strawberries as pyramids.

What I would probably do is talk about my own interest in this
method and tell the class a little about a poem I recently finished on
Florence Nightingale, possibly even read it to them (though not in a
first class). I would certainly suggest to Cole that in his next poem he
write in longer lines, because I find the already slight material of
"Rochford Burn" further attenuated by such lines as:

```
          like this
          for years.
```

I'd also talk a bit about words which are intrinsically interesting and
those which are not . . . "those which are not" being a fine example of
the latter. This would probably lead to a discussion by the class as a
whole about their views on line lengths and breaks, possibly continuing
on to questions about the difference between using words of Latin or
Anglo-Saxon derivation.

The more I write about these imaginary reading assignments,
imaginary writing assignments, and criticism in which the imaginary
class participants are necessarily mute, the more I feel the way I did
when I complained about the enormous cockroaches in Houston and a
friend suggested I might want to get a geiko (phonetic spelling) lizard
because such lizards eat roaches. When I said I might get one, he replied,
"Of course, then you have to clean up the lizard shit." Am I accurately
anticipating the problems and the solutions and the problems caused
by the solutions of these imaginary students?

"By His Stripes"
Well, Helen Williams does not have to be imagined by me. She
participated in a real workshop of mine for two semesters, and "By His

Stripes" was discussed there. Helen has been writing for many years
(she was a student of Howard Moss at Vassar), and I would, and did,
comment on this poem as coming from an experienced poet, though one
who has trouble making substantial revisions. I like much of her work
but feel she loses many potentially excellent poems because she will
only change a word or two, that is, she revises before bringing a poem
to class but then resists changes. "By His Stripes" seems to me mostly
right as it is. The only major change I would suggest, as did several
others in the workshop, is that she not state, "the tiger is love." What
the tiger represents should come out in the poem rather than being
spelled out at the end. "But that's the whole point of the poem," Helen
said. Perhaps. But I think the tiger is love and something(s) else.
Suppose the poem stopped at "filling the room"? Would the love omitted
at the end need to be introduced somewhere else, not as a word but as
an attribute of the tiger? Or as a secondary emotional presence like the
pickpocket? Or is another ending needed if the two lines are cut?

I asked two other less important questions: (1) You, Helen, know
there are echoes of Blake and Hopkins in this poem. Do you want to
acknowledge these connections in any way? (2) Is there any way of
indicating less ploddingly, "I know the tiger is not meant"?

But even if Helen makes no changes, I like "By His Stripes" and
will read it from time to time, especially for the *frisson* I get from:

```
Things split open in the living room
last week, and the tiger stepped in through
    the crack,
shining like aluminum foil,
```

I do not give Helen Williams reading or writing assignments, as
she is an intrepid explorer who needs neither.

Now that I've talked about an actual situation, a real workshop, I
feel more sanguine. Perhaps I could train the geiko lizard to use the
cat box.

Cynthia Macdonald was born in New York City, and except for four
years in Southern California, spent her childhood there. She received a
B.A. from Bennington College, married, had two children, and realized
her ambition of becoming an opera singer. In 1961, after she had been

singing for six years, she began to write poetry. She continued to write and sing while following her husband to Vancouver, B.C., and Tokyo. On her return to the New York area, she enrolled in the graduate writing program at Sarah Lawrence College and received an M.A. She has been a faculty member there for six years and is now a visiting professor at The Johns Hopkins University. She has published *Amputations* (1972) and *Transplants* (1976). In 1973, Ms. Macdonald received a grant from the National Endowment for the Arts; she has had two Yaddo residence grants and, in 1976, a CAPS grant.

Group XI

PHILIP BOOTH
LARRY LEVIS
JAY MEEK
LAWRENCE RAAB

Group XI consists of Philip Booth and three of his former students at Syracuse University. Levis teaches in the writing program of the University of Missouri, Columbia; Raab at Williams College; and Meek at Wake Forest University. Booth provided the student poems, and only he knew the student-poets. All four worked independently.

SONNET
Larry Rapant

The self is such a subtle weaponry.
I cannot count the times I've tried to free
my voice before Love's smile could fade away,
but kept it to myself, as if the day-
light shone for nothing but to be a cloud
and build in heat one dark oppressive shroud.
And so the tongue begins to fork and drool
a storm of words electrified and cruel

that seem to be but uttered out of art
they come from lips that are so far apart.
This must be where we get our battle rites:
our wars of nations, our wars of nights
and our battles of sexes must all have their start
in a motionless hand and an unspoken heart.

Larry Rapant, born in 1947, studied creative writing at Syracuse University with W. D. Snodgrass and Philip Booth. He is a communications specialist for Syracuse Model Neighborhood Facility, Inc. and an instructor at Syracuse University.

WADING HORSES
(After a Photograph by Paul Strand)
Susan Shetterly

Four horses nose
the lowest tide. Their withers
drip
cool as a seal's
belly. Under the heels of
guillemots,
the far, black water rears.

A beast breaks
from the loosening dark,
breathes
and settles down.

From her weedy crevice,
the ancient fiddler, with pale,
myopic stalks, observes hooves
rehearse
a slow kick at the shallow surf,
sees the rise
and beckon of the cobalt
fluke.

Susan Shetterly was born in 1942 and attended Skidmore College, the University of Madrid, and the Harvard School of Education. She lives with her husband and two children outside a small village in Maine, where she teaches at a local elementary school. She has been writing for the past two years and has been published in various poetry magazines.

THE VANISHING MAILMEN
Charles Agvent

Today, all my letters
are blank; stacked in my pouch
like fried eggs, each one
flat and bright as the afternoon.
I am on a strange route;
it is my last day.

People open their doors
on this warm and dogless day.
Only screen doors separate me
from young wives in negligees,
tired schoolgirls, jewelry boxes,
trays of fat plums and ripe melons.

But this is my last day
and any connection made would be worthless
now. Televisions tuned to game shows
send me on my way. I am no Charles Atlas;
I'll miss this job. My muscles will soon
atrophy, wilt into powder and blow away.

This is my last house;
I approach it with short steps and empty pouch.
Termites scramble over the porch and boarded windows.
I sit. My hair stops growing. I am done.
Termites, busy unbuilding, crawl over me.
They've lost another one.

Charles Agvent, born in 1953, studied writing at the University of Bridgeport and Syracuse University with Dick Allen, Philip Booth, and

W. D. Snodgrass. He is a part-time instructor of English at Syracuse University and an English tutor at University College.

PHILIP BOOTH

"Sonnet"

I've seen good poems from the poet who wrote "Sonnet." He's good enough, in his own voice, to deserve telling that almost nothing is right about "Sonnet." From its Emily-first-line to its Yeatsy-last-couplet, it's a poem a computer might write. Plug in the program called *sonnet,* and out comes this "drool / . . . of words" and mechanical rhythms. This print-out is almost totally without language, without voice. It begins with a fair idea and pads it to death. All of which seems to me to come, in this case, from some terribly wrongheaded notions about the nature of language and the possibilities of formal structure.

The poem pads its language to fulfill its meters; the doubled ad-jectives ("dark oppressive") and abstracted comparisons ("so far") are prime examples of how easily a poem can lose its voice. In reaching for pentameter lines, in stretching for rhymes, the poet loses himself: the individuality of his own rhythms and human perceptions. Look, for instance, at how impossibly dehumanized the second sentence is. The syntax overextends itself, almost literally to death.

To see how even a sonnet can hold a highly individual voice, take a small look at Cummings's "next to of course god. . . ." Or to see how a sonnet can explore even foreknown narrative and dramatically make good on it, take a long look at "Leda and the Swan." Look at that about a week—the deepening imagery, the pace. And then go back down to, say, Edna St. Vincent Millay's "On Hearing a Symphony of Beethoven." That's about as bad as a sonnet can get. It's tactically surer than this "Sonnet" we're looking at, but its abstractions are even more vague, and its generalizations are even more general.

The prime trouble with this poem is that it's *typically* bad, not *individually* bad. Typically bad isn't much worse than typically good; if you're ever going to write any poem that's better-than-good, you've got to risk more individual depth than this poem even approaches. I risk saying that to this poet about this poem, because I've seen poems from him that are toughly individual. But even in so formal a structure as a sonnet, he has to learn—first of all—to keep his own voice in shape.

"Wading Horses"

A fine photograph often makes a fine exercise for a poet: to work out from, or in toward. In what direction the poet of "Wading Horses" intends to move her poem isn't clear to me. Like Paul Strand, she seems to love contrast; and she's surely in love with the images single words offer. I instinctively trust a poet who knows the right names for things: "withers" or "guillemots"; I'm taken, too, in the first strophe, with the poet's ear for consonance and assonance. She builds in some finely quiet resonance.

Beyond that first strophe, the poem doesn't build much. "A beast" that may be visually specific in the photograph is insufficiently specified in the poem. After those four specific horses with parts specifically as "cool as a seal's / belly," and after the intense concentration on "the heels of / guillemots," the abstracted "beast" seems practically non-existent. Something's out of balance here, out of proportion, out of *scale*. My early worry that the poem's lines seemed random ("drip" given weight equal to "guillemots"—not to mention to how "the far, black water rears") is confirmed by the poem's increasingly random focus.

I can see the poet unhappy with my worry. *She* can see Paul Strand's photograph when she looks at her poem. And it's naturally hard for her to see that she hasn't *shown us, in the poem*, the evidence Strand's photograph presents. The photograph, by definition, presents to the viewer what the poem must *make present* to a reader. Fine photographs can be fine exercises for a poet: not least as they show in what ways writing with ink is a different gift than writing with light.

What this poem most needs to make present is the poet's sense of the *relative* importance of her images (hers to the extent—literally— that they are "after" Strand's). I don't have in mind this particular photograph of Strand's, but I know enough of his work to know that he uses all sorts of tactics to present some sense of scale. The tactics may be as simple as selective focus, or as complex as developing the film for previsualized ranges of contrast. All such tactics emphasize this or that element of his composition. Not that the tactics should be apparent; tactics in a poem, too, are only a way of making the subject more transparent. But in this particular poem there's an absence of tactics, particularly of those tactics which might give the reader a stronger sense of perspective.

How a photograph is composed is, obviously, a major part of what it's "about." This is easier to see in a photograph, or any visual art, than it is in a poem. Delacroix said a long time ago that "position is the essence of composition."

In "Wading Horses," the poet's positioning of verbs like "drip," "breathes," and "rehearse" already shows how much she's yearning to compose the scene's energies. She instinctively knows that the shape a poem takes, and makes, is part of what it says. Fine. But what the poem most needs is a more secure line, a line that will give her voice more space, a line that will give the poem more of a base to compose from. Or *within*. The poet is so intensely devoted to individual words that she never quite finds a line for those words to be part of. Given the way the poem now starts, I'd think that a three- or four-stress accentual line might be a norm. To work with or against. To try as revision. Not only as reseeing, but also as rehearing how the whole poem may move.

A stronger sense of scale, a more open presentation of relationships; these are what I feel this poem needs. Through a more controlled line, I think it can build to greater depth, and to more climax, than it does now. The fiddler crab is a stretch for depth, all right; I feel with the poet that the poem wants depth. But to claim, as the poem claims, that the stalky eyes of the crab feel the "beckon of the cobalt / flukes" is too much for me to believe. I want to believe, but the end of the poem—like its middle—is too easily abstracted and undemonstrated. I'd guess that the poem may finally be claiming more than Strand's photograph presents.

So far as I know, this is the first poem this poet has ever heard discussed in a workshop. I hope she'll bear with all sorts of comment. She wants tactical knowledge, and her poem needs it. But below the poem's faults there are real strengths to work with: an ear with lots of potential, a concerned eye, and a yearning to give words a life of their own.

"The Vanishing Mailmen"

Somewhere between its title and first line, "The Vanishing Mailmen" gets confused about what it's about. Even if the plural title is only a typographical slip, that slip is symptomatic: the poem vacillates between being specifically human and wanting to be widely general. Or just generally wild. The specifics are, in effect, catalogued, but they never add up to more than themselves. Or say that they are additive, in the sense of $1 + 1 + 1 + 1 + 1$ and so on. Still, they never add into groups, or multiply with or against each other as—say—3 and 4 can: to become 7 or 12. This poem doesn't much allow itself such incremental possibilities. In trying to discover where it may go, it doesn't pay sufficient attention to where it has been.

There are some bright images here, but even those fried eggs seem more decorative than functional, strangely horizontal when looked at in terms of a postman's deeply vertical pouch. Imagery most becomes imagination in the second strophe; I like the play on a "dogless" dog-day and the barely screened sexual imagery. But nothing gets *done* with all this, the poem doesn't evolve from it. Look at how quickly the third strophe disintegrates: the facile diction of "any connection," the flatly forced run-on of "worthless / now." Even though the poem is usually accomplished, line by line, it's finally static. The end of the poem dissolves in what I can only think of as Workshop Surrealism.

Perhaps there's some mimetic fallacy here. The poem, like the postman, gives up too easily. Somewhere within the impotent envy of the second strophe, and the Charles-Atlas-sadness of the third, there's a considerable poem, a poem which can happen if the poet puts this version away and, in effect, starts again out of some deeper necessity than this poem shows. The new poem has to build its specifics more demandingly; it has to resolve itself from more evolving, and not just make modish images. It has to do more justice to this one mailman if he's to touch, in effect, the mailman in all of us. The poem, for me, doesn't come close to doing justice to its subject. I'm not sure that I know what the poem's subject is, or that the poet yet does. But doing justice to one's subject is still, for me, Rule One. All of which is easier said than made good on. You've got to make your own poems. You've got to make the poems your own. This poem is too anonymously modish. To get beyond what workshops can teach you is what workshops finally are for.

Philip Booth, born in 1925, grew up in New Hampshire and Maine. He received his master's degree from Columbia after graduating from Dartmouth. He taught there briefly, as well as at Bowdoin and Wellesley, before moving to his present position as Professor of English in the creative writing program at Syracuse University. He has published five books: *Letter from a Distant Land* (1957), *The Islanders* (1961), *Weathers and*

Edges (1966), *Margins* (1971), and *Available Light* (1976). His work
has been honored by a Lamont Prize, by Guggenheim and Rockefeller
fellowships, as well as by awards from *Poetry*, the *Virginia Quarterly
Review*, *Poetry Northwest*, and the National Institute of Arts and Letters.

LARRY LEVIS

"Sonnet"

Despite an acceptable and interesting opening line, "Sonnet" fails
to distinguish itself as a poem at all. The faint music of its meter, when
present, serves primarily to disguise the poem's evasions of diction,
imagery, and imagination. Most of these problems, I believe, are the
result of a form poorly handled by an "ear" too easily deceived. For
example, the flashily hyphenated attempt at a run-over line here (line
3) does not prevent the poem from remaining resolutely and leadenly
end-stopped by its couplets, and there is a preponderance of lines writ-
ten to a *metronomically* regular iambic pentameter. Neither these lines
nor their subsequent demise into the accentual lines that presume to re-
solve this sonnet, amount, really, to rhythm.

It is possible that any real rhythm is absent because any genuine
speech is absent also. It is difficult to imagine, today, that anyone could
use seriously a phrase as hackneyed as "Love's smile," either in speech
or in poetry. Yet here it is, archaic, indulgent, and flagrantly here. Now
it seems entirely possible that, to the poet, the unfamiliar appetite of the
sonnet form has produced this: when a poet must concentrate so totally
on his measure, counting his stresses like a trombonist just before he
puts the horn to his mouth, the diction and imagery fail to secure
enough of his attention. Therefore, "Sonnet" displays a number of
clichés, archaisms, and merely hackneyed phrases: "Love's smile,"
"fade away," "lips that are so far apart," "shroud," "motionless hand,"
"unspoken heart"—all these tend to deaden the possibilities of imagery
and imagination in the poem. They also seem to encourage the poet to
indulge in the very general speculations that flourish rhetorically at the
poem's end. These speculations comprise, anyway, a disappointingly
familiar, and not very convincing, idea: that wars are started because
of a lack of communication and affection in intimate, human space.
Maybe. But the presence of a Hitler or the desire to obtain oil rights in
the Malaysian peninsula can do quite a lot, politically speaking, to

engender wars and turn lovers into soldiers. I remain unconvinced by
the poem's resolution, however, not because the idea is *necessarily*
faulty, but because the diction holds so little reality, so little actual
speech as it might be really used, or made useful. There are also, in
"Sonnet," phrases that are simply confusing: I do not know why the
tongue should both "fork and drool." Elsewhere the poet can be merely
fanciful, facile, and archaic, as when the words seem "but uttered out
of art." I think Yeats was the last poet who could have made that
phrase live.

I notice no real lovers in the poem at all. Unlike that fine sonnet,
in couplets, "To Speak of Woe That Is in Marriage," by Robert Lowell,
where the idiosyncrasies of the spoken voice are wholly and eccentrically
within the poem's awesome and monstrous experience, "Sonnet" supplies
us only with ideas, not people. Viewed from this perspective, the poem
is not an experience at all; it is a feeble essay, disguised in verse and
written to easy rhymes by a less-than-sophisticated versifier.

And yet, looking at two fine half-lines that somehow managed to
find their way into such enemy territory, I believe there is hope for this
poet, if not for "Sonnet." If it were mine, I would begin the poem again
with the honesties of speech that *are* here in both instances:

>   If the daylight shone for nothing,
>   I kept it to myself,

All the poet needs to do now is to come down, out of his stucco tower,
and write as if his life depended on it, which, for a poet, it might.

"Wading Horses"

"Wading Horses" is more technically accomplished as a poem than
"Sonnet," if only because the poet has a more secure grasp of what her
craft can do. At times, even this fails her, as when she tries to make
"drip" do as a whole line, and the verb calls an excessive amount of
attention to itself, as a word. But most of the craft here is genuine, and
the music manifests itself interestingly in the tensions it poses through
verbs which, at the same moment, describe the stillness present in the
photograph: "the far, black water rears."

The middle verse paragraph of the poem, however, is certainly one
that contains the weakest and vaguest writing in the poem, and a work

of only nineteen lines cannot afford to include such a blemish. The
"beast" refers me, as reader, to Paul Strand's photograph in an attempt to
find *which* beast this is, and the Yeatsian or Roethke-like "loosening
dark" is simply too grand and unearned to occur in the poem.

It is also unfortunate that the middle of the poem is insufficient
preparation for what is intended at the poem's close, and I am made,
uncomfortably, to wonder about the intended significance of the crab
observing the flatfish. What importance should I attach to the "fluke,"
which so gracefully rises and beckons, and how does this subjective
inclusion on the part of the poet have any connection with the afore-
mentioned horses and rearing water? If it is merely scenery, the poem
undergoes a failure to resolve *itself*, as poetry, and a failure to recuper-
ate its subject, the photograph. As it is here, the poem is forced to
include items and animals that remain extraneous and unconnected.

Ultimately, I believe there are really two poems here. The first is
merely begun and is "Wading Horses," about a photograph. The second
poem is not only about the sea, but *takes place* under the sea. It is also
about the poet, about her consciousness.

Throughout this short poem, I have been impressed by the poet's
use of imagery: she exults in detail, and her talent and seriousness are,
for me, entirely evident. She also displays a passion for *naming*, from
"guillemots" to the less fortunate choice of the last word in the poem,
"fluke." Even though neither poem is written yet, I believe in the poet's
genuine "ear": "rehearse / a slow kick at the shallow surf, / sees the
rise" in which the poet's hearing is mimetically sure, and the assonance
works. I wish her luck.

"The Vanishing Mailmen"

"The Vanishing Mailmen" is symptomatic of a *kind* of poetry that
has enjoyed a certain frequency and popularity over the past few years.
It is, for me, less impressive because it contains a facetious, surreal
veneer that is more than faintly familiar. Yet the poem demonstrates a
sureness in its craft, a number of fine lines, and genuine talent.

If the initial simile of "fried eggs" is largely uninteresting and even
careless, "flat and bright as the afternoon" works well enough. I would
rather not have to read "dogless day" in a poem about mailmen, where
it is metonymic for the tired joke of dogs versus mailmen. Elsewhere,
in a poem without mailmen, it could be interesting.

The best writing in the poem, which should be salvaged and used in another, less limited poem, occurs toward the end:

```
            My muscles will soon
    atrophy, wilt into powder and blow away.

    This is my last house;
    I approach it with short steps . . .
    Termites scramble over the porch and boarded
        windows.
    I sit.  My hair stops growing.  I am done.
```

This is so well handled that I believe it should be used in a subsequent poem, a poem of someone unemployed or unemployable. As is, the poem, with its tired, attendant jokes of "televisions tuned to game shows" or "young wives in negligees" seems to become, increasingly, a strategy invented when a poet "wants to write a poem," rather than a concept that evolves necessarily from the fine images the poet can create from fully imagined or real experience.

Beyond this, the poem is much too short and quick to explain adequately why the mailmen are disappearing at all, or why they are taking our abodes with them. The correlative idea of the demise of the speaker, his inability or lack of desire to participate in sexuality or even in a hunger for plums and melons attests, for me, to a strongly forced, and confused, utterance. The entire poem seems haunted by what Stephen Dobbyns has called "the reek of meaning." My suspicion is that the poet distrusts his images too thoroughly to make them do more than participate in a poem already patented by several other good poets. If the entire experience were less playful, less allied to the "Let's Pretend" school of poetry, and if the poet's ideas were tested on his pulse, and in his feelings and desires, his work would be much more vital, and more certain of its metaphorical and formal decisions. The whole thing, really believed in, would be stronger and less harmless.

For the poem—and I can only speak generally about it just now—*is* harmless, though it masquerades as finished work in a certain prevailing style. This makes me glad, however, that the poet is so obviously more talented, more serious, and more subtle in places than the whole

of his poem is. Because if the poem is simply too minimal and cute to
survive, the poet is not.

Larry Levis has published two volumes of poems: *Wrecking Crew,* which
was the 1971 U.S. Award Winner of the International Poetry Forum, and
The Afterlife, the 1976 Lamont Poetry Selection. His recent work has
appeared in *The American Poetry Review, Antaeus, Field, The Iowa Re-
view* and other magazines. He teaches in the Writing Program at the Uni-
versity of Missouri.

JAY MEEK

"Sonnet"

I must admit I find sonnets endearing, even when they turn out to
be open couplets decked out in the title of "Sonnet." And the opening
line, in its best possibility, proposes a voice that seems to delight in
the incongruities of "subtle weaponry." I'm encouraged, and want to
go on.

But there's maybe only one other line here that's equally at ease
with itself: "This must be where we get our battle rites." Why? The two
lines are similar: each makes an assertion, complete in its sense and
syntax, on one line. Moreover, each line opens the rhyming couplet it
appears in, so each is free to shape its own context without having to
lock in on a rhyming word. And that tells me something. For often the
lines that contribute least go most out of control, are those lines con-
taining the sounding word; this is evident in line 6, which does com-
plete the formal requirements with a rather heavy-handed rhyme, but
presents nothing in "dark oppressive shroud" that "cloud" hasn't al-
ready presented succinctly.

So too, in lines 7–10, an ease of clarity and pacing is given over in
the pursuit of form. Without caesuras, and with the doubling up of verbs
(line 7) and adjectives (line 8)—sure signs that language is serving as
metrical filler—each line hurries toward its rhyme. And without end-
stopping until after the fourth line in this set, the lines breathlessly race
toward some point of rest, just when the poem wants to be more de-
liberately paced. For along the way, the sense gets blurred: does the
speaker intend "art," or something like "artfulness," in the contemporary

idiom an altogether different matter? And just how many lips does the speaker have in mind? Where the opening lines speak of *"my* voice," the diction here becomes impersonal: *"the* tongue." And that strikes me as a significant shift, for it suggests that the poem, in those places where it most labors on behalf of its form, loses the fullest contact with its voice. Even the imagery becomes distant and rhetorical: "Love's smile" and "a storm of words" are ornamented abstractions rather than radiantly concrete details.

I want to like this poem because I think the poem wants to be game. And because the voice, when it's there, seems committed to its persuasion. But my sense is that the poem struggles with its formal properties—with heavy rhymes, with anapests that shorten the meter in the last three lines—and in that struggle the ease of language is lost. And when language goes, the voice that's predicated upon it goes, too. So what had the possibility for being agreeably charming—with due seriousness, of course—begins too early to take itself seriously. And that's when things go wrong, only the least of them, maybe, being the borrowing from Dylan Thomas of "fork," or—in the last couplet—the Yeatsian resonance from "The Circus Animals' Desertion."

"Wading Horses"

The title and subtitle prepare the reader for a poem that is perhaps small and essentially presentational: verbally transparent, detailed, in sharp focus. And the opening lines nicely establish that clarity: "Four horses nose / the lowest tide. . . ." The image engages a reader in an act of perception through the accuracy of its language.

But such a focus is demanding, for when it blurs even a bit it blurs noticeably. I'm troubled, for example, by the wayward precision of "Their withers / drip / cool as a seal's / belly." The syntax is ungrammatical, and the image seems loosely distributed through the lines. Beyond that, I'm just not sure the comparison heightens my sense of the horses any. And "Under the heels" not only is difficult to place spatially, but comes, following the seal, as a second aside to the horses.

Horses, birds, crabs, seals, whales: my feeling is that the poem now is overpopulated, that it too often has to take account of its different directions, so that a focus on the horses, and indirectly on the photograph itself, tends to be lost. And as the poem extends beyond its opening image, and through the more generalized material in the second stanza ("beast" instead of horse, for example), the focus becomes in fact lost in the last stanza.

No longer is the point of view working from outside the poem. The reader is not looking at the crab: he is asked to become the crab. That, or have his line of vision deflected by the crab's seeing. And though it might be crabbing on my part, I suspect the fiddler sees less well. The final image is not immediately clear: does "fluke" refer to a flatfish or to one lobe of a whale's tail? I think the sense of the image suggests the latter, but why is only one fluke visible when the whole tail seems to be rising? In either case, as the crab sees it, the earlier integrity that allowed things to exist in themselves becomes violated: "rehearse" and "beckon" seem intrusive poeticisms—there because they sound good, not because they're accurate. Look how far the poem has come from where it started!

The poem seems worth pursuing through continued revisions, continuing that clarity with which it opens. And I'd be interested, too, in seeing what further discoveries might come from the patterned energies of rising and falling that are presented here: in the water falling from the horses, in the black water as it rears; in the horse settling down, in the flukes of the whale rising as it sounds.

"The Vanishing Mailmen"

Because this poem presents the reader with one mailman as its speaker, I'd find the voice somewhat more compelling if the title weren't plural. Such a generalizing title—because it seems to point not to an event, but to a thesis—suggests there is a mechanism, a discernible intent, behind the disappearances, that the *mysterious* instance is part of a *rational* design.

The poem for me suffers from such a separation of its intelligence and its sensibility. In the first stanza, the opening image means to be strange, I think, but succeeds in being only a formula for strangeness, which I suppose is to say that it succeeds in being familiar. The enjambment in the first line gives undue emphasis to the assertion that the letters "are blank," but there is nothing strange in the notion of a blank letter; it is merely the logical opposite of what one expects.

My sense is that this sort of separation comes about when a writer hasn't worked out an agreeable relationship with his speaker. One in writing might well choose to be distant, objective, reasonable; but the voice here needs to speak with an immediacy which the confusion of roles isn't allowing for. The writer's intelligence says, "Put in some blank letters." But the speaker says, "Gee, I didn't open any envelopes, how do I know the letters are blank?" Another instance: in the largely digressive third stanza, "atrophy" and "wilt" are not synonomous, nor do they follow one another in a continuous process; the language is inaccurate, I think, because the intelligence is working at a remove from sensibility. Similarly, I think the voice should simply present its images, rather than go on inductively to organize them as declarations: "I am on a strange route," "They've lost another one." Again, it seems to me, the speaker is put in a position of abstracting his experience. Where there might best be an intelligence that works itself through the speaker —that inheres in his sensibility—it instead separates and then confuses the writer's detachment with the speaker's verbal contact with experience.

I do not mean to come down especially hard. But I do feel the poem unhappily tries to ask the reader to undergo the strangeness the speaker presents, at the same time it asks that he be conscious of his experience as strange. And I'm afraid that's a self-defeating move, not only because it robs an image of its vitality, but because it deprives the voice of its persuasion. Where the poem works best for me the voice speaks within the image, and the image within its dramatic moment: "Only screen doors separate me / from young wives in negligees, / tired schoolgirls, jewelry boxes. . . ." But I think it representative of the poem that the following line deserts that ominous and thrilling moment merely for "trays of fat plums and ripe melons."

Jay Meek, born in 1937, teaches at Wake Forest University. A graduate of the University of Michigan and Syracuse University, he has published two collections of poems: *The Week the Dirigible Came* and *Drawing on the Walls.*

LAWRENCE RAAB

"Sonnet"

"Sonnet" strains terribly to move from the simple "I" of line 2 to an unbelievably all-knowing "we" at the conclusion. I wish the poet hadn't felt this was necessary, but had held to and developed the individual

"I" which is so quickly abandoned. The "self" which is "such a subtle weaponry" in line 1 is already a step removed from the poet himself, or from any conceivable personal speaker.

"Sonnet" begins with a pronouncement that leads me to believe that the poet is already in hiding, and throughout the poem he continually withdraws and conceals his own personality behind all those grand abstractions ("battle rites," "wars of nations," "Love's smile"), clichés (that forked tongue) and insistently mixed and confused metaphors (the forked tongue that drools an electrical—and cruel—storm of words). I would be more interested in the smile of one clearly imagined person than in "Love's smile," which is no real smile at all, more interested in what the speaker sees as the "battle rites" of his own life, the gestures of his own hand, what he himself might have said or wished to say. (Or: if not the poet's actual life, then an invented one, but actual nevertheless for the sake of the poem.) But the poem he writes about being unable to free his own voice is itself spoken in no individual voice at all. It is intent on developing Large Meanings, and the table-pounding assurance of the final couplet—"and our battles of sexes must all have their start / in a motionless hand and an unspoken heart"— seems not only unearned but untrue.

Reticence, mistrust of language, withdrawal in the face of emo-tion—what I see as the poem's most human and truest subjects—surely don't account for *all* our battles, both national and personal. This in-sistence on too much should have been a sign that the poem was grounded in too little: much too little—nothing, in fact—about all those times the speaker "tried to free / my voice." That's what interests me here, not international warfare or the battle of the sexes, but those painfully real moments when what should have been said remained unspoken.

"Wading Horses"

I'm baffled by the language of this poem. At times, as in the opening sentence, the voice is simple and inviting. But then those fancy words come along—"withers," "guillemots." Is this shift of vocabulary a con-scious tactic, or merely language and learning calling attention to itself? And what kind of voice would use these words? Other constructions— "myopic stalks," that "cobalt fluke" at the end—also seem intentionally distracting and confusing. (What is a myopic stalk? The way the fiddler walks? Why "pale," then? Or should "stalks" be read as "stems"? Then, why "myopic"?) But I'm not even sure that fiddler should be in the poem. Is she necessary? Isn't she, in fact, an insubstantial stand-in for the poet?

The subtitle tells us that the poem is based on a photograph by Paul Strand, but the poem doesn't make anything out of the fact of that photograph. Of course, it need not, although the confrontation between the poet as viewer and the picture which the poet's art attempts to animate seems intriguing. Perhaps this is the essential subject of the poem— the tension between what is frozen in that picture and what comes alive again in the imagination. Yet that fiddler only "observes." And as observation the poem never returns to the accuracy of its opening sentence. Instead, the sea rears like a horse. A Yeatsian rough beast "breaks / from the loosening dark." (One of those four original horses? Another horse? Another kind of animal altogether? Or just the sea pretending to be a horse? Isn't the answer important? I think it is.)

If the poem wants to be more than observation—and I think it does— I wish it had tried to grapple with the problems of how things are seen and transformed by sight, changed by what the imagination needs to see, the wading horses altered by the composition of Strand's art, and then changed again by the poet's perception of the photograph. If the poet had chosen to push her poem further in this direction she might have discovered a more consistent (and a more consistently interesting) voice. Then we might be able to judge the effect of "withers" and "guillemots." Distracting, fancy writing? The poem gone out of control? Or could this kind of language become a necessary part of the voice of a particular speaker we could hope to understand?

"The Vanishing Mailmen"

Of the three poems, I find this one the most appealing, if only because it has a sense of humor and tries to tell a story. The poem raises some potentially interesting dramatic questions. Finally, however, it raises far more questions than it answers.

Why is the mailman vanishing? (The plurality of mailmen indicated by the title is a twist that doesn't seem to go anywhere.) Why is this his last day? Why is he on a strange route? How is the initial routine of this day different from all others? Why are all his letters blank? How does he know they are blank? And so on. Of course, we can say that all

of this is simply a jumbled metaphor for dying. But that doesn't seem
to be a very interesting answer. In fact, it's no answer at all, only a
Meaning. I think this insistent sense of death robs the mailman of any
actual life. Nor does the end help, which I find merely confusing. The
mailman resigns himself to his fate, his dissolution, his death: "I sit. My
hair stops growing. I am done." The termites (not acting like any
termites I can imagine, unless the mailman has turned to wood) "crawl
over me." They are "busy unbuilding," just as the mailman has been
unbuilt. Why, then, have the termites "lost another one"? Wouldn't
they have won?

I've said that the mailman resigns himself to his apparent death, but
I don't know if that's really accurate, because the poem withholds so
much. He says, "I'll miss this job." Is he giving up his job—and his life
—willingly? Or is some more powerful necessity drawing him away
from himself? What is won and what is lost? The poem stumbles into
a particularly unconvincing statement in stanza 3 that might well be
emblematic of the various problems here: ". . . any connection made
would be worthless / now." But this is precisely what the poem needs:
connections. I don't mean to suggest that all of my questions have to
be answered precisely and unequivocably, but I want to feel the pres-
sure of the poem's voice making connections in the face of what seems
like certain loss.

The details offer few clues, if any. I'm interested in those blank
letters, but nothing is done with them. How they might be stacked in
the mailman's pouch "like fried eggs . . . flat and bright" strikes me
as merely ridiculous. If the poem is after a certain sense of mystery—
and I think it is—this image is not mysterious, just silly. Nor is any-
thing done with the people in stanza 2. The cliché porno fantasy of
"young wives in negligees" passes by like an unintentional aside. Is the
mailman interested in sex, in the obvious erotic possibilities of those
"ripe melons," in thievery (those jewelry boxes)? Are all these possi-
bilities part of what makes his job interesting and what he will miss? The
poem doesn't say.

Another potentially troublesome aspect of the poem is its similarity to
Mark Strand's beautiful poem "The Mailman." Strand's poem is also
mysterious, right from the beginning when the mailman arrives at mid-
night, but Strand's mystery is always grounded in facts, the facts of the
poem which come to resemble (though never precisely) the real facts

of our lives. Moreover, Strand's mailman has to be a mailman. He is an incarnation of the ancient bearer of bad news, now pleading for forgiveness. But this vanishing mailman doesn't have to be a mailman at all. He has a route and a routine, that's all. He could just as easily be a milkman, a delivery boy, or an Electrolux salesman. Nothing is ever made of the fact that he is none of these but a mailman, except for the notion of the blank letters. This interests me, but I want those letters to be real letters (as real as the poem can manage) before they become symbolic. I believe that a genuine, unsettling sense of mystery is created by subtle displacements of the real world, not by an indifference to what we have all come to assume is real.

One possible tactic for returning to the poem might be to develop another character (perhaps out of the sketchy figures suggested in stanza 2), a "you" to whom the mailman might speak. This would provide the poet with a more immediate dramatic tension—someone speaking not just to himself but to another person, speaking at a particular moment and for some reason, out of some fear or longing perhaps, speaking as the poem might best speak, out of necessity.

Lawrence Raab, born in 1946, is assistant professor of English at Williams College. He has studied writing at Middlebury College and Syracuse University. His published work includes *Mysteries of the Horizon* and *The Collector of Cold Weather*. He has received a Creative Writing Grant from the National Endowment for the Arts and was a Junior Fellow for three years in the University of Michigan Society of Fellows.